A Field Guide for Organisation Development

To our families – the organisations that matter most

A Field Guide for Organisation Development

Taking Theory into Practice

Edited by

ED GRIFFIN

MIKE ALSOP

MARTIN SAVILLE
and

GRAHAME SMITH

Routledge
Taylor & Francis Group

LONDON AND NEW YORK

First published 2014 by Gower Publishing

2 Park Square, Milton Park, Abingdon, Oxon OX14 4RN
711 Third Avenue, New York, NY 10017, USA

Routledge is an imprint of the Taylor & Francis Group, an informa business

First issued in paperback 2016

Gower Applied Business Research
Our programme provides leaders, practitioners, scholars and researchers with thought provoking, cutting edge books that combine conceptual insights, interdisciplinary rigour and practical relevance in key areas of business and management.

British Library Cataloguing in Publication Data
A catalogue record for this book is available from the British Library.

Library of Congress Cataloging-in-Publication Data
A field guide for organisation development : taking theory into practice / [edited] by Ed Griffin, Grahame Smith, Mike Alsop and Martin Saville.
    pages cm
Includes bibliographical references and index.
ISBN 978-1-4094-4049-9 (hbk)
1. Organisational change. 2. Organisational behavior. 3. Organisational effectiveness.
I. Griffin, Ed, 1965-
HD58.8.F5187 2014
658.3--dc23

                                                                    2013035198

ISBN 978-1-4094-4049-9 (hbk)
ISBN 978-1-138-24788-8 (pbk)

Contents

List of Figures

List of Tables

About the Editors

Ed Griffin is an international HR Director and experienced Organisation Development consultant, who has worked across many sectors and organisational types, including Marketing, Financial Services, IT, Pharma, Education, Regulatory bodies, Retail, Energy and Not-for-profit. Internationally, his work has taken him across Europe, the USA, Brazil, Middle East and Singapore.

His experience from working in Finance, Organisation Development and HR roles gives him a unique perspective that combines performance and human factors. His work is based on the belief that it is possible to develop successful and sustainable organisations where people can fulfil their potential. He has undertaken research and writing in the fields of HR, OD and Leadership with articles published in *HR Director*, *People Management*, *Strategic HR Review* and *Training Journal*.

Mike Alsop was, for several years, the global Head of Executive Development for Securicor plc. In 2004, when Securicor merged with Group4Falck, he was appointed to the same role for the newly-created organisation, Group4Securicor (now known as G4S plc) which rapidly became one of the largest 'non-state' employers in the world, with over 600,000 people. He was instrumental in the design and practical implementation of many of the global integration processes for senior executives that contributed to the success of the merger. In 2007 Mike set up his own independent practice, and has worked on executive learning and development, talent management and organisational change initiatives (across a range of sectors) in the UK, Europe, Africa, the Middle East, Asia and the Americas. A lot of his work with individual leaders takes place in the outdoors, walking in the fresh air, often amongst beautiful scenery... helping people find a 'space to breathe' away from the relentlessness of organisational life.

Martin Saville is co-founder of Mayvin, a specialist consultancy with a mission to nurture the human spirit in organisations. Formerly Director of Strategic Planning and Operations at London Business School, Martin is known for the work he does in developing the knowledge and capabilities of OD teams and practitioners. He is on the faculty of a number of leading OD practitioner development programmes and is a regular conference speaker on OD. From 2005 to 2009 he was a Senior Consultant at the Roffey Park Institute. Martin's early career was spent in opera management and he currently serves as Deputy Chair of British Youth Opera, the UK's opera training company. He is an Honorary Visiting Professor of the Faculty of Business and Law, part of London Metropolitan University.

Grahame Smith is an experienced Organisational and Leadership Development Consultant working with public, private and voluntary sector organisations. His industry sector experience spans Telecommunications, Mobile Communications, Security Services, Retail and Financial Services. His professional background is in sales, marketing and general management gained in the fmcg sector with Cadbury, Kelloggs, General Mills and British Sugar. As a successful senior line manager, he saw OD as core to his role; 'Why would I let anyone else do this stuff for me?' sums up his philosophy. Now, as a consultant, his pragmatic approach helps executives face up to the fundamental changes and developments necessary to really deliver on their strategic intent. 'Skills development may feel like the right thing to do, but without creating the right context first it can also be a highly ineffective use of budget'. Grahame has co-written articles for the *Strategic HR Review* and *HR Magazine*.

About the Contributors

Angela Baron spent 25 year working for the Chartered Institute for Personnel and Development (CIPD). Starting as conference manager in 1987, she moved to the research and policy directorate in 1990 where she was responsible for a number of major research projects including the much quoted and recognised people and performance (Black box) work. She has also written extensively, publishing books on Job Evaluation Performance Management, HR Strategy and Human Capital as well as numerous articles and research reports. Angela left CIPD in the summer of 2012 to pursue a career in academia and is now lecturing and researching at a number of Universities and Colleges as well as delivering management training in leadership and performance managers in the education sector.

Sue Belgrave worked in healthcare, community development and television before joining The Body Shop International where she became the uniquely titled General Manager for Company Culture. As such Sue was responsible for ensuring that the experience of those who worked for the company was aligned with the high-profile external image. Having held internal responsibility for OD, Sue then went on to consult on OD and to set up 'Hot Brushes', a business specialising in using the visual arts in organisations before joining Roffey Park where she became Director of their OD Practitioner Programme. Creating an environment in which voices can be heard is central to Sue's work. She specialises in participative ways of working, and has run more than 100 large group interventions across all business sectors. Sue is now launching a new business, finding delight in working in Asia, thinking about compassion in healthcare, sustainability and getting young people into work.

Paul Brewerton is co-founder and Director of Strengths Partnership, an HR consulting firm providing strengths-based leadership development, coaching and talent management solutions. He is a Chartered Occupational Psychologist and Doctorate in Organisational Psychology with around 20 years' experience in individual, team and organisational development. Paul has had a fascination with organisational culture and its relationship with business performance and employee engagement throughout his professional career, and his doctoral research focused on this topic. He has worked across a wide variety of sectors; recent clients include Takeda Pharmaceuticals, Tesco, Bank of England, Legal and General, Panasonic, Police Service of Northern Ireland, Royal Air Force and many more. In recent years, Paul has dedicated his business activities to helping organisations translate a strengths-focused approach to bottom-line business performance, via an OD paradigm. Paul is a regular speaker on the practical application of psychology to business, in particular applying the strengths approach in business and has contributed to a wide range of academic, business and professional publications in this area.

Niki Dalton is the Director of Apical Consulting Limited and an experienced Organisation Design & Development consultant, having worked with clients to design and deliver complex, cross-border change programmes in a wide variety of industries and organizational environments for over 15 years. She is an expert in functional transformation and HR Strategy and believes in marrying the business objectives with people's skills, interests and motivations to deliver high-performing organisations that play to individual strengths and result in inspirational work environments. Niki is also a strong proponent of exploring new working practices from remote and flexible working to portfolio careers, for the benefit of both the business and the individual. When she's not consulting, Niki has a keen interest in garden design, home renovation, sailing and other watersports.

Liz Finney was, until 2011, Principal Researcher at Roffey Park Institute in West Sussex where she developed a particular interest in OD, authoring an influential research report on OD evaluation, speaking on the subject at conferences and on development programmes in the UK and USA and contributing articles to a number of journals. Liz has also researched, written and presented widely on related areas such as employee engagement and the transition of technical and professional experts into leadership roles. Now an independent consultant, Liz combines small and large group facilitation with applied management research. Her interests continue to be in how organisations can build and maintain the healthy human systems that bring success.

Jo Hennessy was for several years the Director of Research at Roffey Park Institute where she set the global research strategy and worked with an excellent research team to deliver and author studies on leadership and management trends, how experts succeed in leadership roles, employee engagement, HR business partnering and, of course, evaluating OD interventions. This thought leadership gave Jo many opportunities for platform speaking, extensive press coverage, and journal articles and informed her leadership and OD development interventions in business. As a Chartered Occupational Psychologist, Jo has worked in consulting for many years working internationally in a number of different sectors. Building on this international experience, in 2009, Jo oversaw Roffey Park's entry into Asia Pacific and set up of a successful overseas operation. More recently, as Managing Director for JCA (Occupational Psychologists) Jo has deepened her experience of general management which she now uses to inform how she leads her own consulting business. Hennessy Consulting Ltd specialises in enabling employee engagement and successful business change through leadership development and wider OD interventions.

Penny Lock's interest in organisational development was stimulated through leading major change, including the management merger of two acute hospitals. Why it can be so difficult to work across team, organisational and cultural boundaries and why many groups fail to operate at their full potential are the questions that continue to interest her. Since 2002, Penny has specialised in developing teams, organisations and leaders using techniques such as board development, facilitation and coaching supervision. At the heart of her work is a determination to help people engage productively and creatively in organisational environments. Penny's business builds on her early career in social research and management in the UK and Spain. Her approach is client-centred, pragmatic and evidence-based. She works independently and in collaboration with other development specialists in the UK and internationally. Penny retains her academic interest and is on the faculty of the Roffey Park master's programme in People and Organisational Development. Alongside her consultancy work, she is a member of BP's global leadership faculty and of the faculty of the NHS Leadership Academy.

Kate Mulcahy is the founder of Change Unlimited, an OD consultancy with a strong track record for designing and delivering leadership development programmes that lead to significant behaviour change. Clients include market-leading organisations in telecoms, IT, pharmaceuticals, financial services and broadcasting. Prior to establishing her own business at 29, her career began at HP where she held a number of internal consulting roles. As UK Learning and Development Manager, she had overall responsibility for providing a comprehensive training and development portfolio resourced largely by external consultants. Having worked inside an organisation procuring and managing external consultants, and now a long-term external partner to organisations herself, Kate is perfectly placed to understand what it takes to establish and maintain effective and seamless partnerships with external providers so that an organisation can benefit fully from the value of an external contribution. Kate has a first class business degree and an MSc in Organisation Behaviour from Birkbeck College.

Andy Smith has 25 years' experience as a consultant and leader. He works at Roffey Park, an OD centre of excellence in Europe and combines his leadership role on the executive team with that of a practising consultant. His focus is leadership and organisational development and he has facilitated a range of leadership and organisational development programmes, both in the UK and internationally. When Principal Consultant for Organisational Development, Andy was jointly responsible for the launch of Roffey Park's OD Practitioner Programme. He has also been Director of the Roffey MSc in People and Organisational Development, a unique self-managed programme, and a leading OD qualification in Europe. He is a regular platform speaker and writer, co-authoring Roffey Park's A–Z Guide to OD. Most recently he has contributed sessions at the USA OD Network Conference and the inaugural European Conference. He has a keen interest in gestalt, complexity theory and group facilitation.

James Traeger is co-founder and Director of Mayvin, (which means 'trusted expert' in Yiddish), a company specialising in the development of heartfelt wisdom in the workplace. Following a career in management in the photographic industry, James specialised in organisational and leadership development from 1996–2006, with clients including the Metropolitan Police Service, Newham NHS Trust, Surrey County Council, Thus Plc and the University of Cambridge. He created the Navigator Men's Development Programme and won acclaim for his work on the Metropolitan Police's 'gender agenda'. James was a Senior Consultant at Roffey Park from 2006–2010. Here he was recognised for his work in facilitation, action learning, cooperative inquiry and large scale interventions. He is a member of the new Ashridge Centre for Action Research and is a faculty member of the Ashridge Doctorate in Organisational Change. He completed his own PhD, researching masculinity in organisations, at the University of Bath in 2009.

Foreword

Linda Holbeche

This book is a timely contribution to Organisation Development (OD) practice literature. As a set of disciplines and a field of practice, OD has been around a long time and there is already a rich seam of (mainly US) literature on OD. So why is more needed? I would argue that there are several reasons why this book is not only needed but particularly relevant now.

Firstly, as Edgar Schein (2006) points out, much of what we now understand as aspects of OD practice, such as teamworking, has become so mainstream as to be invisible – and yet OD is still little understood, especially by leadership teams. Thus OD's broader 'game-changing' potential may be underestimated. And while much of the theory and practice continues to originate in the US, in Europe and elsewhere OD practice is evolving in its own vein to reflect local needs and different inspirations. This book seeks to not only demystify what OD is about but also to reflect some of the latest developments in OD thinking and practice outside the US.

Next it could be argued that OD's time has finally come. As we emerge from chronic economic crisis in the West, the ethics, role and purpose of business have come into question. In this context, OD becomes all the more vital for taking stock of what 'better' might look like and for building healthy and effective organisations. After all, the economic crisis has laid bare some of the economic and philosophical assumptions and values underpinning the current model of global capitalism – the ultimate instrumentalism and short-termism of market-driven practices which privilege the needs of shareholders over those of other stakeholders. With its humanistic values, OD provides a counter-flow and has the potential for sustainably transforming organisations for the better.

More generally, as organisations shift shape and as the nature of work evolves, so the OD agenda grows ever more important. In service- and knowledge-based industries in particular, people – their skill and goodwill – are the source of production, yet work contexts are often far from conducive to good work. Indeed it could be argued that the needs of business and those of employees are frequently in dynamic tension. After all, constant change and restructurings, neo-Fordist approaches to people management and technology used to make work flexible to the disadvantage of employees, can undermine employee well-being, 'engagement' and performance.

As a field of practice, OD is itself in flux and this book captures much of the spirit of contemporary debates. At one level OD focuses on improving the organisational system from within, for instance by diagnosing and addressing causes of employee disengagement or attempting to close the gap between intended strategy and actual implementation. Therefore OD has always been in the business of seeking 'solutions', usually by engaging people in the quest. Yet today there is a growing confluence of thinking about the importance of 'going upstream' to challenge the mindsets which produced the problems in the first place. This means working with leaders in particular, helping surface the questions that raise awareness and creating the basis of more informed choice.

OD's history, its many different roots and approaches, ranging from the classic planned change methodologies to today's preoccupation with the dialogic, are explored in the book. What shine through as consistent and distinctive about OD are its underpinning humanistic values. OD is thus at the intersection of countervailing (business) forces and (humanistic) value sets. This can often create dilemmas for OD practitioners such as whether to attempt to improve the system as part of the system or to be on the outside; whether to pursue more and better 'solutions' or to be agent provocateur to change the system.

The editors and contributors recognise the importance of practitioners developing the field by learning from and with each other. In providing different angles on OD practice, the book's contributors demonstrate the value of an experimental approach to intervening – ranging from the small-scale and individual to large-scale and whole system change; where the spur to intervention ranges from the opportunistic and serendipitous to the deliberate and strategic. Making a difference in these ways requires courage as well as insight. As thinking practitioners these authors illustrate how OD can help reset the organisational moral compass, enable constructive action in the here and now and create contexts where people can willingly and sustainably give of their best.

Reference

Schein, E. 2006. Foreword in Gallos, J.V. *Organization Development*. San Francisco, CA: Jossey-Bass.

Acknowledgements

The Editors and Contributors gratefully acknowledge the following people and organisations who have, in their different ways, provided support, encouragement, feedback, learning, practical assistance and inspiration.

In alphabetical order:

Ashridge Centre for Action Research
Julie Beedon
Anne-Marie Bell
Louis Bickler
Gabriel Bickler
Jane Brodrick
Anne Brookes
Mee-Yan Cheung Judge
Paul Cox
Glenda Eoyang
Jean Floodgate
Robert Gibson
Katie Hogg
Linda Holbeche
Sally Hulks
Carol Jefkins
Q5 Partners
Roffey Park Institute
Learning Resource staff at Roffey Park
Pip Rowson
Denise Smith of SABMiller
Ralph Stacey

Caroline Stearman
Martin West and the team at Gower

Clients, colleagues, students and programme participants, past and present, from whom we continue to learn so much.

> *Ubicumque homo est, ibi beneficio locus est.*
> [*Wherever there is a human being, there is the occasion for a kindness.*]

Lucius Annaeus Seneca

Introduction

A Note from the Editors

This book offers a variety of perspectives and experiences from a group of practitioners and researchers who all share an interest and involvement in Organisation Development (OD). You will find in it multiple voices, mindsets and practices – not all of which necessarily agree with each other. We like to think of it as a collection of essays from the field.

Why, you might ask, have we chosen to create an OD field guide in this way? Wouldn't it be clearer if we had offered something more cohesive? Well maybe, but we wanted to offer something that authentically reflects our own experience of the field of OD, and our sense is that this is anything but clear. OD, as a field, is messy, imperfect and hard to get hold of. As one of our clients recently said, it is like nailing jelly to the wall.

We don't necessarily regard that as a bad thing. It could be that it is in this very messiness that the power of OD can be found. After all, the vast majority of the challenges which twenty-first century organisations face are not resolved by simple, prescriptive solutions. We think that OD, with its fuzzy edges and its contradictions, can help.

So we have tried to give you a book that reflects OD as we experience it, but we also want you to have something that is useful and practical. Whether you are working in OD or in a line management role we hope this book will, if nothing else, encourage you to try out some of the specific suggestions offered in the various chapters. Making a start is, in our experience, the best way to get good at OD.

As editors, we have been very taken by the idea of OD as a field practised by 'ordinary heroes'. Clearly there is a place for deep, expert knowledge, but we think that what today's organisations need are better questions rather than the 'right' answers. This seems to fit well with an OD approach, with its emphasis on enquiry and its insistence that we always look at the context. ('It depends' is a good first answer to most OD questions. The next question, however, is where the real value is: 'on what does it depend?'.)

So instead of producing an exhaustive 'OD checklist', which, in our view, is an impossibility anyway, we have sought to introduce you to some 'ordinary heroes' who can help you get started and take some new actions in your organisations. In so doing, we hope also to have contributed to the ongoing debate about the future of OD, focusing in particular on what we see as distinctive in the thinking and practice of OD outside of North America.

Each chapter has been written to stand alone, so you can go where your interest takes you. In sequencing the chapters we have started with chapters that in various ways look at the history, mindset and role of OD (Chapters 1–3). We then move onto chapters on the realities of organisational life (Chapter 4), emergent approaches to consultancy and change (Chapter 5) and the art of using data skilfully (Chapter 6). Chapters 7–9 cover subjects that have impact across OD, such as team development, large group work and culture; the final chapters of the book (Chapters 10–12) look at OD approaches to large, complex change programmes, working with external OD consultants and the evaluation of impact.

To make the book 'yours', we would encourage you actively to seek out the connections between what you read and your own world. In other words, do bring your own specific questions to the book, based on your professional needs and agenda. You might also want to take note of which chapters speak to you and which ones challenge you most. There may be useful data here for you about your own practice.

Ultimately, it is our sincere hope that in engaging with the competing perspectives and approaches in this book, and adding your own questions to the mix, you will find a creative space in which you and other 'ordinary heroes' can perform extraordinary feats of growth, learning and development. OD is about finding ways to nurture the human spirit in organisations, while at the same time helping organisations to fulfil their core purpose. It is important work. We wish you well on your journey.

Ed Griffin, Mike Alsop, Martin Saville and Grahame Smith

1

What is Organisation Development? An Introduction to the Field

Ed Griffin

The motivation for writing this chapter has come from two key sources; my experiences of working with and developing practitioners, and my own beliefs about Organisation Development (OD). In particular, this can be characterised by:

- Noticing that senior leaders in organisations rarely refer to 'Organisation Development' or the abbreviation 'OD'.

- That describing ourselves as 'OD consultants' often required further explanation to clients.

- Seeing an increasing number of OD roles and departments emerging in many organisations in the UK.[1]

- Noticing an anxiety amongst many HR professionals about the need to know about, and be able to 'do OD'.

- Our personal beliefs that there has rarely been a time that organisations have a greater need to get the benefits of what we understand to be OD.

---

1 Specific references to the UK reflect a particular anxiety that seems to exist there about the meaning of OD and a perceived need in some organisations to have teams or roles with the OD label. This is not an anxiety we have noticed outside the UK.

These experiences have led me to write this first chapter to help students, practitioners and managers create a clearer understanding of the history, thinking and research behind the field of OD, in order that practice can be improved, and ultimately more organisations are able to become better places to work and more effective.

There can be few two-letter abbreviations in organisational life that have, in recent years, caused as much confusion, anxiety and turf warring as 'OD'.

These two letters are, of course, part of the reason for this book coming into being and the diverse range of contributors offering their, at times, differing perspectives on the implications and practices of this thing called 'Organisation Development'. Specifically, in this first chapter I will:

- start by providing my own definition and model of OD;

- explore the history and development of OD;

- present an overview of the practice of OD; and

- put the case for why a different approach to OD may be more relevant for these times and, in particular, for the UK.

A Working Definition of OD

In 2011, when running an introductory programme on OD, I spent time with participants exploring the questions they had about OD. These form a useful backdrop to define OD as they reflect the needs and concerns of practitioners who have an interest in OD.

- What are the most important things to know about OD?

- What are the 'principles' of OD?

- Do we need to be knowledgeable and skilful in everything? It's very daunting ...

- Does it help to be a good project manager when working in OD? What skills are most important?

- What personal skills should I hone to make me a more effective OD practitioner?

- What is the future of OD – why is it not a fad?

- How do you start to develop a strategy?

- How do you get started?

- How do we tailor and be industry specific?

- When is the time to change strategy if it doesn't work?

- Is there any difference between OD now and when it first started?

- What is good OD?

- How do we get other people excited about OD?

- How do we know when we have completed an OD intervention?

- How have we seen OD applied with great results?

- How do I prove, with tangible evidence, what difference OD can make?

- Where is the evidence that OD works?

- It's so far-reaching; can one function (HR) facilitate and lead effectively?

- Where does OD belong? HR/independent/other departments?

- Practically, what does it mean in different areas of a business – HR, Finance, IT, Technical management, Ops management, Production line operation?

- I am struggling with why you would have an 'OD' department – is it not a tool to help address change/implementation?

- How will OD fit into my organisation, i.e. which people/areas should be enacting it/accountable for it?

What was striking for me in hearing these questions was the reminder of just how challenging it could be for anyone wanting to learn about and practise OD, and how to know where to start. This reinforced a particular challenge that reflected my own experiences of the first time I had a job title that included 'OD' in it. As Organisation Development Manager I was responsible for a Total Quality Management programme, leading on market research, doing work on employee engagement, running leadership development programmes and getting involved in performance management. Every time I was asked what my job involved I struggled to give a clear simple message that explained *why* my role existed, rather than giving out a list of potentially unrelated activities.

In answering the question 'What is OD?', I have noticed from my work with OD practitioners, that OD may be used interchangeably to describe one or a number of the following:

- A discipline.

- A field of practice.

- A role.

- A function.

- A profession.

- A department.

Given the range and inconsistency of definitions in practice, it has been suggested that it may be more helpful to think about OD as a *field* rather than a discipline, and a *purpose* rather than a particular set of activities.

As a practitioner I now describe OD as:

> How an organisation develops and implements strategy with the full involvement/engagement of its people.

I have arrived at this simplified definition as a way of encapsulating that OD is about the longer-term performance of the organisation, it involves change because strategy implementation typically requires change of some kind, and it reflects a belief in people and the importance of their genuine involvement in the decisions and actions that impact the future of the organisation. Defined in this way, OD becomes the responsibility of everyone in the organisation, rather than a specific department or those in particular roles. I use the term strategy in the sense that Rumelt (2011) describes it:

> *a good strategy does more than urge us forward toward a goal or vision. A good strategy honestly acknowledges the challenges being faced and provides an approach to overcoming them. And the greater the challenge, the more a good strategy focuses and co-ordinates efforts to achieve a powerful competitive punch or problem-solving effect.*

This requires real attention being paid to what may be difficult and threatening, and not simply getting tied up in the excitement of a new corporate vision. I also see strategy as operating at every level of the organisation, from individual through to team, department division and whole organisation. Taking this view of strategy into account means that the work of OD can start from any level of the organisation and can be the responsibility of any individual in the organisation.

From the work we have done in running programmes and workshops on OD we have then developed a more detailed definition that reflects rather more of the history and development of OD. This definition breaks down into four key elements – a purpose, a philosophy, mindset and behaviours, and a field of practice. We make this distinction because we have noticed an inconsistency in what people are describing when they talk about OD. There is a risk that this inconsistency in using the letters 'OD' may diminish its credibility because it becomes confusing. Our detailed definition is as follows:

- As a *purpose*, OD is the intention to build sustainable successful organisations where people are truly valued.

- As a *philosophy*, OD is about a belief in the importance of growing organisational health, humanistic values, a reliance on behavioural sciences, basing your work on data and diagnosis.

- As *mindset and behaviours*, OD is about looking at the bigger picture – systems thinking, a belief in people, being opportunistic and systematic, being courageous, staying open-minded, being collaborative, having an improvement focus.

- As a *field of practice*, OD is about the use of a diverse range of tools, practices and approaches to enable sustained and sustainable organisational performance through the involvement and collaboration of the people in and around the organisation. This may include Large Group Interventions, Learning and Development activities and a focus on culture change.

'Classical' OD

Through this section I will compare some of the definitions that come from what could be described as the 'classical' school of OD. I see the classical school as deriving from those thinkers and practitioners that have strong links to the development of OD in the USA, particularly through the National Training Laboratory (NTL). (This connection is explained later in this chapter in the section 'Where does OD come from?') It is helpful to explore some of the different definitions of OD as it can help to explain assumptions that may lie behind the way different thinkers and practitioners use the 'OD' abbreviation. The reader may also find it helpful and inspiring to explore further some of the wider biographies of contributors to the field as this can create an understanding of what may have shaped the thinking and approach of key influencers.

One of the most widely used classical definitions of OD comes from Richard Beckhard (2006), it was originally used in the 1960s and is still used now when organisational life, organisations and the expectations of those in them have changed dramatically (of which more later). This is then followed by other definitions that come from a similar background or perspective. Our advice to anyone practising or wanting to practise in the field is to become more aware of the different ways that OD is described and to find a way of describing their OD work that is clear, consistent and helpful for those they engage with.

Beckhard's Definition – 'Organisation Development is an effort *planned, organisation-wide,* and *managed* from the *top,* to increase *organization effectiveness* and *health* through *planned interventions* in the organisation's 'processes', using *behavioral-science* knowledge'.

> *Organisation Development is a planned process of change in an organisations' culture through the utilization of behavioural science, research and theory. (Burke, 1982)*

> *Organisation development is a system-wide application of behavioural science knowledge to the planned development and reinforcement of organisational strategies, structures and processes for improving an organisation's effectiveness. (Cummings and Worley, 1997)*

I have focused on these three definitions as representing particularly influential thinkers/practitioners from the twentieth century. The themes that stand out as running through these definitions are the *planned* nature of the work of OD and the use of *behavioural science*. *Planned* is potentially paradoxical as it may suggest approaches that are more than conscious and reactive. In many organisational contexts *planned* comes to mean that this is work that can be controlled or project managed. This is in contrast to the experiences of many where OD efforts that seek to engage people often develop a life and momentum of their own that moves beyond the control of those at the top of an organisation and out of the reach of a Gantt chart.

In this context behavioural science can be thought of as the field of study that helps us understand human interaction, group dynamics, decision-making, leadership and other related topics.

A more current definition of OD comes from the Chartered Institute of Personnel and Development (CIPD). In the UK, the CIPD has played a significant role in increasing the interest in OD through the provision of training programmes, conferences, qualifications and the inclusion of OD in their HR professions map.

> *Organisation Development is about ensuring the organisation has a committed, 'fit for the future' workforce needed to deliver its strategic ambition. It plays a vital part in ensuring that the organisation culture, values and environment support and enhance organisation performance and adaptability. Provides insight and leadership on development and execution of any capability, cultural and change activities.*
>
> *Includes these topics:*
>
> - *OD strategy, planning and business case development.*
> - *Organisation capability assessment.*
> - *Culture assessment and development.*
> - *Organisation development intervention and development.*

- *Change management and communications.*
- *OD methodology.*
- *Project and programme management.*

What is significant about their definition is that the CIPD may also argue that HR should be the guardian of OD in the organisation. This is contrary to previous trends in the USA where the OD function was more likely to report into the CEO. In the CIPD's factsheet on OD, they state:

> *OD does not replace HR but it does draw heavily on many of the processes of HR. As a people and problem centred activity, it requires sophisticated people management skills and can enable HR to develop the deep organisational insight that is required if they are to fulfil their potential in terms of ensuring the people asset of the business are fully and most effectively utilised. Effective OD should also have the support and the involvement of senior executives and hence, if HR is not operating at the strategic level, it will be more difficult for them to implement OD interventions.*

I argue that for OD to be most effective, it needs to be seen as the work of everyone in the organisation and the responsibility of managers at all levels.

A current definition from someone with a very strong connection to the classical school of OD comes from Cheung-Judge and Holbeche (2011):

> *What? – A field of knowledge to guide the development of organisation effectiveness, especially during change.*
>
> *How? – Using group and human dynamic processes from applied behavioural science methods, research and theories to facilitate movements of groups and organisations.*
>
> *Outcome – To improve the health and effectiveness of organisations and people that work within them in a sustainable way.*
>
> *Values – Respect for human differences, commitments to all forms of social justice. Belief in lifelong learning – emphasis on 'self-renewal ability' of the individual and the organisation.*

What is distinctive here is the explicit reference to the values of OD that can be so key in informing how practice develops and, in particular, how one practitioner may see their work as 'being more OD than someone else's OD'. Often our values are not vocalised in organisational life but can frequently be the source of much conflict and contention.

In their recent study into the history and development of OD Garrow, Varney and Lloyd (2009) found that:

> there are a number of concepts which practitioners tell us are at the heart of OD:
>
> – *Change and the pursuit of organisational effectiveness.*
> – *An organisation-wide scope and a systemic approach.*
> – *Working in partnership.*
> – *Taking both a humanistic and a business-focused approach.*
> – *Being facilitative and challenging.*

What is, perhaps, most helpful about this is that rather than trying to define OD, they have described the characteristics of OD that are observed or experienced by practitioners in the field. That seems to be an approach very much aligned with one of the core humanistic values of OD, that of valuing and honouring the experience of the individual.

Where Does OD Come From?

Through this section I will look at some of the roots and sources that have, and are, shaping the theory and practice of OD. An understanding of this is helpful to the practitioner in making sense of the ways in which different people see and practise OD. It is also important to recognise that this is not a single conscious, unbroken line in the evolution of OD. The roots of OD are rather like copies of a jigsaw puzzle owned by many different people that appear at first glance to be the same, but on closer inspection may have some different pieces and be put together in different ways.

In exploring the history, sources and influences on OD thinking and practice, it would be quite easy to write an entire book. That is not our intention. The challenge comes in trying to identify what may be seen as legitimate sources for OD today and what constitutes 'proper' OD work. As a field of practice that draws from many places there may be some practices that seem at odds with the values of OD that we explored earlier.

Most recently Cheung-Judge and Holbeche (2011) identify five sources as the foundations of OD, these are:

- Systems theory – von Bertalanffy, Katz and Kahn.

- Action Research theories – Lewin.

- Change theories – Field theory, Group dynamics, Three step model of change – Lewin.

- Social constructionism: AI – Berger and Luckman.

- Complexity Theories – Stacey.

Burke (1982) identifies as sources:

- Sensitivity Training – linking NTL's development of T-groups and the Tavistock's human relations training.

- Socio-technical Systems – Trist and Bamforth at the Tavistock Institute – 'the premise that an organisation is simultaneously a social and a technical system'.

- Survey feedback – based on the work of Rensis Likert.

Burke then identifies three key groups of what he refers to as 'mini-theories' that have gone on to influence the development of the field of OD – individual perspective, T-group approach to change and the total system approach to change

Cummings and Worley (1997) identify 'Five Stems of OD Practice', these are:

- Laboratory Training – T-Groups, Lewin, NTL.

- Action Research/Survey Feedback – Lewin, Harwood Manufacturing Company.

- Participative Management – Rensis Likert.

- Quality of Work Life – Trist.

- Strategic Change – Beckhard's open system planning.

One of the strongest threads through all of these sources and influences is the work of Kurt Lewin. Many others have identified him as having great influence in Social Psychology, Sociology and clearly the same is true of his influence on OD. It is useful to understand a little of Lewin's life to appreciate how his work has impacted not only the practice of OD, but also the values that many practitioners hold dear. Lewin was brought up in a Jewish family in Germany and suffered the anti-Semitism that existed during the 1920s prior to the rise of the Nazis. He was forced to flee from Nazi Germany in 1933 and moved to the USA. It was here that his work started at MIT and then the establishment of NTL. Possibly at the root of much of his research and practice was the thought that his 'Jewishness was his own social problem, and it made him generally sensitive to social problems' Gold (1999).

Schein identified Process Consultation as underlying the 'broader concept of organisation development and is the key philosophical underpinning to organisation development' (Schein, 1988):

> PC is a set of activities on the part of the consultant that help the client to perceive, understand, and act upon the process events that occur in the client's environment in order to improve the situation as defined by the client. (Schein, 1988)

The focus on human processes in organisations represented a move away from the traditions of scientific management based particularly on the works of Taylor, Fayol and the emergence of Fordism, where the worker was seen as part of the machinery of the organisation that could be allocated and applied to specific tasks in ways that maximised output and efficiency. Schein highlights that the study of human process in organisations was rooted in the work of Lewin and subsequent developments at NTL.

The jigsaw represents one personal way of seeing some of the key influences and foundations of OD based upon my own experiences, learning and beliefs about OD. The references for each chapter provide a range of sources that will enable the reader to further explore in detail some of the key sources, thinkers and theories that have informed the development of OD over the years.

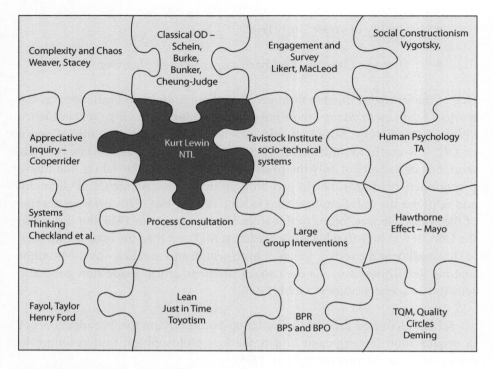

Figure 1.1   A 'jigsaw' of OD sources and history

How Do we Understand Organisations?

How you define and make sense of organisations may reveal much about the way in which OD has developed. Gareth Morgan (1996) provided different 'lenses' through which to view and understand organisations, ranging from machines to organisms. How we fundamentally view an organisation is likely to directly impact upon how we view OD and how, as practitioners, we will approach our work. It may highlight, too, our beliefs about employees and the values that we bring to bear as OD practitioners. Whilst there are still many organisations employing a traditional hierarchy, there seem to be many more organisations that have adopted more flexible matrix and networked structures that reflect the complexities of the world in which they operate. The relationships between businesses, their suppliers, their customers and employees continue to change and the boundaries around organisations have become less distinct.

There are many models and frameworks available to help make sense of what is happening in an organisation and what changes may need to be made.

For example, the Investors in People standard sets out desirable practices in the management and development of employees that could contribute to an organisation being more effective and successful. Another is the EFQM model that takes the traditions and practices of Total Quality Management and 'facilitates definition and prioritisation of improvement plans to achieve sustainable growth and enhanced performance'. There are a number of models that are strongly associated with the classical school of OD, for example, the Burke-Litwin model and Galbraith's STAR model.

More recently De Waal (2008) has identified the components of High Performance Organisations, highlighting the importance of Openness and Action Orientation, Management Quality, Continuous Improvement, Workforce Quality and Long-Term Orientation. These in turn can be broken down into individual components that can allow for the assessment of current performance and to identify areas to improve. In practice, what I notice is that different people and different organisations prefer different models. This is not a case of right or wrong; rather it highlights our potentially differing beliefs about what makes an effective organisation. This in turn may indicate the kind of actions that we take as OD practitioners. In the same way that a 'map is not the territory', the model is not the framework and it is only a tool to aid our understanding of the complexities of an organisation.

What is the Work of OD?

Through this section we will start to explore the practices, behaviours and approaches that typify the work of OD. Reading some definitions of OD may lead us to believe that OD work is only happening at the level of the whole organisation and if it is being managed top-down. For example, Jones and Brazzel (2006) state that certain forms of change or development interventions that focus on the performance of the individual should not be viewed as OD interventions.

In practice, what we see is that internal consultants may have narrowly defined responsibilities that, on their own, do not meet this description of what constitutes OD work. However, if the mindset and behaviours of that individual lead them to look for how the work they do can be connected or aligned with other work in the interests of developing the organisation, then I would argue that is exactly in line with the purpose of OD and worthy of being described as OD. It is my belief that one of the most important tools for an OD practitioner is the art of dialogue. Having deep, effective conversations vertically and horizontally in the organisation is a vital way of overcoming organisational politics and creating a collaborative and coherent approach to OD. From working with practitioners across many organisations it is clear that many feel they cannot do 'real' OD because their role does not have a whole system responsibility. It requires the practitioner to have an ambition for their organisation and the courage to look and work outside of the confines of their role.

It may be helpful to think of OD interventions in a number of different dimensions:

- Individual to whole organisation involvement – this concerns the scale of an intervention in terms of the numbers of people who are engaged in it, for example, coaching an organisational leader through to a Large Group Intervention involving all employees in developing strategy.

- Individual to whole organisation impact – this concerns the breadth and depth of impact that an intervention is designed to have, for example, giving feedback to a director through to a programme of organisation re-design.

- Spontaneous to Planned – the work of OD needs to happen both in the moment and in ways that are structured and organised. The discipline of an OD intervention is the intention behind it, i.e. that it will help in the development or delivery of strategy and do that in a way that is involving and enabling of sustained performance. For example, an unexpected conversation with a key person that encourages a different way of doing things through to the use of a Programme Office to manage a range of business projects.

- Human to Technological – this is about the style of the intervention and the extent to which it is based upon process (as defined by Schein earlier) or on the 'hard' components of organisations such as IT systems or supply chains. For example, an interpersonal skills training programme through to a Business Process Re-engineering exercise.

The challenging of defining OD interventions is that the list is potentially endless, as it could be any activity that can assist in the development or delivery of strategy in an involving way. The work of OD and specific interventions are described in detail in subsequent chapters.

Challenges for OD Today

It is helpful to examine the social and economic context in which organisations are operating and the challenges faced with new generations in the workplace. This can raise questions of the relevance of OD and how it may need to continue to change and develop. If organisations and the people in them are changing, does this also mean that OD has to change too? In recent years there has been a growing understanding of the potential impact/conflict caused by new and different generations entering the workforce, and their often very different expectations and needs. Today we also see looser boundaries around many organisations, often driven by the need for organisations to be more flexible and dynamic in response to their customers, suppliers and employees, as well as the need to take greater account of the environment in which an organisation operates.

As one OD director challenged, has the work of OD focused on group work partly because it has grown up with a more libertarian generation who believe that everyone should have the opportunity to have his or her voice heard? This was then overtaken by the Generation X folk who have been used to a rather more ruthless focus on cost-reduction and standardisation with approaches such as Business Process Re-engineering and outsourcing. And now we have the Net Generation and beyond, for whom waiting for an intervention may take too long as their comfort with Web 2.0 means that if they want to contribute, question or complain they do it immediately, they do it online and they tell others they've done it and that they should do it too!

A Simplified Approach to OD

As identified at the start of this chapter, it often seems that 'becoming' an OD practitioner is a daunting possibility with the potential need to *know* so much and *do* so many different things. It can also feel that there are many great people from the field of OD that should be honoured to do their traditions justice.

Today organisations are facing some very different challenges from those faced in the 1950s and 1960s when OD was starting to develop as a field.

The kind of organisations that existed in the period when OD was developing, and were the focus of early OD practices and research, were often manufacturing-based and hierarchically structured. Perhaps we are now facing challenges that require the work of OD more than at any point previously? The impact of the global credit crisis, the growth and impact of countries such as Brazil, India and China, greater instability in some sectors and countries suggest that we could benefit from greater thoughtfulness going into the management and planning of organisations, and the ways in which people are involved.

Based on how I defined OD I have described an approach to the *practice* of OD that I believe is simple, coherent and works at the level of the individual, team and whole organisation. This is in contrast with some of the history, underpinnings and practices of classical OD, without, I hope, criticising them.

So, if we start with the idea that OD is 'how an organisation develops and implements strategy with the full involvement/engagement of its people', we need to identify the approach that can enable this to occur. Given that the individual is the basic unit of any organisation, it seems logical to test any OD framework for how it can apply to individual employees as well as the groups that they are organised into to make teams, departments and whole organisations. I think it is also important to question whether OD can be delivered on an enduring basis for a whole organisation – one colleague talks about 'helping to light candles around and through the organisation', i.e. a more emergent and subtle approach than top-down driven.

From working across many sectors, different scales of organisations and different cultures, I have identified four components for a simpler approach to OD. These components or practices represent what I see as the 'essence' for building sustainably successful organisations that genuinely treat 'people as their greatest asset'. They are:

1.   Defining what 'Well-being' (Seligman, 2011) means for the whole organisation. This is more specific and tangible than the older concept of organisational health, and broader and deeper than traditional forms of business outcomes.

2.   Creating an enduring 'Space to Think' (Kline, 2010) for those who are part of, or who interact with, the organisations, e.g. employees, customers and suppliers.

3. Maintaining the means of connection, e.g. space, technology, time, commitment, etc. that allows people inside and outside of the organisation to sustain the dialogue that allows a 'Space to Think'.

4. Sustaining access to operational capability, i.e. ensuring that the means of delivering the work to be done, the products to be produced or services delivered is available inside the organisation or outsourced through contracted external parties.

These four components are described in more detail below, together with the examples of the questions that may need to be addressed.

ONE: WELL-BEING

Whilst Seligman's work has focused on defining well-being at an individual level, I believe it has the potential to help organisations define a condition that is more desirable and sustainable than simply focusing on profit, yield growth or similar measures. This is not to provide a watered-down vision for an organisation; rather it is to find a way of more deeply engaging people in the work of organisations. This also specifically helps to address issues of defining organisational health, something often referred to as an intention of the work of OD but is often not described in ways that are possible to measure and record.

Seligman defines well-being as:

- Positive Emotions – these are feelings that are often associated with pleasure and warmth. Team climate could be one direct way of assessing the emotional experience of employees. Many engagement surveys ask questions about the feelings of employees at work.

- Engagement – this is based on Csíkszentmihályi's (1997) identification of the experience of performing an activity when the level of challenge matches the top level of the individual's skill. In an organisational context this raises questions of how well people are matched with the demands of their roles and the importance of job design and selection processes.

- Relationships – Seligman identifies relationships as being an almost hard-wired requirement of the 'social brain' of us a species.

- Meaning – being part of something that has significance beyond our individual existence.

- Achievement – this is often the starting point in business planning and strategy development as it is how success is often defined or assessed.

At a whole organisation level, the route to defining Organisational Well-being may come through addressing:

- What do we need to achieve? This can encompass traditional organisational goals.

- What is important/meaningful about this?

- How effective are the relationships we have?

- What does it feel like to be engaged in/with this organisation?

- How do we support our people in working at the top end of their capability?

- How will we as leaders role model our own well-being?

TWO: 'SPACE TO THINK'

Nancy Kline defines ten factors that enable people to pay deep and real attention to each other. I believe this condition is critical because it is the most fundamental demonstration that people are valued and respected. It is also the way in which what is most important can be revealed. In organisational life truth is often obscured by fear, corporate KPIs, jargon, or perhaps market research that is designed to deliver only certain answers.

Kline identifies ten factors that enable the creation of a Space to Think. These are:

- Attention – listening with respect, interest and fascination.

- Incisive Questions – removing assumptions that limit ideas.

- Equality – treating each other as thinking peers.

- Appreciation – practising a 5:1 ratio of appreciation to criticism.

- Ease – offering freedom from rush or urgency.

- Encouragement – moving beyond competition.

- Feelings – allowing sufficient emotional release to restore thinking.

- Information – providing a full and accurate picture of reality.

- Place – creating a physical environment that says back to people, 'You matter'.

- Diversity – adding quality because of the difference between us.

At an individual level, I think this is about the willingness to give deep attention and to treat with respect everyone that we come into contact with. With these values and this behaviour demonstrated individually there is the potential for a feeling in others of being more deeply appreciated. This seems to lead to greater levels of trust and a willingness to speak openly. All too often the realities of organisational life are not understood or communicated at senior levels because of the fear of delivering 'bad news'.

At a team level, this will be most apparent in the nature of team meetings and the extent to which everyone is given the opportunity and encouragement to contribute. A deeper level of attention within teams may encourage team members to be more appreciative of diversity and difference, and to take the time to understand and be prepared to think and act differently.

At a whole organisation level this may be engendered by the behaviour of managers at every level, the way in which corporate communications are managed and the practices associated with employee engagement. It seems plausible that organisations that adopt this approach may be more likely to spot opportunities and notice the threats or changes that face them. Perhaps it is this kind of approach that enables what Collins (2001) described as the 'Stockdale Paradox', the ability and willingness to face the stark realities facing your organisation, and yet never give up the belief that things can be better.

To enable the development of 'Space to Think' may require people asking themselves and each other:

- How do we enable our employees, customers, suppliers and partners to have an enduring voice?

- How do we pay deep attention to those voices?

- What kind of leadership behaviour do we need for a thinking culture to develop and thrive?

THREE: MAINTAINING THE MEANS OF CONNECTION

In order for organisations to work effectively it is critical that the means are available for people to connect inside and outside the organisation. Technology risks giving us the illusion of being able to be constantly in touch and yet at the same time employees in many organisations refer to the tyranny of mobile telecommunications. This is also about addressing the more obvious issues of working across different locations and time zones.

The fundamental question to explore here is what needs to be in place to enable us to engage with employees, customers, suppliers and partners on an ongoing basis?

FOUR: ACCESS TO OPERATIONAL CAPABILITY

To fulfil its purpose any organisation will need to perform certain key functions that may range from the extraction of raw materials to the production of products or the delivery of services. Whatever those functions are, the organisation will need to ensure that it has secure access to them either because it owns that capability or it has a robust and secure supplier relationship to deliver it on its behalf.

Operational capability needs to reside at every level of the organisation to ensure effective delivery:

- The individual employee able to carry out the tasks required of their job.

- The team or department that delivers a key function for the organisation.

- The organisation as a whole able to fulfil its purpose through its most basic functioning.

To develop in this area organisations need to be clear about the systems, process or tools needed to deliver on organisational purpose and to the level that organisational goals and objectives require.

What Does This Approach Require of Those Working in the Field of OD?

These four components do not immediately offer a prescriptive process to be followed for OD work, nor do they define a set of standard interventions to be utilised. Rather, they identify a combination of commitments to a way of working together and focusing attention on what matters most to the people of an organisation. This seems to be consistent with much of the work of OD; a strongly held belief that a particular approach can yield extraordinary benefits. My own experience in organisations and in working with other practitioners is that there is rarely a time that an OD approach is adopted by an organisation and used comprehensively for a sustained period of time. It seems to be used more in periods where transformation is needed or there is a particular need to bring most of the constituents of an organisation together.

My aspiration is that those practising in OD and seeking to develop themselves and others, do so with a deep understanding and connection with their own values and beliefs that do so much to shape our practice.

As individuals we need to honestly ask ourselves:

- How effectively and consistently do I pay attention to other human beings?

- Do I understand and practise well-being for myself?

- How do I stay connected and committed to those I work with and for?

- Do I have the operational capability to deliver in my role?

References

Beckhard, R., 2006. *Organization Development – a Jossey-Bass Reader*. San Francisco, CA: Jossey-Bass.

Browning, G. and Worman, D., 2008, *Gen Up – How the Four Generations Work*. London: Chartered Institute of Personnel and Development.

Burke, W., 1982. *Organization Development: Principles & Practices*. New York, NY: Little, Brown & Co.

Cheung-Judge, M.Y. and Holbeche, L., 2011. *Organization Development – a Practitioner's Guide for OD and HR*. London: Kogan Page.

Chartered Institute of Personnel and Development OD factsheet. Available at: http://www.cipd.co.uk/hr-resources/factsheets/organisation-development. aspx

Chartered Institute of Personnel and Development Professions Map. Available at: http://www.cipd.co.uk/cipd-hr-profession/hr-profession-map/ professional-areas/organisation-development.aspx

Collins, J., 2001. *Good to Great*. London: William Collins.

Csíkszentmihályi, M., 1997. *Finding Flow*. New York, NY: Basic Books.

Cummings, T.G. and Worley, C.G., 1997. *Organization Development & Change*. Stamford, CT: Cengage Learning.

De Waal, A., 2008. *The Secret of High Performance Organisations*. Available at: http://www.andredewaal.eu/pdf2008/MORE2008.pdf

Garrow, V., Varney, S. and Lloyd, C., 2009. *Fish or Bird? Perspectives on Organisational Development (OD)*, Research Report 463. Brighton: Institute for Employment Studies.

Gold, M., 1999. *A Kurt Lewin Reader – The Complete Social Scientist*, Washington, DC: American Psychological Society.

Investors in People, 2013. Homepage. Available at: http://www.investors inpeople.co.uk

Jones, B. and Brazzel, M., 2006. *The NTL Handbook of Organization Development and Change: Principles, Practices & Perspectives Unknown*. Hoboken, NJ: John Wiley & Sons.

Kline, N., 2010. *Time to Think*. London: Ward Lock.

Morgan, G., 1996. *Images of Organization*. Thousand Oaks, CA: Sage.

Rumelt, R.P., 2011. *Good Strategy Bad Strategy*. London: Profile Books.

Schein, E.H., 1988. *Process Consultation Vol. I*, Addison-Wesley OD Series.

Seligman, M., 2011. *Flourish*. London: Nicholas Brealey Publishing.

Wikipedia. Map-Territory Relation. Available at: http://en.wikipedia.org/wiki/ Map–territory_relation#.22The_map_is_not_the_territory.22

2

HR and Organisation Development: A Match Made in Heaven or the Odd Couple?

Angela Baron

The concept of Organisation Development (OD) is relatively intangible, therefore getting across what it's about can be difficult and as a result some HR practitioners have been slow to fully realise its potential. OD should be about developing organisational capability that involves reviewing behaviours, business processes and structures to inform and influence future strategic requirements and as such provides a useful vehicle to ensure people management is embedded in organisational strategy.

Introduction

OD has been around for 50 years or more but for much of that time was viewed by HR professionals as some kind of mystical science one step removed from the operational reality of ensuring people were managed and motivated to deliver the needs of the business. It was often seen as an external resource to be brought in to manage one-off change interventions rather than a core part of people management and there was a sharp distinction between the role of the HR professional and that of the OD consultant.

But in recent years the HR profession has made efforts to get close to OD as organisations and indeed people management becomes ever more complex with an increased need to gather, analyse and use data to inform both what actions need to be taken to drive change and to assess the impact of the actions themselves to develop the most effective model of people management.

One of the reasons for this is the accelerating pace of change in all aspects of business life not least of which is the expectations and aspirations of workers about how they will be managed and motivated. Added to this, cost pressures, particularly in the public sector, are causing many organisations to redefine and refocus their business model and look at how they can deliver in a more effective and efficient way. All this means that HR professionals need better understanding of the context in which their organisation operates, of what drives value for the organisation and how they can respond with appropriate people management practice, which will trigger performance through people.

As a result the essential elements of OD, data generation to inform planned action and change, have become increasingly attractive tools in all areas of management, particularly HR. Its behavioural approach with a focus on people and organisational effectiveness, is increasingly putting OD tools and techniques in the spotlight as HR people look for ways to both develop their own strategic awareness and demonstrate and maximise the contribution of people to the business.

This chapter will look at the evolving relationship between HR and OD, how the two disciplines work together, and how HR practitioners are both using OD as a tool to drive effective people management and manage change. It will consider the role of OD specialists and other disciplines and how they interact with HR professionals to put together effective OD solutions.

Evolution of OD and HR

Human Resource Management and OD have very different histories. HRM began in the early twentieth century as a transactional function focused on administering all aspects of the employment cycle from recruitment to retirement. In the 1970s and 1980s the function was focused on managing industrial relations and as such took on a negotiation role. However, this role was largely negated by legislation limiting the power of the unions and from the 80s onwards the HR profession has been struggling to redefine its role in terms of adding value through people rather than maintaining operations.

During this time we have seen the development of new models of HR, not least of which is the Bath People and Performance model (Purcell et al., 2003), which demonstrates how HR adds value through enabling people to perform by providing them with ability, motivation and opportunity to perform through the development and implementation of HR practice. We have also seen the devolution of much of the transactional element of HR to line managers, who are increasingly responsible for implementing practices to recruit talent, manage performance and identify development needs.

Increasing use of technology has also transformed HRM enabling much of the administrative element of HR to be delivered through dedicated software programmes or even outsourced either externally or to in-house shared service centres. This, many practitioners argue, frees them to concentrate on the strategic aspects of HRM to become a valued participant in determining the strategy and effective operation of the organisation. The evidence does indeed suggest this may be the case. The Martell and Carroll study (1995) of 115 subsidiaries of Fortune 500 companies found that a majority had integrated HRM and strategic planning systems, discussed HRM issues in strategic plans and recognised the role of HRM in implementing business strategies.

OD has a shorter history rooted in behavioural science, psychological concepts, and social and human values related to openness, trust and harmony. Typically OD practitioners 'intervene' to address an organisational issue, problem, or opportunity, often as process consultants.

The history of the two disciplines suggests different agendas – personnel management (later becoming HR) concerned with the technicalities of the employment cycle, compliance, legal constraints, and getting the right skills in the right place at the right time. And OD concerned with understanding and managing organisational change through a focus on behaviour and analysis of information.

OD and HR Coming Together?

One of the outcomes of HR taking a more strategic role is that it is now increasingly common to find HR people taking on responsibility for OD-type interventions or approaches to manage their organisations effectively. There are a number of factors that are contributing to the growing use of OD by HR people. The first is the recognition that people management reliant on process can no longer serve the needs of the twenty-first century organisation, which demands flexibility and agility to change direction in response to the myriad of factors which are impacting on them. Increasingly there is a need for people management to operate in a context of a values-driven culture where innovative, forward-looking behaviour is valued and processes put under constant scrutiny and review. Ed Griffin and Grahame Smith (2010) writing in *Strategic HR Review* argue that in challenging economic times OD can provide HR with the appropriate tools to take a longer-term focus and involve employees in the change process.

The Chartered Institute of Personnel and Development (CIPD) have embraced the concept of OD in their map for the HR profession which describes HR leaders as providing insight and leadership in cultural and change activities. Their work investigating the evolution of the HR role (CIPD, 2010) describes HR as becoming insight 'driven' which is described as:

> *The translation of a fresh understanding of the organisation into creative and relevant solutions in the areas that matter most.*

It is no surprise then to find many ambitious HR professionals anxious to add value in their organisations seeking to develop OD skills. Equally it is no surprise that the value of such skills to organisations is rising as they seek to steer their way through continuous change whilst trying to build their capability to sustain performance into the future.

With the adoption of the business partner model of HR delivery and human capital management thinking, HR has shifted towards a more analytical approach to people management. HR people have had to become increasing skilled at collecting, analysing and acting on information – a traditional description of OD – particularly to inform management action around engagement and performance of individuals.

In addition the increasing complexity of organisational life is putting more and more pressures on organisations, which might impact upon their performance. Many of these pressures require a greater degree of understanding and the ability to interpret complex data and they include:

1.   Employment trends: the push for 24/7 service and more flexible working patterns requiring more sophisticated rostering and resource planning.

2.   Availability of skills, and other structural changes in the labour market such as the influx of migrant workers and an ageing workforce requiring better talent planning and forecasting.

3.   The drive for more social responsibility from organisations and the demand from employees and customers that they behave ethically and fairly requiring impact analysis on a range of environmental factors.

4.   Technological advances driving new products and new ways of working requiring scenario planning and constant scanning of business horizons.

5.   Customer expectations for better and cheaper products requiring constant reviews of price, quality and innovation.

6.   Business education encouraging managers to be coordinators more than controllers, and cultivators of individuals rather than commanders of 'followers' requiring a new set of skills around the understanding of individual needs and aspirations.

These trends require the skills to help people through rapid and continuous change, involving new behaviours, cultures and social norms. As a result whereas OD has commonly been seen as the preserve of the one-off change initiative it is now increasingly becoming embedded into everyday actions which require constant review, analysis and feedback that can be acted on for continuous improvement.

This has significant implications for HR who still need to manage the operational or transactional elements of contract and compliance whilst recognising the transformational nature of these trends and the impact for behaviour. This is requiring a whole set of new skills to be embedded alongside the existing knowledge and expertise associated with the day-to-day activities of acquiring, developing and managing people.

Practitioners generally see OD as being about developing organisational capability and therefore the exact nature of the OD/HR working relationship would depend on the context and requirements of individual organisations. However, this would usually involve identifying relevant positive behaviours, business processes and organisational structures needed to deliver future strategic requirements and informing the actions required to deliver these. As a result OD practitioners might evolve from a variety of backgrounds including project management and IT where they might gain a useful understanding of process, and OD might well be delivered by a cohort of individuals from different disciplines working together to share their specific skills to drive change. In truth it matters little to the organisation what function is delivering OD as long as it is generating insights that can make a difference to long-term organisational effectiveness.

How Does OD Add Value?

The measurement of OD is dealt with in another chapter but evaluating the contribution of people and the impact of HR are both concepts preoccupying HR practitioners and demonstrating added value is essential for the credibility of both OD and HR. A 2009 Roffey Park research report, *Best Practice in OD Evaluation,* by Liz Finney and Carol Jenkins opens with the words:

> We approached our research aware that there are many practitioners in the field of OD who believe that its systemic nature makes it hard to measure.

However, they go on to argue that the discipline will lose credibility if its effectiveness can't be demonstrated. As organisations struggle to remain ahead of the game, it's important that they have the right information to enable them to decide what strategies will work best for them and how they can leverage the best value from all their resources particularly their people resources. It therefore becomes imperative that they have better understanding of how value is created. In 2003, the UK's Accounting for People Task Force reported on:

> The widespread need for better Human Capital Management (HCM) reporting. [Because] we believe that greater transparency on how value is created through effective people policies and practices will benefit organisations and their stakeholders.

In the seven years since this report was published, HR have got a lot better at identifying and introducing strategic HCM metrics as well as continuing to monitor the more standard operational ones such as turnover, absence, retention and accidents rates. This has been driven by the need to answer questions such as:

1.   What would be the impact on the business if the executive team was able to use human capital measures to significantly increase their strategic decision-making capability?

2.   Are the people measures supporting the achievement of each of
      your business's key strategies?

3.   How does your workforce become a key strategic differentiator for
      you?

The point being that the most important metrics are those that match the
business objectives. The key is for HR to work closely with senior management
to understand those objectives, devise strategies for HR to help deliver them,
and then measure how well it achieves those objectives, which starts to bring
them into the territory of collecting and analysing information to develop
insights to drive the business.

The ability of HR to collect and analyse good-quality, meaningful data
has increased rapidly in recent years and work on human capital by Baron
and Armstrong (2007) suggests there is now a much greater degree of comfort
among practitioners with handling data to demonstrate impact and inform on
action. Many practitioners have been actively collecting and reporting human
capital data for several years and are finding greater internal appetite for
information that can inform on key performance indicators.

HR people have access to a range of measures and data that can help them
to build the case for OD interventions, the impact of which might be described
in people management terms such as improved engagement, readiness for
change or increased capability. Although care needs to be taken as to the actual
measures chosen to ensure they adequately reflect the context and business
needs of organisations, communication and explanation is the key to ensuring
measures are really informing on outcomes.

OD and HR in Partnership

All of the available evidence both from research and practical experience
suggests that there are many management models where OD is making a
valuable contribution to organisational success. In relation to HR, the business
partner model of HR delivery puts the emphasis on practitioners working in
partnership with line managers to review and analyse processes and behaviour
where clearly they need a developed understanding of the full range of issues
that might be impacting.

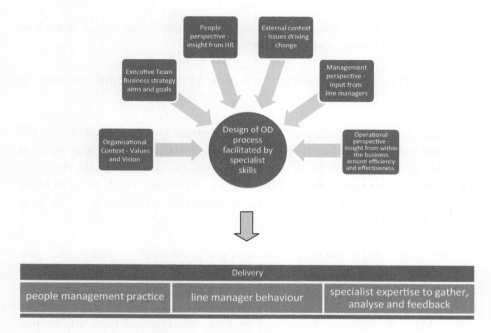

Figure 2.1   OD design and delivery model

It is questionable, therefore, that there will ever be a strong case for OD to be subsumed within HR departments as some elements of the HR profession have suggested. There is a much stronger argument for a multi-disciplinary approach to OD where people from all parts of the organisation input into the design and implementation of OD either to drive change or deliver insights to inform strategy. In practice many practitioners across OD and HR identify with this approach which they find attractive because it ensures that change is led from the executive board and draws upon all the expertise available across the organisation. Such a model of OD design and delivery might look something like Figure 2.1 above.

In this model the HR role in delivering OD is multi-faceted. It stresses the importance of OD reaching into all parts of the business whilst remaining a people and behaviour centred approach. The model could make use of external specialist expertise to facilitate the design and delivery of OD but alternatively could draw upon internal skills from HR/OD and other functions possessing systems, IT or programme management experience. In this model it would be wrong to compartmentalise or functionalise OD and HR. OD is about taking the organisation forward in a strategic direction and therefore is by default an executive-led function. Any member of the executive board could act as an OD consultant. As you drill down into practice then individual functions need to adopt the appropriate behaviour to make it work but ultimately OD is the responsibility of everyone in the business.

Combine HR and OD Strengths to Leverage Performance

It would be naïve to suggest that all HR departments or indeed practitioners can rebadge themselves as OD specialists. Whilst there are many parallels a more positive approach is to combine the strengths of both disciplines in a way that delivers the best interventions to leverage performance.

A simple model of OD and HR working together put forward by some parts of the literature is that successful OD is underpinned by positive and proactive HR practices and that HR deals with the day-to-day activities of managing whilst OD takes a more long-term and hence strategic view. In reality new forms of HR delivery such as business partnering and greater involvement of line managers in people management are blurring the boundaries and it is increasingly difficult to see where HR stops and OD begins.

Many of the insights generated from this work suggest that the relationship is much more complex with HR needing to maintain an appropriate balance between the operational requirements of the business such as rigorous management of resources in difficult times with the strategic intent such as developing organisational agility to enable the organisation to keep moving, changing and adapting.

A more positive approach may be to design a relationship which plays to the relative strengths of both disciplines to identify a new set of skills. These strengths, as discussed in the literature, can be found in Table 2.1.

If we are indeed moving out of a phase where the emphasis in organisations has been on transactional leadership into a phase of transformational business where people need to get much more deeply engaged with helping the business achieve its long-term strategic priorities, then clearly both HR and OD need to play to their strengths to come together to deliver this. Many HR practitioners are therefore finding the OD working model of change management an attractive antidote to the past over-reliance of HR on a process-driven approach.

Table 2.1   HR and OD strengths

HR Strengths	OD Strengths
Business partner model integrates HR across the business.	Future focussed.
Ability to collection analyse and understand people data.	Able to take a 'whole organisation' view.
Influencing and negotiating.	External OD consultants have more freedom to challenge the status quo.
Maintaining robust systems and processes.	Is not necessarily constrained by the need to maintain operational business requirements.
Ability to use insight to drive action through people directly focussed on performance.	Diagnosing and initiating change requirements and actions.

Conclusion

There is little doubt that OD and HR have grown closer together in recent years with many HR professionals looking to OD tools to generate the kind of insight and understanding necessary to manage people through turbulent times and build a first-class people management function. This shift has been driven by the steadily mounting pool of evidence concluding that if HR is to equip itself to become an insight-driven function, offering a proactive response to business intelligence, real understanding of business need and with a good grasp of the drivers and levers of sustainable performance it needs to become better and better at generating, analysing and enabling action from data.

Leveraging the strengths of OD and HR to come together in partnership with line managers and business leaders potentially paves the path to driving sustainable organisation performance. However, there are some issues around how this relationship might work in practice with a number of different approaches being used at present. What would work best for individual organisations would be determined by organisational context, external factors driving the need for change and the delivery model of HR.

References

Baron, A. and Armstrong, M., 2007. *Human Capital Management: Achieving Added Value Through People.* London: Kogan Page.

BIS, 2003. *Accounting for People Task Force Report.* Available at: http://www.bis. gov.uk/files/file38839.pdf

Chartered Institute of Personnel and Development (CIPD), 2011. *Next Generation HR Insight Driven*. London: Chartered Institute of Personnel and Development.

Finney, L. and Jenkins, C., 2009. *Best Practice in OD Evaluation*. Horsham: Roffey Park.

Griffin, E. and Smith, G., 2010. Recession: A shot in the arm for HR. *Strategic HR Review*, 9(1), pp. 17–22.

Martell, K. and Carroll, S.J., 1995, How Strategic is HRM?, *Human Resource Management*, 34(2), pp. 253–67.

Purcell, J., Kinnie, N., Hutchinson, S., Rayton, B. and Swart, J., 2003. *Understanding the People and Performance Link: Unlocking the Black Box*. London: CIPD.

3

The Practitioner at the Heart of OD: The Role of the Individual

Martin Saville

Introduction

As Chapter 1 makes clear, OD is not really a professional field of activities. It's more like a philosophy and mindset – a way of viewing the world. In fact it seems to me that OD is not actually defined by a set of activities at all. Let me illustrate the point.

> I was working with the UK National Health Service (NHS), consulting to over 20 people from different NHS organisations. All of these people were involved with OD, but none of them had the same jobs. Some were in HR, others in leadership development. Another ran the Improvement team, responsible for introducing LEAN, a methodology designed to streamline their hospital's processes. Someone else was responsible for infection control. Someone else still was responsible for helping demonstrate that their organisation deserved to become a 'Foundation Trust'. There was nothing that all these activities had in common in terms of the job role.

If there was no single activity that united all these people, what was it that made them OD practitioners?[1] My view is that the essence of OD is not to be found in 'things people do'. Rather, I believe the answer lies in the mindset of the practitioner. For example, most seasoned OD people would say that OD is defined by ideas such as:

---

1   Note that in this chapter I use the terms 'OD practitioner', 'OD consultant' and 'OD person' interchangeably to mean anyone involved in an OD role.

- A whole-systems mindset: looking at the *relationship* between the parts of an organisational system not just at the parts themselves.

- An open systems orientation: paying attention to the 'big picture' and to the relationship between an organisation and its environment.

- A focus on human dynamics and processes.

- An emphasis on humanistic values, such as participative decision-making and helping organisations become more self-sustaining.

- A curiosity around organisational patterns.

If we look again at what my NHS people do in light of the bullet points above, then they do start to have something in common. For example, the work they do benefits greatly from a whole-systems mindset. They will most likely succeed by engaging with human dynamics and helping their organisations become more self-sustaining. Viewed in this light, all the people on my list are indeed OD people, but only because they were thinking about their roles in an 'OD way'.

OD is All in the Mindset

So by this definition, we are 'doing OD' if we think about our role or project in an 'OD way'. Consider then the task of putting in place a new performance management system. Is this OD? According to my definition, it depends on how we think about it. One approach is to see the task as a technical job needing to be 'done right'. This would lead us simply to focus on implementing an excellent performance management system as effectively and efficiently as possible. There is nothing wrong with this, but it is not OD because there is no whole-systems outlook.

On the other hand, we could think about this new performance management system as an opportunity for a wider conversation. We could start engaging the organisation around what is needed for future success; this could lead us into discussions around strategy, leadership and culture. We could then design the performance management system in light of these discussions. This is what I mean by thinking about a role in an 'OD way'.

We can go further: the new performance management project might be an opportunity to foster and embed new, desirable cultural values. Imagine, for example, that the organisation's leadership wants a more participative culture. In such a culture, power is shared widely and people are trusted to make decisions. This implies a different attitude to information sharing, accountability, risk, failure and learning. An OD approach would see the performance management project as an opportunity to practise and reinforce this culture of the future. The way in which the project is designed, people are consulted and so on, could all support the new cultural values. At this point, the project (and its success criteria) stops being just about performance management and starts developing the organisation much more broadly. That is OD.

By this definition, virtually any activity or project can be OD. For example, a person who is a Management Accountant can also be an OD person if they think about their role in an OD way. Indeed, many OD practitioners believe that in an ideal world, no OD team should be needed in an organisation because the values and mindset of OD are so strongly embedded that specific OD input is unnecessary.

Local, Timely and Specific OD

From what has been said so far, it follows that OD will look very different depending on the organisational context, and the role and experience of the practitioner. Part of the function of OD people is constantly to ask the question: 'What does OD in our organisation need to look like now?'. It is the answer to this question, carefully thought through in light of the wider context, which underpins an organisation's OD strategy. This explains why OD looks so different across different organisational settings.

One implication of this is that OD, as a set of activities, will always be local, timely and specific to its context, rather than general and universal. Not only will OD vary from organisation to organisation, but it will vary in the same organisation over time as things change. This focus on context is very much part of the OD mindset.

This explains why OD is sometimes regarded as slippery and opaque, a reputation which can be challenging to practitioners. There are a number of different ways to respond: some OD teams make skilful use of the ambiguity, building a brand for themselves as 'useful people who make things work better'. Others develop a very clear OD strategy grounded in the organisational context. They then engage their stakeholders in focused communications around this. Choosing how to position OD to the organisation is a critical role for internal OD people and calls for an astute assessment of the wider context.

OD Practitioners Work with the Mindsets of Others

We have seen that OD is defined by the mindset of the people who practise it. In my experience, effective practitioners also engage with the various mindsets and 'mental models' of their clients and stakeholders. Whatever OD looks like in a given context, its practitioners are often helping their clients 'loosen their grip' on their own particular way of seeing things. This enables them to get alongside the perspectives of others and create a shared mindset that takes in the multiple perspectives of all concerned. It is this that enables teams, groups and whole organisations to move forward together. Consider this example.

My consultancy, Mayvin, was working with the UK Board of a successful global manufacturing organisation. The company operated in a dynamic sector of the Fast Moving Consumer Goods (FMCG) market. They were looking at whether to invest millions of pounds in a new manufacturing plant and the decision was proving tough. To recommend a 'go' decision the Operations Director required multi-year customer projections. The Sales Director was not willing even to predict demand for the company's product next month, let alone in several years' time. The relationship between these two directors was particularly challenging. Although polite and cooperative in meetings, privately each blamed the other for the Board's inability to decide on the new factory. Faced with this situation, the Chief Executive found himself acting as an 'honest broker' stuck between his colleagues, both of whom he regarded as central to his organisation's success.

The OD work needed here was to support each of these competent, successful people (and those around them) in seeing the situation differently. People needed to loosen their grip on their own mindsets and start creating a new, jointly-owned mindset. Having spent time with the key players individually, we organised a day-long strategy session in which we started by looking at the environment in which this company was operating. We then facilitated a conversation, helping people to talk increasingly openly and honestly with each other. This enabled them to see each other as multi-dimensional, real human beings rather than objectified and hostile caricatures.[2] They began to see that their difficulties were caused by the unpredictable nature of the world rather than in terms of the incompetence of others. This process of making sense of things together enabled the Board to generate ideas that no one person would have thought of alone. It started with helping the various actors to enquire into each other's mindsets.

OD Practitioners Work with Their Own Mindsets

In the example above, the OD work was about engaging with the mindsets of others. Accomplished practitioners also work with their own mindsets. We have already seen that they bring a systemic mindset, a focus on values and human dynamics. These elements of organisational life tend to be invisible to busy, pragmatic leaders and managers orientated towards getting things done. By drawing attention to these unseen but vital aspects of organisational life, the OD practitioner makes it possible for them to be considered and included in decisions. This connects to the concept (from the philosopher Martin Heidegger) of 'transparency'. We might say that certain aspects of organisational life are transparent (i.e. invisible) until the OD practitioner draws attention to them.

In general terms, therefore, the 'OD mindset' is useful in helping decision-makers see things they may have missed. However, the specific mindset of individual practitioners is also important. For example, some people, because of their life experiences or personality, may be particularly sensitive to issues around inclusion of diverse points of view. Others may be particularly sensitive to issues around emotional intelligence and relationships and so on. The other side to this is that individuals may have particular areas of over-sensitivity and bias. Of course OD people are no different from anyone else in this regard; however, experienced practitioners are sufficiently self-aware to make productive use of this in their practice. They do this both by drawing attention to things that others may have missed, and by helping groups become more aware of their own areas of sensitivity, blind spots and biases. Consider the following example.

> I was working with a senior team in a local government organisation. We had spent several hours thinking through their future strategy in light of major changes in the environment. We then turned our attention to leadership. 'What

---

2   The relationship moved from what the philosopher Martin Buber would have called 'I/It' towards 'I/Thou'.

kind of leadership style and culture is going to be needed to deliver this strategy?' I asked. The answer came quickly and clearly: one in which power was shared, and appropriate risk-taking encouraged and supported. A shift was needed to an 'enabling culture of empowerment', rather than one of 'command and control'.

By this time, I had been working with the organisation for some time, and had noticed a pattern: whenever I asked a question of a group, the most senior person in the room always answered it. This happened whether or not they were best placed to give the answer. That answer was then rarely challenged. I decided to take a risk and point this out to the group. Had they noticed this pattern before? There was a long moment of silence, followed by laughter. No they hadn't noticed it (at least not explicitly), but now that I'd mentioned it, they could see my point. This led to a useful conversation about how this team could start to model a different style of leadership.

The point here is that because of the kind of OD practitioner I am, I was particularly sensitive to the issue of whose voice was heard. In the example above, I was able to use this sensitivity to help my client. Over time, I was also able to support individual members of that team to become more aware of their own sensitivities and mindsets, and where these could be put to productive use on behalf of the group.

There have, however, been times when I have assigned more importance to whose voice is heard than the situation warranted. In such situations, my sensitivity became more of a bias. As I have grown as a practitioner, I have developed my self-awareness and have learned better to calibrate when this aspect of my mindset is serving me and when it is getting in the way.

As well as noticing what others miss, there are a number of other ways in which OD practitioners can use their own mindsets to serve their clients.

SPOTTING PATTERNS

In the example above I offered feedback to the client group on a particular pattern of behaviour. This pattern was not restricted to the one group. It was discernible all over the organisation, implying it was an aspect of the culture. See Chapter 9 for more on culture.

Everyone could see it as soon as it was pointed out. Such patterns in organisations are always there to be noticed. Other common examples include a habit of leaving things incomplete, avoiding difficult conversations or a tendency for top leaders to suck up too much responsibility. More positive examples include a commitment to the organisational mission, a willingness to help other colleagues and a desire to do the right thing. An interest in repeating patterns, positive and negative, is a hallmark of the OD mindset. OD practitioners help their clients to see these patterns, allowing them to deliberately accentuate the helpful ones and damp down the destructive ones. (See Chapter 5 for more on the importance of patterns in OD.)

EMBODYING AND STANDING FOR SOMETHING DIFFERENT

As well as shaping the way we see the world, our mindset also shapes the way we 'show up' in the world and the impact we have on others. Continuing with the example of the local authority, we have seen that my particular sensitivity to whose voice is heard impacts on the kind of OD practitioner I am. This affects not just what I notice and talk about, but actually how I operate. We might say that I stand for and embody an approach to OD which ensures that everyone's voice is heard.

Often, OD people in organisations add value by standing for and modelling something important that is a little different to the mainstream of the organisation. Whether it's a 'big picture', whole-systems orientation, a focus on people and values or some desirable aspect of the organisation's culture, the OD person often becomes a standard-bearer for it. This is not always a comfortable place to be. It can feel lonely and carries political risks. Wise OD practitioners develop strategies for resilience and support.

BEING THE OD INTERVENTION

Because as OD people we often embody something different and challenging to the prevailing way of doing things, there are times when simply by being at a meeting we have an impact, intended or otherwise. For example, if we are seen as the standard-bearer for the 'big picture' or for acting courageously, our presence in the room may be enough for people to think or behave differently.

The questions we ask and the conversations we hold will also change the way people think about a subject. As Appreciative Inquiry practitioners are fond of saying, 'All questions are fateful'. (See Adams, Cooperrider and Schiller (2004) for more on this.) For example, if I ask you about your levels of engagement as part of an OD diagnostic activity, that might start to create expectations and curiosity about engagement. It may change the conversations you have with your colleagues. In some small way things will be different, even though my intention may have been to 'diagnose' rather than 'intervene'.[3] So it can be said that in many ways the OD practitioner *is* the OD intervention, and the mindset of the practitioner is therefore crucial to this intervention.

Holding our Mindset at Arm's Length and Helping Others Do the Same

So far I have described a number of ways in which the OD practitioner can work with and use their own mindset to be useful to their client. Sitting beneath all of these examples is the principle that our mindset shapes our interpretation and understanding of the world. In this way it informs and motivates the actions and decisions we take.

One implication of this principle is that the world is not made up of absolute, objective truths. Rather, it is made up of multiple truths: I have my truth based on my way of seeing things and you have yours. They may be different but neither is right nor wrong. Or as the ancient Jewish commentators (apparently) put it in the Talmud, 'we see the world not as it is but *as we are*'.

This is especially important because it is very easy to create self-fulfilling prophesies through our mindset and beliefs. We all know that we perform best for the colleague or manager who thinks we are fantastic. Conversely it is always with the one who thinks we are no good that we mess things up. Research into the placebo effect has established very clearly that a person's beliefs about a situation can have a profound impact on the outcome of that situation. For example, in the world of medicine, clinical outcomes will be materially affected by the patient's beliefs about whether a treatment works or not. Not only that, but the doctor's beliefs have also been shown to have an impact, even when these beliefs are not shared with the patient. (For more on the placebo effect, see Ben Goldacre's entertaining book entitled *Bad Science* (2009: 63–85) and Chapter 6 of this book.)

> As a thought experiment, consider your reaction to this chapter so far. Most probably you have responded in terms of whether you like what I have to say (or not), agree with it (or not), find it interesting (or not) and so on. Whatever your response, try and take a step back and ask yourself what your reaction says

---

3   This, of course, creates challenges for a linear notion of OD consultancy where 'Diagnosis' and 'Intervention' are seen as different phases in a cycle of activity. See Chapter 11 for more on this.

about what is important to you, what you find interesting, what you think about the world. We see the world not as it is but as we are. So what is it about you that shapes your response? Now, consider how someone who values different things might have a different response.

This little thought process should lead you into thinking less about the nature of this chapter, and more about yourself and others. In essence you have started to hold your own mindset at arm's length so that you can enquire into it. 'Being right or wrong' gives way to 'being different'.

So as practitioners, we need to take a great deal of care to recognise that our beliefs and opinions about something or someone are neither true nor false, right nor wrong. They are simply beliefs and opinions. However, while this is all very well in theory, it is very difficult to do in practice, especially in the heat of the moment. How many of us can honestly say that we always maintain an open, curious mind to those with different views to ourselves? We may be able to in some circumstances, but what about when those views are anathema to everything we hold dear? It takes practice to develop this capacity. With practice, however, OD people can bring a degree of 'reflexivity' to their work, holding their own perspective at arm's length, enquiring into it, learning from that and enabling others to do the same. (See Chapter 6 for more on this.)

Beyond Mindset

So far in this Chapter I have focused primarily on the mindset of the OD practitioner. This section looks at other aspects of the importance of the individual in OD.

WORKING WITH HUMAN DYNAMICS

One of the hallmarks of OD work is a focus on 'how' rather than 'what'. For example an OD practitioner will often consider *how* decisions get made in their organisation, rather than the decisions themselves. To do this they will evaluate the effectiveness of formal mechanisms for decision-making, but they will also look at informal processes. In particular, they will be interested in human dynamics such as the quality and nature of the key relationships, levels of trust, political behaviours, who wins out when there is conflict, etc. (Think back to the example of the UK Board of the FMCG company.)

These aspects of human behaviour are typically regarded as 'no go' areas in organisational life. People tend to act as if they do not exist. It is also precisely these issues that usually hold the key to success or failure, a fact that most people readily acknowledge in private conversation.

Edgar Schein, one of the founders of the OD field, refers to these kinds of issue as 'process' issues. He has written extensively on 'Process Consultation' – see *Process Consultation Revisited* (1999). This is a collaborative approach to OD consulting characterised by a shared diagnosis of the problem between OD practitioner and client. This enables process issues to be addressed in a helpful way.[4] The key point here is that the best OD practitioners do not shy away from issues of process, they head towards them.

USING YOURSELF AS A 'DIAGNOSTIC INSTRUMENT'

Another way in which the individual is central to the practice of OD is through the notion of the 'Self as Diagnostic Instrument'. The key idea here is that it is possible for the practitioner to use his or her own experience of engaging with the client as diagnostic information. In other words, the practitioner's experiences say something important about what is going on in the client's system, often out of people's conscious awareness. Consider the following example.

I am facilitating a group of senior executives, all of them highly effective in their domains of expertise. The conversation is stilted and punctuated by long silences. I notice my tummy rumble and feel a flutter in my belly. Anxiety? Or am I just hungry, in spite of the good breakfast I recently enjoyed? I consider the matter in hand. I need this session to work. Will my needs be met? And then ... will this group feed my needs?

My attention is taken by a sigh on my right. 'This is feeling really stodgy, like ... treacle sponge', says a man. I decide to take a risk. 'It's funny you should mention food', I say, and I share my daydream about needing to be fed. This leads to an interesting conversation. It turns out that everyone is feeling anxious about getting their needs met. The group relaxes a little. We start tentatively, but soon we are in an animated conversation, getting bolder about where we do and don't trust each other, the blockers and enablers, and what it would take to be more open. I breathe a sigh of relief.

---

4   You can learn more about OD Consulting in Chapter 11, and more about human dynamics in organisational life in Chapters 4 and 7.

This phenomenon, in which a person experiences something 'on behalf' of a group or individual they are trying to help, is discussed widely across various traditions of psychotherapy, coaching and consultancy. It goes under different names; however the term from psychotherapy is 'counter-transference' – see, for example Casement (1990). What is common to all the descriptions is that the practitioner experiences things that do not belong entirely to them. In the story above, it was a daydream. There is also data in emotions, for example frustration or fear, in physical sensations like heat or trembling, in a particular piece of music, phrase or image popping into mind. If we can cultivate the capacity to notice these internal experiences as we engage with our clients, we will spot something useful. Here is another example.

> I once enjoyed a lunchtime conversation with a client, an OD manager, in which we found ourselves creating an 'alternative world' for her company as if it was an airliner on a long-haul flight. This was no ordinary airliner because whenever the pilot tried to change airspeed, heading or altitude, unexpected things happened. For example pushing the throttle forward caused all the toilets in the aeroplane to flush. Meanwhile the controls for the reclining seats in First Class were connected to the engine and main control surfaces so that passengers were inadvertently causing mayhem. Yet somehow this aeroplane was still in the air, getting where it needed to go, albeit spending half its time flying upside down or dangerously close to a stall.

This conversation started out as a bit of irreverent fun: we needed to blow off some steam after running a tough workshop. But as we talked it became clear that our alternative world contained some useful insights about leadership, decision-making and culture. Our fantasy also acknowledged the fact that while imperfect, the organisation was successful and that we had to be careful not to disrupt what was working well. Subsequently, another realisation came to light. It dawned on us that the most useful insights from this 'alternative world' were contained in the elements that caused us the most hilarity at the time. It was as if the funnier (and perhaps edgier) they were, the more they contained something important that could not be talked about in some more 'normal', rational ways.

It is clearly important not to get too attached to any one experience or story. These internal experiences cannot be thought of as 'true or false', and any one experience is open to multiple interpretations. Also it is not always easy to separate out what belongs to us and therefore has nothing to do with our client organisation. But offered tentatively, with curiosity, these 'self as instrument' experiences can be very helpful in pointing to something important that might otherwise be overlooked. (For more on the 'Self as Instrument' see Mee-Yan Cheung-Judge and Linda Holbeche's excellent book *Organization Development* (2011) and articles by McCormick and White (2000) and Cheung-Judge (2001).)

Powerful OD Practice

So far I have discussed the ways in which the individual OD practitioner is central to the field of OD. In this section I look at the personal qualities, capacities and skills of the most powerful practitioners. For the OD practitioner thinking about their development or that of their team, this section offers a 'map of the field'. At the end of this Chapter I discuss ways in which the OD practitioner can start to develop these qualities, capacities and skills.

SELF-AWARENESS

Many of the examples discussed in this chapter rely on the OD practitioner having high levels of self-awareness. If we are to support our clients working with mindset, group dynamics and our 'self as a diagnostic instrument' then we need some familiarity with our own emotional and psychological landscape. We need to know our own biases and blind spots, our own particular lens on the world, our ways of seeing and not seeing. We need to understand our personal, social history, and how this has influenced our outlook on the world. Remember, we see the world not as it is, but *as we are*.

This in turn links to our ability to create psychological safety for our clients. As I was constantly reminded in my own professional training, we can't take a client to a place we have not been to ourselves. As OD consultants we often find ourselves 'making it okay' for individuals or groups to express feelings such as anxiety, fear or anger. This process of 'making it okay' is what psychotherapists call 'containment'. Before we can provide containment to others, we need to work on our own areas of sensitivity and blindness, our own needs, our own trigger points. This enables us to manage our emotional responses to challenging situations, a necessary prerequisite to helping others manage their own responses. For more on containment, see Brown and Stobart (2008).

Developing self-awareness also enables OD practitioners to appreciate the difference between their own psychological and emotional issues and those of their clients. The practitioner who can't tell the difference is, in effect, reading from an unreliable internal 'diagnostic instrument'. At worst, this can lead to a practitioner unwittingly working through their own unresolved issues while purporting to help the clients with theirs. This is arguably an abuse of power. For a full treatment of this subject, I recommend Adolf Guggenbühl-Craig's excellent book, *Power in the Helping Professions* (2005).

UNDERSTANDING OF HUMAN PSYCHOLOGICAL PROCESSES

It follows that an understanding of human psychological processes is very important to the OD practitioner. Not only does this build self-awareness, it also helps with understanding others. There are many ways for developing this understanding. My own practice is rooted in a mix of therapeutic approaches combined with a body-based, 'somatic' tradition. For more on somatic approaches, see the ground-breaking book by Pete Hamill, *Embodied Leadership* (2013).

The world of coaching also has much to offer here, especially those approaches that are designed to help people get beneath surface issues. The key thing is to embrace a rich set of perspectives that will enable the practitioner to understand and engage with their experiences and those of their clients.

IMPACT, CREDIBILITY AND POLITICAL WISDOM

The OD role is often that of 'critical friend'. Practitioners need to be able to 'speak truth to power' and help people hear difficult but important things they would rather ignore. The ability to have an impact, to influence and to build credibility is therefore crucial, the more so when the OD practitioner has little formal authority to call on. Political wisdom is also an essential part of the mix. Successful OD people are usually well-versed in reading organisational dynamics, building coalitions, fostering trust with many people, spotting opportunities and choosing the right moment to act. Without these capabilities OD people are rightly charged with having nice ideas that don't make any real difference. (See Chapter 4 for more on this.)

COMMUNICATION, TRANSLATION AND SHAPE-SHIFTING SKILLS

Earlier in this Chapter I discussed how the local, timely and specific nature of OD means no single set of activities belongs exclusively to the field. An implication of this is that developing an OD strategy means working out 'what OD needs to be round here'. Having done this, the practitioner must develop a communications and stakeholder engagement plan that 'translates' their strategy into language and examples that make sense in their clients' everyday setting.

Communication and engagement skills are part of doing this well, however, there is a further element that can be described as 'shape-shifting'. This denotes the skill of flexing how we 'show up' in order to match and blend with (or sometime mismatch and challenge) the people we are trying to engage. Shape-shifting means taking on the mindset of the target audience, changing the language we use, the examples we give and the underlying assumptions about what matters most. This skill is especially important to OD people because of the field's reputation for being slippery. Paradoxically perhaps, it is through shape-shifting that we make OD tangible in the minds of our stakeholders. (For more on shape-shifting, see Chapter 6 in this book.)

AUTHENTICITY, EMOTIONAL INTELLIGENCE AND RESILIENCE

Equally paradoxically, as well as being effective shape-shifters, skilful OD practitioners also maintain a strong connection to who they are, their values and what they stand for. It is as if this is the stable core that allows them to shift their outer shape while remaining authentic and credible. This leads on to ideas around emotional intelligence and resilience. Successful practitioners have developed the capacity to experience and manage their own moods and emotions, work with those of others and stay centred and grounded under pressure.

ACCESS TO OUR 'INTERNAL OBSERVER'

Much of what I have discussed requires that OD practitioners have the capacity to notice and reflect on their responses to events 'in the moment', in other words, as they are taking place. It is this capacity that enables practitioners to hold their own mindset at arm's length, to use their experience as a diagnostic instrument, to suspend judgement and so on. Doing this well requires splitting our attention so that we are both acting in the world, and simultaneously observing ourselves in action. Different traditions have different names for this idea. Sigmund Freud in *The Interpretation of Dreams* (1900) described it as maintaining a quality of 'free floating attention', while spiritual (and other) traditions focus on Mindfulness, helping people to exercise more choice over where they direct their attention.

ENQUIRY SKILLS TO COMPLEMENT ADVOCACY

Another important capacity of the OD practitioner is the ability to maintain a curious, enquiring perspective, one that can sit alongside advocating a point of view. When we adopt an enquiry-based mindset, we ask questions of the people we disagree with in order to understand how they see things the way they do. We start from the assumption that as intelligent, well-intentioned human beings, they must be seeing something that we are missing. We therefore enquire in order to understand and then invite them to do likewise with us. In so doing we get alongside people who see things differently from us, building empathy, trust and understanding, and influencing and being influenced through 'soft power'. This is how we create together a shared mindset that takes in the multiple perspectives of all those involved.

The ability to enquire is also connected to the ability to learn, particularly from mistakes. When things go wrong, if we can let go of our own defensiveness and help others to do likewise, we can have a conversation that may generate powerful new learning.

Enquiring is not the same as being 'nice'. In my experience, genuine enquiry has often led into some of the toughest conversations of my career, but also to some of the most profound and useful learning for me and for my clients.

ACTION AMID UNCERTAINTY

We have seen that the role of the OD practitioner is complex, subtle, ambiguous and at times, paradoxical. So, of course, is the world of organisational life in which the OD practitioner operates, as Chapter 5 makes clear. In spite of this, we do need to act, and with as much wisdom, integrity and heart as we can muster. Powerful OD practitioners make decisions and take action.

Of course the same applies to powerful twenty-first century leaders and managers. In fact, arguably, all of the qualities, capacities and skills described in this section belong as much to leadership as they do to OD. For a fuller treatment of this subject see James Traeger's thought-provoking article on twenty-first century leadership (2011).

Developing as an OD Practitioner

Having discussed the central role of the individual in the field of OD and the qualities exhibited by the most powerful OD practitioners, I now offer some practical suggestions to support OD practitioners to develop and grow. Think of this section as 'Martin's top tips' based on my own personal journey and on the work I have done to support many OD teams and individual practitioners. I hope it is helpful.

GET STARTED

OD is an enormous field and it is easy to feel paralysed by the sheer size and scope of it. People will avoid OD work because they feel they don't know enough to get started. In my experience this is a trap. Learning to be an OD practitioner is like learning to swim: the only way to 'know enough' is to start doing it. To be clear, I'm not encouraging people to do things for which they are not competent or trained. In my view, however, newer practitioners do well to give their 'inner perfectionist' time off and find appropriate ways to get started.

I have discussed above how OD will always look different depending on the context in which the practitioner is operating. Developing an achievable OD strategy is a combination of a rigorous organisational diagnosis and a wise reading of the political environment. These can then be overlaid onto a realistic assessment of the capability, passions and experience of the OD team.

In other words, to get going in OD, work out what the organisation needs and what the OD team can offer. Then, work out how and where to start, engage the appropriate stakeholders and get going. As events unfold, course correct, maximising learning en route.

This pragmatic approach can also be used to prioritise the learning needs of the OD team. Instead of feeling it is essential to know everything about OD before starting, practitioners can ask what they need to know now to take the next step. They can make this assessment in light of the current OD strategy and the kind of OD practitioner they are and wish to become.

KEEP GOOD COMPANY

Working in OD can feel lonely, regardless of whether we are the only OD person in the organisation, part of a team or an external consultant. The nature of OD requires practitioners to eschew being part of a tribe and to hold themselves at the margins of the organisations they are supporting. It is this that that gives them their useful difference but it can be tough emotionally. Successful OD people invest in building networks with like-minded colleagues they respect (whether or not they have 'OD' in their job description). They do this within their own organisation and outside it and they use this network for support, challenge and as a source of new ideas and perspectives.

As they manage their careers, OD practitioners will also benefit from thinking carefully about the teams they join. We have seen that 'OD' can mean many different things, so before accepting a new job, look beneath the title and job description. Get clear about what the role actually involves, what learning is available and from whom. Then choose wisely.

REFLECT AND LEARN

Supervision, mentoring and peer coaching processes can be enormously helpful as ways of enabling OD practitioners to reflect, learn and develop. This applies to people at all levels of experience and knowledge. Through reflecting with other practitioners on our work, we come to see how our own blind spots and biases might be getting in the way. We also get the chance to articulate what we did well, ensuring that we can do it again and that the story gets told.

The supervision model comes primarily from the world of psychotherapy and more recently, coaching. Typically the practitioner pays another (usually) more experienced colleague to support and challenge them in their practice, helping them to see the situation from a more detached perspective. In the OD context, supervision can sometimes blur into 'shadow consultancy' in which the supervising practitioner offers technical support that is invisible to the end client.

By comparison with supervision, mentoring is less structured, though some organisations have developed quite formal mentoring processes. The idea is to connect practitioners with more senior, experienced people. This enables the mentee to benefit from the mentor's experience, while the mentor has the satisfaction of giving something back and learning from another's perspective. Mentors will often support their mentees politically, for example through introductions to people in their networks. Sometimes a practitioner's mentor will be part of the same organisation (though not part of their formal reporting line), and sometimes they will be from outside the organisation. Mentors often find they learn as much from this process as their mentees.

Peer coaching can take place informally, as when two practitioners meet for an occasional coffee, or in a more structured way, for example through facilitated action learning sets. Compared to supervision or mentoring, the peer coaching relationship is more two-way. The idea is that each person both contributes and benefits from the varying perspectives, skills and experiences of their colleague(s). Peer coaching works best when over time, each participant gets approximately equal 'airtime' to talk through their issues and practice. While one person has their 'airtime', the other(s) provides support and challenge (but not advice) and thus practises their coaching and questioning skills. Peer coaching is generally most effective when the conversation focuses on one person's issue at a time, rather than jumping about.

PERSONAL GROWTH AND DEVELOPMENT

We have looked in the previous section at the importance of self-awareness. In my view any OD practitioner wishing to operate in the ways discussed in this chapter should have ongoing practices around personal growth and self-awareness. Here are some of the key routes that I am aware of, though there are doubtless many others.

The world of psychotherapy has a great deal to offer. There are a large number of therapeutic approaches, ranging from 'psychodynamic' traditions which pay particular attention to unconscious processes, through to more 'humanistic' approaches such as Gestalt and Transactional Analysis. There are also 'somatic' or body-based approaches that take an holistic perspective to the relationship between mind and body.

For the OD practitioner looking to engage in therapy, one possibility is simply to start working with a therapist as a client. Getting some foundation training in psychotherapy from a reputable organisation is also a powerful way to build core skills and gain self-awareness. Another option with more of a group focus is to participate in a Personal and Professional Development group facilitated by a reputable psychotherapy organisation.

An alternative to the world of therapy is that of coaching. Available methods range from those focused on behaviours and performance through to deeper, ontological and integral approaches in which clients look at the fundamental questions, assumptions and dilemmas underpinning their lives. Once again there is the possibility of engaging with coaching as a client or seeking training.

A third option is to seek out development in working with group process or organisational consulting. There are a number of reputable organisations offering academic and practitioner programmes in these fields.

In all cases, I strongly recommend that people explore and try out a number of possibilities to see what fits best before making a choice. Above all, only work with reputable organisations and practitioners.

Finally on this subject, it is worth pointing out that the process of personal growth and development is an ongoing journey rather than a destination. My advice is to stay curious and open, try out different things, and keep looking for that next step. Few practitioners regard themselves as truly 'cooked' when it comes to personal growth and those that do are best avoided.

DEVELOP YOUR INTERNAL OBSERVER

It is the capacity to split our attention between acting and observing ourselves in action that underpins much of the OD practice I have discussed in this chapter. This is not easy to do and requires that we have some choice over where we direct our attention, rather than just getting caught up in whatever is happening.

Simple meditation practices can help here. There are many rich spiritual traditions for those who are interested to explore, but here is a simple practice that can have a powerful impact.

- Sit in a quiet room in a comfortable, relaxed position with your back straight, your arms and legs uncrossed and your feet in contact with the floor. (Some people like using chairs for this, others prefer sitting on the floor with their legs crossed or in a kneeling position with a cushion.)
- Close your eyes and pay attention to the physical sensation of your breath entering and leaving your body. Typically this is best done by focusing on the sensations at the nostrils or the abdomen.
- Every time you notice that your attention has wandered away, gently bring it back to the breath.
- 'Success' in this practice does not mean maintaining your attention all the time on your breath. What matters is the noticing that your attention has wandered and the bringing it back.
- Whatever happens (within reason), do this until the time you have decided to spend on the meditation practice is up.
- Start with three to five minutes. Over time, work your way up to 15–20 minutes.

This practice won't have an instantaneous effect, but by repeating it four or five times a week, over a few months you will start to develop far greater awareness and control over your attention. As an added bonus, you will probably also feel calmer and clearer about what matters to you.

PRACTICE

OD practice is an embodied skill, like learning to swim or to speak a new language. Embodied skills are about 'doing things well' rather than 'talking about them knowledgeably'. As such they take practice. So to get good at OD, make a start and then practise with the support of colleagues you respect, learning from your and their successes and mistakes. After all, given that we are always practising something whether we like it or not, we might as well make some proactive choices about what we would like to be practising. See George Leonard's wonderful book *Mastery* (1992) for a fuller treatment of this subject.

Conclusion

This chapter has focused on the role of the individual practitioner in OD. I have argued that the field of OD is inseparable from the mindset of the OD practitioner. I have also discussed how powerful OD practitioners work intensely with their own mindsets and those of their clients, as well as with their own experiences of events as they unfold. The latter part of the chapter focused on the qualities, capacities and skills of seasoned OD practitioners. I then offered some suggestions for how to develop these qualities, capacities and skills.

I thank you for your engagement with these ideas and I wish you well in the important work of supporting your client organisations to be more effective, healthy, relevant and sustainable.

References

Adams, M.G., Cooperrider, D.L. and Schiller, M. 2004. With our questions we make the world, in *Advances in Appreciative Inquiry, Volume 1, Constructive Discourse and Human Organization*, edited by D.L. Cooperrider and M. Avital. Oxford: Elsevier, 105–24.

Brown, R. and Stobart, K. 2008. *Understanding Boundaries and Containment in Clinical Practice*. London: Karnac Books.

Casement, P. 1990. *Further Learning from the Patient*. London: Routledge.

Cheung-Judge, L.M. 2001. The Self as an Instrument – a cornerstone for the future of OD. *OD Practitioner*, 33(3), 11–16.

Cheung-Judge, L.M. and Holbeche, L. 2011. *Organization Development*. London: Kogan Page.

Freud, S. 1900. *The Interpretation of Dreams*. Oxford World's Classics edition translated by J. Crick. Oxford: Oxford University Press.

Goldacre, B. 2009. *Bad Science.* London: Harper Collins.

Guggenbühl-Craig, A. 2005. *Power in the Helping Professions.* Putnam, CT: Spring Publications.

Hamill, P. 2013. *Embodied Leadership.* London: Kogan Page.

Leonard, G. 1992. *Mastery: The Keys to Success and Long-Term Fulfilment.* New York, NY: Penguin.

McCormick, D.W. and White, J. 2000. Using one's self as an instrument for organizational diagnosis. *Organization Development Journal,* 18(3), 49–62.

Schein, E.H. 1999. *Process Consultation Revisited: Building the Helping Relationship.* Reading, MA: Addison-Wesley.

Traeger, J.R. *21st Century Leadership: Collective Intelligence.* [Online]. Available at: http://www.mayvin.co.uk/articles/21st-century-leadership-collective-intelligence.html [accessed: 9 January 2012].

4

The Reality of Organisational Life: Working at the Edges and in the Spaces in Between

Mike Alsop

Introduction

The purpose of this chapter is to explore the 'implicit' aspects of organisational life and the 'dark (or shadow) side' of how organisations really operate. It shows the importance of paying attention to these aspects in order to have a genuine and lasting impact.

Key questions:
- How does change really happen in organisations?
- How does an understanding of organisational politics contribute to the work of Organisation Development (OD)?
- How can OD practitioners engage with the realities of organisational life without colluding with the negative?

A Pragmatic Realist's 'Take' on Organisations and Organisational Life

For many years I struggled to accept that OD might actually be a 'real' profession, with proper disciplines and practices. Working as the Head of Executive Development inside a very large, very down-to-earth and very pragmatic international organisation (Securicor plc, which merged with Group 4 Falck to create Group 4 Securicor, now known as G4S plc) in a particularly 'tough' industry (security solutions), I was caught up in the gritty reality of trying to help busy leaders and managers grow their revenues and margins in a climate featuring ruthless competition, challenging labour relations and volatile market conditions.

Whenever I did steal a moment to read about the latest developments in OD, or take myself off to a conference to hear anyone speak on the subject, I tended to be left with a vague sense of irritation and the beginnings of an annoying (even to me) inner dialogue that typically seemed to say, 'That's all very well, but it wouldn't/couldn't work here'. My frustrations (which, in all honesty and with the benefit of hindsight, were probably saying much more about me than they ever were about what I was reading or listening to) stemmed from my sense that the prevailing orthodoxy (or at least the stuff I was reading or listening to) viewed organisations almost as scientific laboratory specimens, suspended in time, and susceptible to the prodding and poking of well-intentioned and thoroughly objective 'professionals' who somehow knew best and who could 'fix' them and 'make them better' via the careful application of top-down 'solutions'.

My 'take' on organisations and organisational life was (and largely still is) very different from this! I see organisations as complex, messy, multi-faceted, constantly morphing and shifting groupings of individual human beings (each with their own complex, messy, multi-faceted, constantly morphing and shifting needs, interests and aspirations). One of the best descriptions I've ever heard came from one of my senior G4S colleagues, who described organisations as 'storm-tossed vessels of compromise and convenience'.

It is probably fair to say that if we were to use a simplified 'Newtonian worldview – quantum worldview' continuum to understand my 'take' on organisations, organisational life and the general business of change, I would naturally inhabit a place well towards the 'quantum' end of the scale!

For me (and I accept that this is a very personal view), anyone who works in the business of OD needs to understand that it is impossible to be effective and, at the same time, to remain 'outside' the dynamics of the organisation. Somewhere in the dim and distant past someone told me that, 'Every intervention changes the course of history', and I have tried to remember that 'truth' in every piece of consultancy, workshop facilitation or coaching that I have ever done. Having said that, I do also believe that anyone working in the business of OD needs to have some rather well-developed skills in the whole area of 'impartial, rational and objective observation', as the Newtonian worldview would have it.

Assumptions about the nature of organisations...
... and how to change them

Newtonian Worldview

- Focuses on things, parts, separate objects
- Linear 'cause and effect' thinking
- Change is manufactured and engineered – unfreeze, change, refreeze
- Impartial, rational objective observation possible
- Control, prediction, harmony, equilibrium
- Intelligence lies at the top of the organisation, expert views predominate
- People as economic resources: human capital

Quantum Worldview

- Focuses on processes, patterns, information flows and connectivity between parts, integrated whole
- Non linear, cyclical, spiral processes of change
- Change, development and adaptability as natural life flows
- Observer always participates in and influences what is studied
- Unknown future, emergence, creative tension between order and chaos, importance of diversity for innovation, dynamic equilibrium
- View from the top is partial, distributed collective intelligence, whole cannot be known from any one place
- Purposeful human beings – mind/body/heart & soul

Figure 4.1   **Assumptions about the nature of organisations ... and how to change them**

I like the idea of the OD practitioner as the 'yeast in the dough'; the quiet catalyst or 'special ingredient' working quietly and without fuss or drama 'at the edges' and in 'the spaces in between' the more obvious and apparent organisational elements, but having a disproportionate effect on the finished product.

Many years ago, when I was struggling to get to grips with the idea of 'executive development' and trying to drag myself out of the world of 'training' and into something less earthbound and more rewarding, I spent some fascinating, challenging and thought-provoking hours in the company of the late Professor Roger Stuart at the Wadenhoe Centre in Northamptonshire ... and I experienced something of a breakthrough. I had been describing the organisation's recently revised international strategy (and the place of my role within it) and was probably complaining about a perceived lack of resources and investment in people and development. After listening carefully and politely for longer than anyone could reasonably have been expected to, Roger held up his hand and said, rather forcefully:

> *Mike, you have to make your mind up now. The time for talking is over. What are you going to be? Are you going to accept the limitations*

> *that you think surround you and just act out the role as some sort of*
> *'creature of the CEO' or are you going to be a bit more creative, and*
> *start acting as an organisational guerrilla? If you choose the first path,*
> *you know what the rest of your career will be like. If you choose the*
> *second path, you will have a very different experience!*

We didn't really talk very much after that about quite what he meant by the term 'organisational guerrilla', as I rather self-indulgently took us off into a different metaphor, describing my aspirations for the role as being more about 'lighting many candles' than 'building one big bonfire', and, sadly, we never had the opportunity to continue our conversation at a later date. When I drove home that day, however, the words 'organisational guerrilla' would not leave my mind, and they have kept coming back again and again over the years.

In the rest of this chapter I will try to put into words what I have been thinking (and to some extent, enacting in my OD career) about OD as a form of 'unequal/asymmetric combat' ever since. I have no military background and I am certainly not an expert in military history, so, to anyone who does and/or is, some of my ideas may appear under-developed, ill-informed or even downright wrong. I am not suggesting, either, that organisational life is necessarily anything like warfare, but I am, however, deeply curious and inquisitive, and have always believed that we can learn massively from history and from other 'spheres of life', so many of the following ideas are culled from my odd and eclectic reading over many years. Rightly or wrongly, wars and conflicts have always been used by intelligent opportunists to create advantage from the disruption of existing systems and orders, and I hold the view that organisational disruption creates gaps and spaces that can be exploited by the alert OD practitioner.

Each of the next short sections describes a different aspect of guerrilla activity that seems to offer value (in a completely different context) to the OD practitioner.

Training, Preparation and 'Mastery'

Over the last twenty years I have been privileged to work with many OD practitioners, from a range of backgrounds. The really good ones, the ones who seem genuinely and repeatedly to make a difference (to individuals, to teams and to whole organisations), all seem to have one thing in common – a real air of 'mastery' that is the result of years of experience, diligent study and training.

When I use the term 'mastery', I use it in the same way that we might use it to describe someone who has worked their way through a profession, or a technically demanding craft such as carpentry or stonemasonry, from novice status, through an extensive apprenticeship, to journeyman status and thence to mastery. Traditionally, in mediaeval crafts, apprentices were indentured to their masters and worked for them for years as they completed their training, whereas journeymen had a higher level of skill and would go on journeys to assist their masters. Masters were viewed by society as 'freemen' who could travel as they wished to work on the projects of their patrons.

Masters would be capable of tackling projects of great scale (both in terms of physical space and across long spans of time) and complexity, and would be able to use a wide range of tools with accuracy, precision and consummate skill. They were often noted for their air of patience, unhurried stillness, concentration, self-control and for their disciplined energy. Equally, they were sometimes held in awe for their apparent stubbornness and lack of deference towards anyone who tried to wield power and influence inappropriately!

Effective OD practitioners certainly need to be able to use a wide range of tools with accuracy, precision and skill, and it has often struck me that the really fine ones own a level of authenticity and unfussy self-assurance that certainly qualifies them for the title of 'freeman'. To borrow a couple of terms from Chris Mruk's (1999) work on self-esteem, it is as if their honest awareness of their '*worth*' (i.e. the value that they bring) and of their '*competence*' (i.e. their range of skills and knowledge) has earned them a measure of what I like to call 'assured humility' – the appreciation that they are truly good at what they do, combined with the understanding that they can always learn more and get even better, without having to worry themselves unduly about the fleeting opinions of others.

Returning to my theme of the OD practitioner as 'organisational guerrilla' engaged in some sort of unequal or asymmetrical campaign, it seems to me that the parallels are fairly obvious. The ability to stay calm, think ahead and play 'the long game' (as opposed to being drawn into 'brave and glorious but ultimately futile gestures') is of huge importance. Many of the real 'architects and agents of change' that I have seen and worked with in organisational life have 'served their time' by committing long years to their own training and preparation, and to developing their 'mastery' (both of the tools of the trade, and of the self), and have the wrinkles and scars to prove it. Having said that, I don't deny the fact that occasional acts of dramatic and youthful revolutionary fervour can have a serious impact … but they do bring with them some serious risks, i.e. heavy return fire, the mobilisation of opposing forces and even potential acts of retribution!

The Importance of Context and Intelligence – 'Appreciating the Situation'

Much like the 'irregular forces' in an asymmetric combat situation, effective OD practitioners (especially in a world of scarce resources and investment) can gain themselves a useful advantage by having a really thorough and well-informed understanding of the organisational 'lie of the land'.

As I said at the start of this chapter, I see organisations as complex, messy, multi-faceted, constantly morphing and shifting groupings of individual human beings (each with their own complex, messy, multi-faceted, constantly morphing and shifting needs, interests and aspirations). If this is the case, it strikes me that, to have any chance of really understanding 'what is going on', the OD practitioner needs to have a really good 'intelligence network' supplying information from as many sources and perspectives as possible. This means taking the time to build and nurture trust with as many people in the organisation as possible in order to get the fullest possible picture. I have often heard internal OD consultants complain that life for them is more difficult than it is for external consultants. In some ways they are right, but in this particular area of work the internal consultant who has pursued a lengthy and thoughtful campaign of relationship-building and intelligence-gathering is much better-placed than the external consultant 'parachuted in' at short notice.

There are a couple of simple but effective tools that I have found useful in this area. The first, which I call my 'Fame Factor' grid, first saw the light of day at a very early stage of my career in OD. I was working as part of a team of internal consultants, and our 'home base' was a delightful converted mansion with its own grounds, set in the English countryside, some twenty miles or so away from the organisation's head office. The surroundings were wonderful, and it was a real joy to be able to wander through the gardens in the sunshine, chatting to colleagues as the birds sang in the background ... but after a while I began to worry that we were becoming a little remote from the realities of the business, and I was concerned that if we allowed this situation to get any worse we would soon become an irrelevance – and a target for some serious cost-cutting! On one particular afternoon I carefully drew up a list of all of the people in the organisation who I deemed to be 'key players', and then I wrote down all of the contacts and interactions that I had had with them over the last week, the last month, the last quarter and the last six months. The resultant grid was predictably 'scary', especially when I made a note of who had initiated the contacts, but it served its purpose. In the next few days I put together a campaign plan (under the guise of a research project) to get myself in front of as many of these 'key players' as possible – not to sell anything specific, but to listen to them talking about their world, their plans, their concerns and their opinions. Not surprisingly (again with the benefit of hindsight) this intelligence-gathering campaign quickly paid dividends, and I was soon finding myself invited in to work on all manner of change initiatives across the organisation.

The second tool that has helped (and which continues to add value in a wide range of OD interventions) is my slightly simplified and bastardised version of my friend from Manchester Business School, Professor Peter Naudé's, work on relationship network mapping, which I always refer to as 'Circles, Lines and Gaps'. This is a great way of getting behind and beyond the bland two-dimensional nature of the typical organogram, and almost always brings useful insights about the real 'lie of the land' when it is used in a spirit of curiosity and inquisitiveness. At the start of any engagement, I like to draw a map of the 'players', to see who is connected to whom, and to get some appreciation of where the various sources of influence and interaction might currently be (and where they might be 'used' to greater effect).

Before I go on to describe how such a map is created, I want to take a moment to answer any questions that might have been raised by my use of the word 'used' in the previous sentence. I sometimes get asked whether my approach to OD, with its overt use of the metaphors of 'guerrilla warfare' doesn't run the risk of becoming somehow underhand and manipulative. My response is that in the wrong hands it certainly could be viewed that way, but in the right hands (hands guided by strong values and a healthy sense of 'right and wrong' and 'good and bad') it is ultimately positive and beneficial. After all, physiotherapy uses manipulation based on a thorough understanding of the human body to bring about healing and well-being … but torturers can use the same knowledge for a quite different purpose! This is why proper, robust supervision is so important in OD – it serves to keep us from crossing to 'the dark side', and helps us resist the temptations of ego, power and material rewards.

Anyway, let us get back to the map. Using the largest sheet of paper (or computer screen) that I can lay my hands on, the first thing I do is write down the names of all the various 'players' (active and dormant) in the particular 'game' or 'drama' that I want to understand. Each name sits inside its own circle, and the various circles are dotted around the paper in some sort of representation of relative 'closeness' or 'distance'.

Circles

- Each person (or organisation) can be represented as a circle.
- Some circles may be larger than others, depending upon their 'importance'.

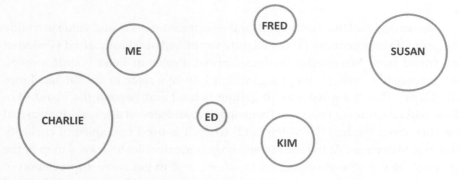

Figure 4.2   Circles – the players in the system

Lines

- The connections between each person (or organisation) can be represented as a line.
- We can use arrows to show the prevailing 'flow' of the relationship.

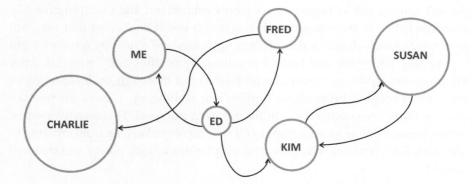

Note, some lines may be thicker than others, depending upon the 'strength' of the relationship.

Figure 4.3   Lines – the connections in the system

Once all of the 'players' have been identified and sit in their respective circles, I then try to represent their various connections to one another by drawing lines between them.

The next (and often the most interesting) step, is where I pay attention to the gaps – the 'spaces in between', where connections do not currently exist, or where opportunity and potential sit waiting for some sort of catalyst to work its magic!

Gaps

- The absence of potentially useful connections between each person (or organisation) is represented as a gap.
- Gaps (white spaces) are often more significant and worthy of attention than existing lines!

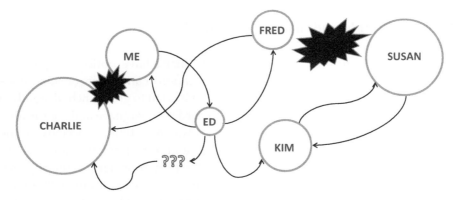

Note, some gaps may need attention and action, where others may not.

Figure 4.4   Gaps – the fascinating opportunities (and potential risks) in the system

In my experience, the best relationship network maps (Circles, Lines and Gaps) are created when a good collection of people, with a wide range of perspectives, get together to share their 'views'. One has to bear in mind the fact that the 'picture' is only ever a 'snapshot' of a moment in time, and that things are always changing and shifting, but, nevertheless, a good, up-to-date map is worth its weight in gold if we hope to have a good journey or a successful 'campaign'.

The two tools that I have described so far focus on people and relationships, but the effective OD practitioner has to understand that these, whilst hugely important, are not the only factors at play in any given context. A full and proper 'appreciation of the situation' requires attention to be paid to other dimensions. A few lines ago I used the terms 'picture' and 'snapshot' and introduced the idea of a shifting, changing image. This is a metaphor which is used to real effect by another excellent OD tool – the so-called Change Kaleidoscope developed by Julia Balogun and Veronica Hope Hailey (2004) in their book *Exploring Strategic Change*. This 'diagnostic framework' encourages change agents to pay serious attention to eight 'contextual features', namely time, scope, preservation, diversity, capability, capacity, readiness and power.

Some of the insights to be gained when a group of people have proper conversations about these contextual features can be particularly useful, and can often prevent over-exposure and dangerous and risky excursions into potentially damaging territory.

Personal Brands and 'Inside Outsiders'

One recurring feature of organisational life that I have noticed, apparently regardless of economic sector, geographical location or any other considerations is the tendency for an organisation's culture (if it is left to grow unchallenged) to develop in a gradual but inexorable drift towards convergence and conformity. This means that similarity of thinking grows over time, especially if the organisation is broadly successful, and the reservoir of creative ideas is not renewed and refreshed, leading to a potentially dangerous state of complacency and comfort. This seems to be particularly the case in organisations that have invested heavily in the promotion of a set of values and have encouraged the development of closely described competencies.

For the OD practitioner, especially the long-term internal consultant, this creates an interesting dilemma, with risks and opportunities apparent in almost equal measure. If they have been diligent in building and nurturing a wide and deep network of relationships inside the organisation over time, as I was suggesting in the previous section, there is every chance that they will have had the ear of some important and influential people ... and may even have contributed to the creation and emergence of the prevailing culture. The risk is that, as a direct result of their success in developing the organisation (whatever that might mean) they might eventually come to be seen as an adherent of that culture, and to be viewed as a protector of the status quo rather than as an agent of ongoing change and growth.

There are ways, however, in which the OD practitioner who is genuinely 'working at the edges' and in the 'spaces in between' can play a vital role in keeping the organisational fermentation going. Partly this is about creating (and constantly updating) a personal brand that is known and recognised for bringing something different and yet valuable, and partly, I believe, it is about acting as the bridge between the known world of the organisation and the unknown world 'beyond the gates'.

Borrowing once more from the world of asymmetric conflict and guerrilla campaigns, the importance of personal brand becomes fairly clear. Whatever we think of their politics (and I am certainly not going to give away any clues about what I might think of them), most of us are able to call up strong visual images of people like Mao Tse-tung, Ché Guevara, Fidel Castro and Nelson Mandela (one-time guerrillas to a man), and could probably even give a reasonably accurate summary of what they stood for or were trying to achieve.

Now, I am not suggesting that any of us as OD practitioners need to start wearing military fatigues and a bandana, or need to start growing a beard and long hair, but I do think that we probably ought to pay some attention to how we present ourselves (as they all undoubtedly did) so that we stand out from the herd and bring a distinct sense of 'valuable otherness'. I propose to use the next few lines to describe a couple of ideas that I have found useful in this area.

The first of these, respectfully borrowed from some very creative and original work done by the Bath Consultancy Group, is to do with how we make an impression with other people by transmitting a sense of 'Authority, Presence and Impact' to create a strong identity. Our 'Authority' stems from our past, and is the manifestation of our unique experiences, learning and qualification. Our 'Presence' is all about how we are 'in the moment' with other people, and the level of attention that we give to others when we are with them. Our 'Impact' is all about whether the people we are with have a sense that we can bring something valuable and different to their future. The skilled OD practitioner is able to weave these three dimensions together when they are with clients (existing or potential) to give a strong and consistent impression of assurance and capability. Without resorting to egocentric 'name-dropping' they should be able to refer to previous successful commissions, and ought to be able to use specific anecdotes as illustrations of their skilled prior use of a particular methodology or approach to a difficult issue. Their assured conversational abilities, involving the use of precise questions, diligent listening and accurate summarising really ought to leave the impression that the client's issue, their business and their problems are (at that moment) the only things that they are interested in, and their thoughtful offering of insights, observations, options and suggestions (but not instant solutions) should leave a sense that their ongoing involvement would bring an extra level of previously unanticipated value!

The second idea, which I think is particularly useful for the internal OD practitioner, is about developing a brand or a reputation for being a source of new, or different or 'left-field' ideas for the organisation that would not normally be part of its thinking. This is what I refer to as being an 'inside outsider'. I was extremely fortunate in my 'internal consultant' career in that the organisational structure, with lots of partly autonomous regions and business units around the world, meant that I was able to move in and out of the consciousness of the various leadership teams at various times. This meant that with a fair degree of careful time- and visibility-management (using the 'Fame Factor' grid that I described earlier) I was able to avoid the worst excesses of the 'familiarity breeds contempt' issue that many 'internals' often struggle with, and, at the same time, ensure that I never slipped completely 'off the radar'. Also, as a centrally funded resource I was largely outside of, or beyond, the direct control of the various reporting structures, and was therefore able to commit a reasonable amount of time to my own development and to making contacts outside the organisation, without the worst of the relentless pressure to deliver against short-term KPIs that so many people inside organisations face. All of this meant that whenever I did reappear in direct view of a part of the business that I had not been with for some time, I was usually able to contribute an idea, or an approach or a useful contact that helped them in some way … and which added to my 'personal brand' as a sort of organisational 'Scarlet Pimpernel'!

Allies, Patrons, Sponsors and Auxiliaries

After the earlier section about context and intelligence, and the importance of properly 'appreciating the situation' it probably comes as no surprise to learn that I am very keen on the idea of utilising the power of others in the pursuit of noble OD aims! I love the Taoist epigram, 'Work without effort; act without doing', and I think that its underlying message is a marvellous prompt to us to find ways of making things happen without necessarily having to do them ourselves.

In another of my earlier sections I wrote about mastery, and the concept of 'assured humility'. I think that the ability to know one's own weaknesses, and to reach out to others who have different and complementary talents is one of the best features of real mastery ... as well as being a sensible and pragmatic way of protecting one's personal brand and reputation. After all, the master does not want to become known as a 'Jack of all trades'. Really good and effective OD practitioners are deliberate alliance- and team-builders, with the ability to group and regroup different types of resource fluidly and responsively, depending upon the nature of the challenge facing them. This is not easy work, as it tends to rely upon one's ability and willingness to commit time and effort to keeping up-to-date with who's who and what is happening – which can sometimes feel like a self-indulgent luxury in the busy results-hungry world of contemporary organisational life.

We must not forget, either, that just as asymmetric conflict and guerrilla combat can be very dangerous in a physical sense, the use of similar approaches in the world of OD can be risky too – albeit in a different way. Picking the 'wrong' patrons or sponsors (sometimes called 'backing the wrong horse') can be seriously damaging, both to the prospects of success for the initiative of the moment and for the reputation and personal brand of the OD practitioner. Unfortunately it is still true to say that people are often judged by the nature of the company that they keep, and it is difficult to retain the reputation for being an 'inside outsider' if one is too closely associated with one or two high-profile sponsors or patrons.

Many of history's most successful guerrillas and proponents of asymmetric conflict have been skilled users of allies, patrons, sponsors and auxiliaries, and I think that we as OD practitioners can gain a lot from following their example. I seem to have heard about lots of initiatives that have come to grief as a result of their proponents taking what I would call a 'head-on' approach to an issue ('brave and glorious but ultimately futile gestures'!) without having done the necessary lobbying and coalition-building before leaping into action.

As I suggested earlier, the real currents of power and influence inside an organisation are not necessarily obvious to us simply as a result of looking at the current organisation chart. Some 'stars' are in the ascendant, despite their apparently 'junior' status, and others may have reached (and passed) their zenith. Some names, for example, may be the representatives of informal 'talent pools' or 'interest groups' which have no formal existence (and leave no obvious trails) within the overt hierarchical structures, but which are able to call upon huge resources through personal loyalty and shared history. The OD practitioner has to understand (and work actively) within the reality of this 'shadow world', and, to be effective, needs to build and maintain contacts in as many of its areas as possible. I would suggest that the steady but deliberate sharing and spreading of ideas by way of these informal connections is a much more effective way of generating real development of the organisation than many of the more obvious and 'traditional' approaches. In a way this is what I meant when I used the 'lighting many candles' rather than 'building one big bonfire' metaphor at the start of the chapter.

Nimbleness (Strategic Opportunism?)

If organisational life is, as I believe it to be, constantly shifting and morphing in response to the actions and reactions of a multitude of factors, then it is definitely important for us as OD practitioners to be able to react and respond rapidly to changing conditions, and to 'seize the moment' as and when it arrives. This sounds like a statement of 'the bleeding obvious', but there is actually more to it than meets the eye!

To be able to know 'when to strike' and, equally, when to remain safely hidden, the effective 'organisational guerrilla' needs to have a clear picture of the ultimate goal or strategic objective, for it is only when they have such a picture that they can make the necessary judgement 'in the moment' as to whether a particular course of action will help or hinder.

For some years now, as an 'internal consultant' and as an ostensibly independent 'external consultant' ('sailing beneath the Jolly Roger', as an old friend amusingly but pertinently calls it) I have encouraged the use of what I call 'touchstones'. These are short, succinct statements, taking whatever form suits the style and needs of my clients, and which somehow express their beliefs, aspirations, values, goals, aims and intents. For some they take the form of whole organisational 'mission statements', whereas for others they might be lists showing a set of objectives or diagrams showing some sort of future state (or way of being) for the organisation. Whatever form they take, they can be produced at any moment and used to 'test' the usefulness or validity of any potential course of action before it is taken.

One of the most effective forms of 'touchstone' that I have come across is the 'Point Of View' concept, which was originally developed by the Bell

Pottinger Group, for use in the world of public relations. This brilliantly simple framework allows an organisation (or an individual, for that matter) to create a succinct expression of:

- What you think and believe about the world you operate in.

- How you behave every day as a result.

- The benefits you are then able to deliver to others.

- How you think others should behave and act, especially towards and with you.

The possession of (and confidence to use) a succinct 'Point Of View' statement also allows the OD practitioner to spring into action whenever the moment arises. It is difficult in this complex, changing, shifting world to 'stage manage' every potential meeting or interaction with the 'key players' in the organisational scene. Sometimes, even with the best-laid plans, we find ourselves in situations of unexpected opportunity. For example, we might accidentally find ourselves all of a sudden sharing a lift or standing in a queue (or in any other random, everyday situation) with a particular senior executive who we have been trying unsuccessfully to 'get to' via more orthodox routes for some time. Without the existence of a deeply held 'Point Of View' such moments might easily pass us by and become moments of regret (an old family friend used to say that 'if you let it, life can be nothing more than a string of missed opportunities'). With a strong 'Point Of View', carefully and sensitively used within a conversation so as not to appear 'clunky' and unnatural (remember the 'Authority, Presence and Impact' idea from earlier in the chapter) these moments can become real opportunities to make connections and to sow the seeds of future success.

Selective Targeting and 'the Long Game' (Tactical Opportunism?)

An old boss of mine (himself a former British Army officer with active service experience), when confronted by my youthful 'bull at a gate' enthusiasm, often used to say, 'Slow down, Mike; it's a long game, and some fights are not worth dying in a ditch for'. Eventually I managed to 1) sit still for long enough to work out what he meant, and then 2) find a way of putting his message into useful (I think) practice in the organisation where I was working at the time.

For many years the business had been led by a relatively small group of people who shared similar backgrounds and had presided over steady and largely untroubled growth. Several of them seemed to be moving into a phase of their career where they had one eye on retirement, and were, confusingly, being very cautious in their approach to change whilst also making some obvious attempts to develop a succession strategy. One strand of their approach to succession management involved the commissioning of a well-intentioned 'Director Development Programme', whereby every single person with the word 'director' in their job title had to attend every one of a series of six externally designed and run residential modules. Although I had no formal role in the programme, these events were all held at the conference centre where I had an office at the time, and very soon I found myself having conversations with many of the delegates in their coffee breaks or at the end of the day. A theme quickly emerged. The younger and/or more recently appointed programme participants, whilst acknowledging the good intentions behind the programme, all seemed to be expressing a frustration about having to attend every module, regardless of its relevance to their role, and were becoming restless because their more individual development needs were not being addressed. It also seemed as though the organisation, with its rather patrician, top-down, one-size-fits-all initiative, was adopting an approach that inadvertently raised people's awareness of the need for change, learning and development ... and yet had no way of addressing the subsequently awakened demand for it! At the time that this was all emerging, and very much on the back of my own experiences, I was developing my thinking about how directors and managers really learn and develop, and I felt that I was getting close to a new approach (which, over the years, has grown into my 'Appreciation, Provocation and Exposure' concept) that might work in practice ... but which needed testing and trialling. As I mentioned earlier, it strikes me that wars and conflicts have always been used by intelligent opportunists to create advantage from the disruption of existing systems and orders, working at the edges of the big 'pitched battles' or in the gaps and spaces opened up by more overt actions. This, then, looked like a situation where opportunity beckoned, but one which needed to be handled with care.

Effective guerrillas are careful not to deploy all of their forces in one pitched battle (unless the odds are stacked overwhelmingly in their favour), and tend to 'keep their powder dry' until it is needed. They tend to weigh up every situation so that they may 'live to fight another day', and in this situation it struck me that any overt public introduction of my individual-focused approach to director development could very easily look like criticism of the 'one-size-fits-all' approach currently being offered, and would put me in a very exposed position. This being the case, instead of using the more usual 'logical and rational' approach to the introduction of OD initiatives – public presentation of a formal proposal with costs, benefits, timelines and overt outcomes, to be approved by the existing 'powers that be' – I took a much more selective approach, engineering conversations where I could listen to the expressed frustrations of individual directors, and then introducing the emerging ideas about my new approach as an opportunity which might lead to mutual benefit. I chose my 'targets' very carefully, avoiding the established 'old school' leaders at the very top of the organisational hierarchy, and deliberately 'going after' the next generation of directors – the ones on an upward career curve, with energy, open minds and a degree of frustration. This was very much about 'the long game', and about building a particular group of allies and patrons/sponsors for (I hoped) later initiatives. Before long, and under the camouflage of a research project, I was working 'one on one' with a small number of directors, but as the word spread about what we were doing, the numbers grew and it became apparent that my new approach would be the favoured means of director development as and when the expected 'regime change' took place.

New Orders and Diplomatic Withdrawal

All guerrillas, whatever their cause or philosophy, tend to seek change and the eventual removal of the status quo. By definition they are frustrated in some way or another under the prevailing circumstances, and work towards some form of renewal. Not all are successful. Some fail properly to 'appreciate the situation' in its fullest sense and mistime their actions through faulty judgement, based on poor intelligence. Others are thwarted by overwhelming odds and either 'go down in a blaze of glory' or lose heart and 'lay down their arms'. Some, however, do achieve their aims, and then they find that success brings a new reality … and discover that they now face life as a member of a new establishment, or a new order. All of a sudden, the person who functioned best in the shadows, working quietly with limited power and resources, finds themselves in the spotlight, with people watching and expecting results.

Politicians often say that opposition is more straightforward than government. I wonder whether it is ever possible for a successful 'OD guerrilla' to become a long-term 'créature of the CEO', as Roger Stuart described the role of the more traditional organisational functional leader, who is expected to use the normal tools of organisational life to build, create, drive and deliver?

The two approaches demand very different sets of skills. The literature of organisational life is full of metaphors that use the circle or a cyclical form as their basis. Perhaps one of the most useful skills of the real organisational guerrilla is the ability to know when the circle has turned and it is time to move on, time to slip back into the shadows?

References

Balogun, J. and Hope Hailey, V., 2004. *Exploring Strategic Change* (2nd Edition). London: FT Prentice Hall.

Mruk, C., 1999. *Self-Esteem* (2nd Edition). New York, NY: Springer.

5

Working with Chaos and Complexity: An OD Practitioner's Perspective

Andy Smith

About This Chapter

There are different parts to this chapter and I have attempted to knit them together as best I can. The parts are:

- A bit about me, and my take on Organisational Development (OD).

- A story of how I got interested in complexity and chaos theory as it applied to OD.

- A philosophical discussion about what the implications of chaos and complexity theory are for the field of OD.

- A summary of some of the theory.

- A description of some models and 'tools' that I have used with clients and groups of learners to make sense of some of these concepts.

- At different stages extracts of a personal account/story of some OD work that I have undertaken, which I think is best explained from a complexity perspective.

- Some pleas and postscripts that both describe how you might use what I write and how I found the process of writing.

I have tried to write this chapter in a direct conversational style.

A Bit About Me and OD

I do think it is important that in reading this chapter you have some sense of where I'm coming from and what I do. I have worked in OD almost since I joined the world of work in 1978 and certainly before I knew what it was. Through my early work in organisations, I learnt about change, communication, and worker and leader anxiety. I was introduced to the world of staff inspection and sophisticated time management systems. I then moved into learning and development, diversity policy and internal consultancy. I have worked on the people aspects of job design, outsourcing, service reviews, performance management systems, job evaluation, competency frameworks and career management policies and structures. However, for the last 15 years my work as an external consultant has focused on leadership and OD. Underpinning most of what I do is a keen interest in groups and facilitation. Groups have been my OD apprenticeship.

At Roffey Park where I currently work, I played my part alongside several colleagues in introducing a successful OD Practitioner Development Programme back in 2004, one of the first in the UK. I have also been Programme Director for Roffey Park's MSc in People and Organisational Development. In the USA I would probably be referred to as a scholar/practitioner.

With all that experience you might think I would be really clear on what OD is. In truth, having studied and practised OD for some time, I think the answer to 'What is OD?' is a complex one. It can mean different things to different people, at different times. However, when asked, I answer that OD is concerned with:

- both organisational effectiveness and organisational health;

- thinking systemically – seeing links and patterns in organisations; and

- change.

As a practice, OD:

- is collaborative and process oriented (attuned to emotions, energy, relationships and power);

- appeals to a common value base;

- is research and inquiry oriented; and

- is characterised by a sense of optimism about people, and what they can achieve together.

Getting Started

I got into complexity theory by accident over 15 years ago. I had until that time been widely involved in large and small-scale change efforts as a manager, consultant, trade union representative and change manager. I had witnessed small-scale changes like a desk move excite huge interest, energy and anxiety beyond that which I could have imagined. I had

> **COMPLEXITY**
>
> 1. Made up of parts.
> 2. Complicated.
> 3. Whole made up of parts.
> 4. Group of unconscious feeling that influences behaviours.
>
> *Collins English Dictionary*

seen large-scale change effort focused on technology and systems that failed to engage with people about what this meant for them. I had witnessed the collective opposition and sabotage that had emerged as a result. I had worked with a manager who, although perceived by his reports and peers as 'soft' and over consultative, achieved huge changes.

My way of thinking and talking about change was the product of the dominant discourse (how people talked) about change at that time and still do. I was part of this discourse, often promoted on management of change programmes that I participated in and ran. The language was all of burning platforms, driving change, managing resistance, vision and Gantt charts. This provided some idealised notion of planned change, delivered on time, to meet pre-agreed success criteria, to align with a clear mission, vision and strategy.

And the models most in currency at that time were ones like Kotter's which seemed to become accepted management orthodoxy. Kotter (1995) talked about why change efforts failed and came up with a model for managing change that suggested you needed to:

- Establish a sense of urgency.

- Form a powerful guiding coalition.

- Create a vision.

- Communicate a vision.

- Empower others to act.

- Plan and create short-term wins.

- Build on the momentum to produce more change.

- Institutionalise the new approaches.

I found the model came to be used in a formulaic way. I experienced it being used as a diagnostic tool by consultants to fault find in the change effort. For example, the vision was found to be wanting, or leaders were blamed for not communicating it sufficiently well and action plans were, as a result, put in place to remedy this. This way of operating seemed rooted in a belief that, if all the ingredients were in place, the change would be managed successfully (in other words cause and effect were predictable).

The commonly held assumptions behind this model were not questioned. Since then I have come to realise the model as presented:

- presupposed that change could be led from the top and 'managed';

- that it was possible to create a sense of urgency and a guiding coalition; and

- that at some time the instability of change was replaced by a period of stability where it was possible to institutionalise the change that had taken place.

I still think the model is useful in some ways: sometimes the change effort was lacking in some areas and talking about these seemed to move things on. But I think it represents a way of thinking that is too limited and, which for me, does not fit in with the reality of change and OD.

So when, in 1998, I went on a consultancy skills programme at Roffey Park and I was introduced to a different way of thinking about change where the language was of 'emergence', 'unintended consequences', 'uncertainty', 'constant change', 'power', 'competing initiatives' and 'fluidity' I found something that spoke to me about my real experience of change, one of organisational mess, excitement and anxiety. Whenever I offer these two ways of thinking about change to groups and clients I work with, almost inevitably the first model is the one familiar to them and the one they try to follow. Whereas the second is much closer to how they really experience the change process. So I became a chaos and complexity convert and, ever since, I have been trying to find ways of using this way of thinking to help me understand what I do and do good work.

How Does Complexity Relate to OD as a Field?

So I do think chaos and complexity theory is important to understanding the field of OD because it represents an alternative to the dominant way of talking about change and OD. This is the paradigm of planned change and interventions, where levers are pulled to deliver predictable outcomes within a given timescale. Like any paradigm, it has its uses and limitations. Not least, the sense of predictability alleviates anxiety for people who are most often charged with delivering tangible results with diminishing resources. For me, this dominant paradigm is also a philosophical position. It makes assumptions about the nature of the world, people and organisations and how we know about these things. It rests on a long history of discourse which privileges 'real' science. This was itself the result of a dominance of one way of thinking that can be traced back to Greek philosophy and more recently Taylorism and Scientific Management (see boxed text below), which, as ways of thinking, still influence the world of OD.

TAYLORISM AND SCIENTIFIC MANAGEMENT

Frederick Taylor (1856–1917) was a key figure in the development of OD. An engineer by background, Taylor applied scientific principles to the processes of management. He was interested in objective data gathering on workflows, worker selection and training and division of labour between managers and operatives. Although thinking has moved on from scientific management, it still influences the field of OD in areas such as work measurement and lean business processes. The metaphor of the organisation as a machine remains associated with Taylor's thinking.

In a practitioner publication like this, I do not propose to expand too much on this but I do want to provide some kind of abbreviated timeline to help you make sense of it all. Of course, it is my timeline, so it is highly selective! This history has contributed to a 'rationalist' view of causality. According to Stacey (2001), this is one that implies the future is determined and enacted by reasoning human beings.

A VERY SHORT AND SELECTIVE HISTORY IN THE PHILOSOPHY OF THOUGHT AND THE DOMINANT DISCOURSE OF ORGANISATIONS

Classical Greek Philosophy Plato (427–347 BC) and Aristotle (384–322 BC)

Plato and Aristotle had in common that they sought to examine the world in a systematic way using reason to formulate general principles. Plato suggested the highest realities, or forms, which existed beyond our senses, could only be understood through reason. Aristotle on the other hand emphasised more what could be known through our experience and senses. Things could be known by structured and repeated experience in a world linked by space and time. What both have in common is this separation of thought and senses.

Rene Descartes and Cartesian Dualism

Descartes (1596–1627) is important to the evolution of philosophy and modern science. His central question was 'of what can I be certain?' In seeking this answer Descartes distinguished between what can be known through the senses and the world of thought. For Descartes the mind and body were separate and thought was critical (I think therefore I am) and was instrumental in a mechanical world. So thought was the 'lever' to influence matter.

Isaac Newton (1642–1727)

The rise of science is most often linked with Newton. The Newtonian view of the world rests on time and space being fixed as frameworks of a mechanical universe within which all other action takes place. In this world particles and atoms behave in predictable ways based on established rules and principles that link cause and effect.

Enlightenment (1650–1750)

A period of history in the development of western thought and culture characterised by a rejection of medieval and more spiritual views in favour of the principles of the scientific method, scepticism and reason. The Enlightenment links to radical developments in the sciences (which undermines previous ways of understanding the world) and politics (the French Revolution for example) during this period.

Positivism (1850 onwards)

Draws on the scientific methods made popular in the enlightenment. It became a foundation for social research rooted in the belief that the methods of the natural sciences could be applied in social research. This meant that human behaviour could be observed and objectively measured to establish principles of people's behaviour that could link cause and effect. In OD this plays out in the emphasis placed on the evidence base of the behavioural sciences.

As far as OD goes, it shows up in language like this. The OD consultant will meet and gain entry to the client system. After a period of relationship building and contracting they will be given access to the client system where through dispassionate data collection they will arrive at a hypothesis about what the problems in the system are, the causes for this malaise and prescribe a solution. Following implementation of this intervention, the OD consultant will leave the system better aligned, healthier and more efficient. This is the classic consultancy cycle (Cockman, 1998) as shown in the diagram below (Figure 5.1).

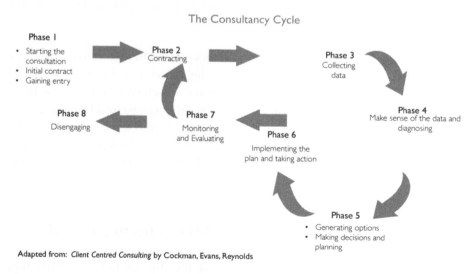

The Consultancy Cycle

Phase 1
• Starting the consultation
• Initial contract
• Gaining entry

Phase 2
Contracting

Phase 3
Collecting data

Phase 4
Make sense of the data and diagnosing

Phase 5
• Generating options
• Making decisions and planning

Phase 6
Implementing the plan and taking action

Phase 7
Monitoring and Evaluating

Phase 8
Disengaging

Adapted from: *Client Centred Consulting* by Cockman, Evans, Reynolds

Figure 5.1   The consultancy cycle

Now in describing this approach, I have exaggerated for effect. But as a practitioner (both internal and external), I have heard myself with clients, and on programmes to develop practitioners, say 'no data, no intervention' etc. I have talked of the consultancy cycle that this way of working represents. I still do. I have used models to diagnose what was to be done and classic models of change management (such as Kotter's) to engineer the solution to be implemented.

So what's wrong with this? Well at one level, nothing much: some of the models are useful for us and our clients. At another level, I think there is quite a lot lacking in this approach. As a way of talking about OD work, it is used time and time again without, for the most part, practitioners really thinking about what they are saying and claiming. It has so influenced our way of thinking as practitioners, that some, in my experience, find themselves incapable of detaching from it. My major issue here is that this way of working does not match my lived experience as a consultant, leader and member of an organisation. Organisational life is messy, not predictable.

Some of the research that underpins the field of OD, and the claims to knowledge we make as a result, also render it untrue. For example, take the Hawthorne experiments. Leaving aside more recent claims about their results, this research examined how changing the ergonomics (lighting) brought about change in worker behaviour. The researchers actually concluded that it was the presence of the researcher, rather than a change in the lighting, that changed worker behaviour and motivation.

My belief is, that as consultants, we are never detached objective observers of the systems we work in. We are part of the action and, in the mere act of turning up, something different happens to that which would otherwise have happened. Our very presence affects patterns, interactions and the operations of rules in ways we cannot predict or often understand. *I think this is key to OD practitioners understanding how they can, with this way of thinking, be differently effective for their clients.* As far as I am able, I describe some ways of doing this in the rest of the chapter.

An Alternative Discourse and How This Relates to the Field

Complexity and chaos theory form part of the mix of developments that challenge the dominant way of thinking and talking about OD and change. There are other theoretical and philosophical schools that have influenced this, for example social constructionism and postmodernism, as well as changing practices that promote dialogue across organisations. Again, I don't propose to explore all of these, but in the text boxes, I have provided some brief explanations.

SOCIAL CONSTRUCTIONISM

The idea that reality is socially constructed rather than an objective truth. Reality is a perception created by people, most often in participation with others, as part of a social process. These realities need to be maintained and reaffirmed if they are to be sustained. In OD, social constructionism (Berger and Luckman, 1979) underpins approaches such as appreciative inquiry and others rooted in conversation and dialogue.

How this might lead to a change in how we see OD work is best set out by Bushe and Marshak (2009). They argue that the classical way of describing OD, and the theory that supports it, is at odds with much of the developments in practice and supporting theory now in use by some. With this type of underpinning knowledge, OD practitioners are more likely to believe that change cannot be managed, rather it is emergent and self-organising. As a result, the role of the OD consultant has changed from one of diagnosis and planned intervention to one of promoting dialogue in support of self-organising processes which may lead to change.

POSTMODERNISM

Postmodernism challenges the acceptance of objective truth as received wisdom, which in turn, is often associated with enlightenment and modernism. It links to social constructionism in that it emphasises the role of language, power and relationships in the forming of ideas and beliefs.

I take issue with some of Bushe and Marshak's conclusions, for example, they do not give sufficient attention to power and anxiety in organisations. By this I mean:

- How those in power influence what is said and those without power are less likely to be heard.

- How unconscious processes in organisations create anxiety and dependence.

However, leaving these two points aside, I think their arguments are pretty convincing. So I am inviting you to take a different philosophical position on the field of OD by engaging with certain aspects of chaos and complexity theory as you read through this chapter.

Barking up the Wrong Tree: Trying to Make Complexity Theory Simple and Utilitarian?

As I have heard Ralph Stacey say 'If you change the way you think, you change the way you act' and, as a practitioner I am inviting you to do the same. However, before I go further, a word of caution. Frustratingly, I think it is wrong to make complexity theory simple, practical and utilitarian. Paradoxically, this is what I have tried to do here. The reason I say this is because trying to make complexity simple misses the whole point. Things are complex because often they are. A practitioner who thinks otherwise may too easily assume that they can readily identify cause and effect and go just with what they know and think is practical and useful, rather than living with the uncertainty of not knowing what is going on and find out more.

What Do we Mean by Chaos and Complexity Theory?

CHAOS THEORY

Chaos theory draws mainly on mathematics and computer modelling and observation of patterns in systems such as the weather. Chaos is a misnomer for this body of theory as it is not about utter confusion. Rather it is about patterns so, 'chaordic' might be a more appropriate term. What might seem chaotic from one perspective is more patterned and ordered than might appear from another. Here are some of the key messages I take from chaos theory.

Firstly, small changes in initial conditions can result in unanticipated and unintended consequences. The two examples most often quoted here are the rounding of the fraction in mathematical modelling leading to an entirely different outcome. In weather systems, this is about the flap of the wings of a butterfly having a significant and unanticipated effect on weather patterns far away. This insight challenges the question of linearity and a clear or proportional link between cause and effect. Rather, there can be multiple causes for an effect and multiple effects for a cause.

Secondly, chaos theory is also about patterns. The nature of these patterns links to attractors. Attractors are not forces or magnets but patterns of where the system is headed or ends up. There are different types of attractors (Eoyang, 1997):

- **Point attractors** are those where the end point is one of stability although the path there may not be identical. The example often used is of placing a marble and rolling it around the rim of a bowl. The marble will end up at the bottom of the bowl but its movement around the side of the walls of the bowl will vary. In an organisation, a project end date could be viewed as a point attractor.

- **Periodic attractors** are those where, over time, a similar pattern repeats itself like the seasons or an annual business planning process.

- **Strange attractors** are the most 'chaotic' in form in that they do not move towards a stable state. Rather, they are unpredictable and have a dynamic of stable instability or regular irregularity (Stacey, 2012). This means that over time we can see that the apparent randomness of the pattern is bounded in some way, so it will not go beyond certain points. The clear example of this is weather patterns. Whilst it is possible to predict weather in the short term, in the long term this becomes much more difficult. We know too that there can be seasonal variations and exceptional weather events. But the weather will not move beyond certain norms – it will not snow in the Sahara, for example.

CASE STUDY 1: A STORY OF CHANGE, CHAOS AND COMPLEXITY

A colleague and I were reflecting on the world of consultancy and learning and development. We had noticed that people's titles had shifted in the recruitment adverts. Learning and Development Managers were being replaced by Heads of OD. In our work on the MSc in People and Organisational Development we had noticed a similar shift, from people to organisational development. That seemed the new thing. Alongside others we started using the language of OD and went and spoke at a CIPD Conference on 2004 on the title 'Is there confusion in OD?' where we mentioned the launch of our new OD Practitioner Programme. After the presentation I got talking to one of the attendees, 'Ben'.

Commentary: What has this to do with complexity and chaos theory?

My colleague and I spotted a pattern that represented some kind of shift in how people in organisations talked about HR, L and D and OD. No one I think planned this. It just emerged somehow but took firm root in the press and literature. We decided this represented an opportunity and speaking at the conference set in train a whole series of different events we could not have predicted.

A final insight from chaos theory is about the unpredictability of patterns and the possibility of sudden and unexpected change. Lorenz, in his observing the dynamic of water wheels, saw that the movement of the wheel was affected by subtle changes in water flow (Gleick, 1997). Movement could vary from none, to slow, to fast, to one, where in a moment, suddenly, the wheel flipped and shifted direction.

Now, I have sometimes heard this moment of flipping referred to as the edge of chaos. This phrase is often associated with chaos theory, as I do in this chapter, and probably wrongly so, as it draws on some different concepts. The important thing though about this idea of the edge of chaos is that it represents a point of transition between one type of pattern and another. Most often at this point, the system will be at its most volatile and unpredictable. Because of this there is often the possibility of change and innovation (Kimball, 2008). That is not to say that beyond the edge of chaos there is stability as some of the models I use suggest, rather a different form of pattern.

My experience is that different proponents of chaos theory's application to organisations will take different positions on how chaotic chaos theory is. By that I mean how or whether it can be used to predict in a different, but still deterministic way, or not, what happens in organisations.

Leaving this aside, in social systems, how do we understand these concepts? The riots in the UK (Summer 2011) provide a possible example. The tipping point for what seemed a spontaneous outbreak of rioting/protest/criminality (depending on your perspective) was the shooting by the police of someone in Tottenham in London. This led to copycat riots throughout London and the UK that were both connected and unconnected. The riots shook the political system and led to the cancellation of an international football match. They probably affected stock prices too. But no one, despite lots of people offering different hypotheses, based on their own view of the world, can explain how and why this happened. And just as quickly as the riots spread, they died down.

CASE STUDY 2: MOVING TOWARDS ANXIETY

At an early run of the OD Practitioner Programme I bumped into someone from Ben's organisation. Ben had suggested they attend. I think I was doing a session on group dynamics or systems thinking but I can recall the atmosphere being a bit edgy in the group and I pointed this out and we talked about it. I thought nothing more of it until sometime later I got the call from Ben's organisation again. I was asked to do a number of things. He told me that his colleague had reported back that she thought I was the kind of person that would be good to work with. I visited Ben's organisation and spoke about change to some senior managers and the HR and Learning and Development Team.

Commentary: What has this to do with complexity and chaos theory?

Well this is about emergence, connection and unpredictability. Someone attended the programme because we had met Ben. I entered the group at a time when I think there was some anxiety that was playing out and I moved towards this rather than avoided it. Somehow the participant was sufficiently impressed by this to say that I was the person to have further conversations with.

In organisations it is perhaps more difficult to explain this phenomenon although people have started to adopt the language of the 'edge of chaos' and 'tipping points' and 'nudges'. My experience of team development and unstructured group work suggests that stripping away traditional ways of relating and ordering conversation and action can have both predicable and unpredictable effects. People often try to reinstall normal ways of operating by forming agendas, rules and procedures. Others resist them. On the cusp between these, often there is a breakthrough moment where people find new ways of operating and relating that they will experience as transforming, without being able to identify the point at which change occurred or became possible.

At its most simple level, it could be where someone decided to break the habitual patterns, for example of being either supportive or suppressing their real view, to say directly and challengingly what they really think and feel. This can give rise to relief, anxiety and some change. To be instrumental in this requires the OD practitioner not to place faith in some overall design for the intervention, rather, in the moment, to notice the pattern, draw attention to it and sometimes model a different alternative way of behaving. For a group that is highly critical, for example, this might be the act of affirming someone, and vice versa. So I am very wary of facilitators who stick to their pre-designed methodology and structure to get to an end point, come what may, no matter what is going on in the group.

My group work has also taught me to expect the unexpected. I have worked with groups whose normal pattern of conflict and challenge can shift suddenly to one of support when stimulated by a small challenge to the team from outside it. I have also experienced groups, seemingly working well and collaboratively on a joint project, suddenly turn on each other and the facilitator. Some theory and patterns of group dynamics may help explain some of this but not all of it.

As a practitioner, I believe you have to move towards these moments, rather than away from them. By that I mean a variety of things depending on what appears to be the group's normal pattern, as examples:

- If divergent views are being expressed, I try to ensure they are heard and held rather than stifled.

- If there is conflict and emotion in the room, to acknowledge and explore it.

- If there is agreement, suggest the group move on rather than carry on talking.

As a practitioner I need as well to be able to live with the uncertainty of my own fear of what might be and is happening, and the fact that the group might prefer if I did something more 'safe' and 'usual'. In acting in this way, I am very much entering the group's life and pattern, rather than existing as an observer outside of it. I therefore become a new variable and even small things I do may make a difference. This possibility of change and the opportunity to do something different can create anxiety. This is why when working in this way I pay attention to how I can create a safe enough environment (a container in the jargon) for people to take risk. Both are needed for people to let go of their normal defensive routines if something different is going to occur.

Chaordic Patterns, Tensions and Polarities

Another way I work with groups and organisations to make this notion of chaordic patterns more accessible is by using the simple model below (O'Connor 1998). This gets people thinking about the relationship between order and chaos; valuing both; and seeing that the scope for change is often at the edge of chaos, where these tensions are held in a way that is useful. It is not about being at one end of the continuum or the other, rather about noticing the patterns between the ends and thinking about ways that these can be influenced or changed. Whilst this represents a deterministic way of thinking about organisations, I think it does draw on some of the concepts of chaos theory as it encourages thinking about patterns and how organisations can have both ordered stability and unstable order. So it does embrace paradox in some way.

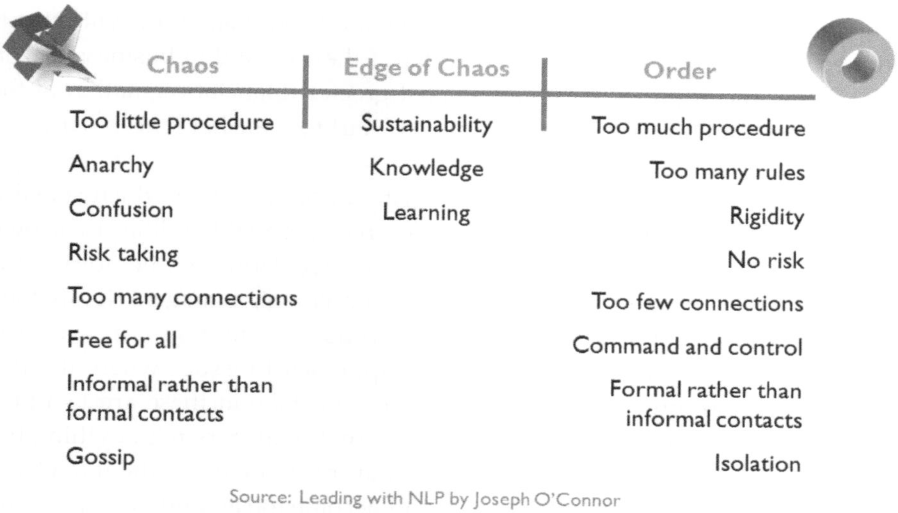

Chaos	Edge of Chaos	Order
Too little procedure	Sustainability	Too much procedure
Anarchy	Knowledge	Too many rules
Confusion	Learning	Rigidity
Risk taking		No risk
Too many connections		Too few connections
Free for all		Command and control
Informal rather than formal contacts		Formal rather than informal contacts
Gossip		Isolation

Source: Leading with NLP by Joseph O'Connor

Figure 5.2   The Edge of Chaos

In terms of the changes they are considering, the questions I pose are:

- What are the forces for order – how are they valued?

- What are the forces for chaos – how are the valued?

- Where does the power lie between them?

- Are you on the edge and if not, do you need to go there?

- If you were to go to/be at the edge what would need to change and what would that be like?

As an activity, you could try this out now with your own organisation. My experience is this can help people understand these patterns and dynamics differently. It also tends to shed light on what really happens in organisations compared with what people say should go on. For example the 'stuff' that goes on in the chaos side is rarely officially sanctioned. It often involves activities where 'mavericks' break the rules and do things differently. Some senior leaders often like the results but can't officially sanction them. Other leaders in the same organisation might not like the rule breaking because they associate this with risk but might not have the power or opportunity to act to stop it. So, collectively, the leadership publicly ignore what is going on. At least until something goes wrong. And when a risk rebounds on them, they will refocus on mechanisms for installing greater order, if they are still in business. If you think about the arguments for and against greater financial regulation of the markets pre- and post-recession, I think you start to see what I mean here.

As another example, I once worked with an organisation which stated it wanted to have an empowered workforce, free as possible within their own responsibilities to take decisions and be innovative. However, because of the industry involved, where there was the risk of accident, managers rightly took such risk seriously and provided lots of procedures to minimise it. The issue for the organisation was it took the same approach to issues where the risk involved was not great. If a manager made a mistake in these areas, a new procedure would be written. The result was that managers felt anything but empowered. I encouraged the client to look at this issue using the model and they realised that their approach to risk had become too accentuated in certain areas. For these areas they could afford to loosen up some of their procedures so that their rhetoric on empowerment was more likely to be trusted by their managers. They audited their procedures to see which ones were no longer needed.

Polarity Management

Whilst he does not reference chaos theory, this notion of working with tensions and different polarities around which patterns form is evident in the thinking of Barry Johnson (1997) on polarity management. The characteristics of polarities are that they:

- have no end point;

- are like breathing: the polarities need each other just like you can't exhale without inhaling;

- are mutually inclusive rather than exclusive;

- are real opposites; and

- exist over time.

The practitioner needs to distinguish between what is a problem that is solvable and true polarities. However, these polarities often have an archetypal quality to them in that many are true of many organisations and form part of the things that get talked about, actioned and bemoaned.

Some examples are:

- Centralise or decentralise.

- Cost and quality.

- Diversity and cohesion.

- Risk taking and risk management.

- Consistency and innovation.

- Stability and change.

- Task and relationship.

Johnson views tensions between these polarities as neither good nor bad. There can be both positive and negative effects to either. The important thing is to notice when forces get out of kilter. Holding them in balance is where the new might emerge. Certainly trying to resolve differences by some process of alignment would be a bad thing in most cases. Rather, it might be better to help people live more productively and effectively with the patterns that emerge between these differences.

To illustrate what I am saying, here is an example from when I consulted to a high-tech organisation. The engineers who produced the technology to support their products were engineers first and foremost. They loved the latest technology. They wanted to make sure the product they produced harnessed the best and latest technology and that this was tested and tested so its reliability and quality were of the highest order. Clearly there were some good things about this approach.

There were downsides too which the marketing and sales force bemoaned. They saw their geeky colleagues pre-occupied in a way that bore no relation to the 'real' world of commerce and fast moving markets. They were concerned how rising costs would affect margin and price in a competitive market for the product. And what most concerned them was that in testing and retesting the products, they came to market too late and, no matter how good they were, market share would be lost. So even though the product was not fully signed off by the engineers, they would sell on its value to clients who were waiting. Of course engineers viewed this behaviour as risky ... and so it goes on.

Both parties were right in some ways and both had legitimate anxieties. The answer to this lay not in resolving the tension but helping them to live with it better and understand it. If either 'side' won out that would be a greater risk.

Johnson puts forward his own way of plotting the positive and negative consequences of polarities which you might find useful to work through with people involved in change so they develop an awareness of these issues.

From Chaos to Complexity

In this next section, I am going to move on from chaos to complexity theory. As with the earlier section on chaos, I want to describe some of the key principles and terminologies and discuss their implications for OD practice. In this way of thinking, organisations are often described as complex adaptive systems. So we are adopting the metaphor of an organisation as a living organism or community rather than a machine, an anthill rather than a car.

The characteristics of complex adaptive systems are normally described as:

- Systems consist of numbers of interacting agents (in organisations this means people).

- Interactions are governed by local rules.

- Agents repeat certain actions and interactions.

- Agents adapt to each other.

- The action of an agent will not necessarily provoke the same action in another so effects and relationships are unpredictable.

- Interaction can be non-linear both because of the above and because some of the rules may be different for certain agents.

- Ongoing variety provides for novelty.

- Systems can both model their environment and influence it.

Simple Rules and Complex Adaptive Systems

I often use a very simple exercise to help people make sense of some of the concepts underlying complex adaptive systems and change. I explain to the

Figure 5.3   Connections

group they are a complex adaptive system (a group of individuals) come together for some purpose, normally learning. I then invite them to follow these instructions.

- Choose two people (but don't let them know you have chosen them).

- When I say go, move to a position where you are equal distance between them.

- When they move (because they have chosen other people), move to a new place of equal distance.

- Stop when you find steady state (i.e. when everybody in the system has found a place where they can position themselves between the people they have chosen).

What ensues follows a similar pattern, but there are always variations. There is laughter, excitement and some anxiety. It starts slowly then gains momentum, people bump into each other. Very soon the 'system' settles down in the room. People stop moving. I then ask people what sense we can make of this activity for organisations and OD. Using this metaphor, the things that normally get discussed or raised are:

- Neither where we ended up overall as a system, nor where people were standing within the system could have been predicted.

- The rules governing the movement did influence and constrain the end point.

- Normally at least one person applied different rules either because they wanted to, or because they misunderstood them.

- Some people were more connected with others.

- Often the least connected people are more towards the edge than the centre of the group (and my personal experience is that this often models reality in that people who are less well known are chosen less as connectors: so the system replicates or models the 'real' environment. For example I worked with one organisation where people in regional offices nearly always ended up as the outliers).

- Despite the initial anxiety and/or excitement (people experienced it differently) it settled down remarkably quickly.

- If you experiment further, by introducing a new person or asking people to connect up to different people, something will happen on the system as a whole (sometimes this can have a significant or slight effect: it depends on how others are connected).

Now if we accept this as a legitimate way of thinking about the work we do with people as they organise, this has real implications. The ones I draw out are the importance and power of multiple connection, difference of perspective from those at the centre to those on the edge, the fact that if you are at any stage 'stuck', do something different and the chances are something different will happen but the outcome cannot be predicted.

Most important, is that as an OD practitioner you are an 'agent'. You can exert influence on the system in different ways. You can seek multiple connections; you can follow or suggest different rules; you can introduce new people; and you can connect people differently; you can choose to stay at the edge. All of these actions and choices will have consequences and have the potential to bring about change. Rarely though will you be able to predict the outcome of what you start off and, always, you are part of the system you are trying to influence. You are not a dispassionate observer but an active participant. Clearly I think this has implications for practice.

CASE STUDY 3: CONNECTIONS AND SIMPLE RULES

As a result of the connection with Ben, we ran an OD Capability programme for the organisation's learning and development and HR team. We introduced models such as Burke-Litwin (2007). The team started to carry credit card versions of the model. We applied it to the organisation to understand it together and to think about next steps. Ben asked me to provide two days consultancy a month. I never quite knew what would happen on these two days. Normally I would turn up and Ben had arranged for a range of people to see me. I did not know what outcomes were wanted even when I asked Ben. Some were coaching conversations and others were just chats. I looked at the competence framework. I designed a 360. And at the end of the day, Ben and I would have a meal at my hotel and talk. He would pose questions he was wrestling with. Like, where should the OD function sit? Should it be a central function or integrated into the business? I spoke of the pros and cons of each but made no expert recommendation. A month later I went back and Ben told me he had re-organised as I'd suggested!

Commentary: What has this to do with complexity and chaos theory?

Well it's all pretty unpredictable. We offered the Burke-Litwin model as just one model but it quickly became the one adopted. There are simple rules at play here. I turn up two days a month. Ben puts people in front of me and we have a chat. Some conversations lead to other things. Some don't. There was no preset agenda. When I asked Ben what outcome he wanted from any conversation I very rarely got one. Just have a chat, see where it takes you, stir things up a little, and talk to them about 360 or change or whatever. The evening conversations were important. There was a pattern and a rare quality to them. We made different sense of the same conversation. I think my 'expert' power influenced the client consultant relationship – so my questions became suggestions and unintended consequences flowed.

Structured Complexity?

What I have described above clearly shows the importance of simple rules and that the effects of simple rules are not always simple. However, building on the notion of simple rules, Glenda Eoyang (1997) through her writing and the work of the Human System Dynamics Institute (HSD) provides some interesting ways of relating complexity theory to organisations (Eoyang and Olson, 2001). For

MEMES

A word that combines notions of memory and genes. In the world of OD I think of memes as the genetic DNA of the organisation. They transmit things like culture, values, the way of doing things around here, out of awareness.

example, HSD promotes a notion that culture is a reflection of how people behave which is in turn the product of simple rules (Holladay, 2005). They see simple rules as the meme-transmitting DNA of the organisation providing guidance for decision making.

This they argue allows for:

- More cohesiveness and consistency in decision making.

- A sense of reduced anxiety and confidence in how to do things.

- A need for less active management.

- Altered structures in support of the rules.

- Greater continuity in periods of change.

They propose these rules can be uncovered by simple conversations and questions like 'What are the rules here? What gets rewarded? What are the publicly endorsed rules and how do they compare with the 'real' ones?' And I would add 'Who makes the rules?'

Eoyang has developed some rules (Holladay, 2005) for making simple rules as follows:

- Rules should reinforce desired behaviours.

- The rules should be short, understandable and transferable across the organisation.

- There should be no more than seven plus or minus two. This is based on psychological research that says we are only able to hold this amount of data at one time.

- The rules should describe how and in what ways people come together to address differences in the group; and finally how people exchange information (this reflects Eoyang's core model of working with complexity, the CDE model, that I describe below).

- Each rule should start with a doing word.

Eoyang goes on to say how the rules can be used by managers to measure and regulate performance. This is where I take some issue with her thinking as I find this too ordered a way of working to be consistent with chaos and complexity thinking. It therefore has more in common with a more rational perspective. For example, I would see 'desired behaviour' as something that is socially constructed rather than an objective truth. However, that may also be why Eoyang's thinking is attractive to those seeking to build bridges between traditional and rational ways of thinking and those supported by the less traditional ones I have described.

And setting simple rules can be an interesting way of organising. I was talking to a former colleague of mine who had inherited a new role in the management of some different teams, with different expertise and different ways of seeing the world. Very quickly she wanted to get them working across boundaries. She set some very simple rules which went something like this:

- Each of you will participate in one of four projects.

- You should self-organise with maximum diversity across these projects.

- Consume your own smoke: don't moan to me about your differences.

- Subject to the above, act as if you have choice and responsibility.

From this, a whole set of interesting interactions and changes occurred. The sense of engagement, empowerment and ownership were palpable and the results excellent. And my former colleague admitted that there were other requisites for working effectively in this way – she had a team of highly experienced, self-motivated and autonomy-liking individuals. The same simple rules, she does not believe would work so well in another setting.

ACTIVITY

Apply the notion of simple rules to your own organisation.

- What are the simple rules in action?
- How are they different from those that are espoused?
- If you had the power to redesign them what rules would you set?
- Try to apply Eoyang's rules on simple rules. How do they stack up?

Eoyang and Olson (2001) also put forward a model for making sense of the patterns in organisations and working with complexity and chaos, the CDE model. These they describe as follows:

- 'C' for container: This is about paying attention to how the system is bounded and held. At its simplest level this could be who is or is not at a meeting or where it takes place, for example at an away day or a scheduled business meeting.

- 'D' is for differences: this is about diversity; opposing views and tensions. Honouring these differences and dialogue between them holds up the possibility of change.

- 'E' is for exchanges: this is about how people exchange information and connect.

Using this model, you can as a practitioner, look at any particular pattern to understand what is going on; have conversations about this; and agree some actions geared towards change.

ACTIVITY

Think of an issue or pattern in your organisation you are seeking to understand or change in some way

What is the pattern? How is it sustained?

- Container.
- Differences.
- Exchange.

Then repeat the activity with the question of how would you like it to be different. What might you change to make this possible?

In this way, by using Eoyang and Olson's model, people can talk about change and complexity in a systematised way to arrive at some joint actions. So this represents a very practical OD intervention rooted in complexity thinking.

From Complex Adaptive Systems to Complex Responsive Processes

What I have written in the last sections about chaos and complexity theory belongs I suspect to what Stacey (2001) would call the school of 'formative causality'. This perspective still implies that the future can in some way be known and created but differs from rationalist causality in that it accepts that self-organisation and emergent patterns may vary this end state. In this last section, I want to move on to an understanding of complexity rooted in what Stacey (2001) describes as 'transformative causality'.

This perspective suggests that movement towards a future state is constantly in a state of construction and the act of construction is what creates movement, but to an end state that cannot be predicted. The foundations for this process are human interaction and conversation. However, even the simple act of conversation is understood differently, as a complex responsive process.

Borrowing from Stacey (2001), how I make sense of this is as follows. A traditional way of thinking about communication is that:

- Person A thinks.

- Person A converts this thought to words/gestures.

- Person A transmits these words to Person B.

- Person B thinks about what is said.

- Person B converts their thoughts to words/gestures.

- Person B responds.

This is a linear, sequential way of communicating where thought and action are separated out and rooted in the individual.

However, if we understand the world of communicating from the perspective of complex responsive processes, communication unfolds between Persons A and B in a way where both parties' gestures and responses feed off each other continuously as they 'go along' together. Whilst there may well be patterns to their interactions, and turns, the way they behave and respond to each other is complex because they are influenced by a range of factors including history, ritual, power, emotions and anxiety and context that belongs to the moment of interacting. Further there is no simple separation between the individual, others and the context in which they show up.

So, at a fundamental level, writers such as Stacey and Shaw are rejecting a dualist notion of communication and traditional ways of thinking about organisations and in so doing they differ from others such as Eoyang. They have adopted the theory of complexity sciences and added to it a greater appreciation of what this means in terms of human relating and organising. For them, people are not the same as other biological systems. They do not follow rules in a simple or rational fashion.

Stacey (2010) believes:

> *Organisational wholes are our own imaginative constructs with no physical existence ... organisational reality is actually just people; the communicative interaction between them.*

Similarly Shaw (2002) says that:

> *The territory of exploration is increasingly understood by managers not as actually 'there' but being formed by the exploration itself.*

When thinking in this way, I shift from using nouns such as organisations and relationships to verbs such as relating and organising. It is these processes that give life to such concepts as organisations.

This way of thinking represents a radical challenge for me on what it is to be human and how we create ourselves through our interactions, let alone to be an OD consultant. I am still coming to terms to fully understand what this means. However, what I have taken from this is that how we are and how we organise, is brought forth in our conversations with others.

It has helped me understand some things better, for example the nature of repetitive patterns of conversations in organisations. In my own organisation there seems to be a particular conversation that is held time and time again (the content is irrelevant in some senses) about the different ways of seeing our work and the purpose of the organisation. I have not only been part of these conversations but I also have seen consultancy reports that are 20 years old that refer to exactly the same kind of conversation, the tension and anxiety between different perspectives, although none of the people involved are the same. So there is something going on here that is important in ways I do not fully understand. I used to get frustrated by the repetitiveness of it but have come to see it as an important pattern, a way of relating that keeps us as we are, which may or may not be a good thing. I suspect as with the question of polarities, it is more important that we have the conversation than the conversation resolves the points at issue. This is why as a practitioner I think we need to be careful in pursuing management orthodoxy of alignment that most OD models imply.

CASE STUDY 4: AN EMERGENT OD STRATEGY

We continued to work across the organisation in lots of different but rarely large-scale ways. We continued to build the capability of the OD Team (as they were now called). I noticed how they seemed to turn up differently at meetings alongside the managers they supported to help identify issues, needs and solutions. It seemed a different level of engagement. They seemed more influential and confident. Several years down the track Ben and I took stock of where the organisation was. We had been involved in delivering 360 for the vast majority of leaders across the organisation. Nearly all had attended some form of leadership development programme (often involving other consultancies that were a better fit). It was clear that across the organisation there had been a range of interventions touching on most of the boxes of the Burke-Litwin model. There was talk of the need for change, of doing more with less, of the importance of culture, leadership and values and of Lean. People were looking more actively at staff and client engagement surveys. There were more plans for development, restructuring and strategising.

Commentary: What has this to do with complexity and chaos theory?

Well a lot happened from the time Ben and I first met. Very little of it could have been anticipated. Certainly, at the outset, I did not intend some form of whole system intervention, yet the reality was something akin to this had happened. We ended up somewhere we had not planned for. The relationships and connections that Ben had with me and those he had across the organisation and with senior leaders in particular were key to this.

So how does a practitioner attempt to use this? Shaw models a practice where she actively enters the conversations of the moment. She constantly inquires into what is happening and is an active participant in what is going on. She leverages her own and notices others' power. She cannot predict where each conversation will lead. There is no sense of her pretending to be an external or neutral servant of the system, as represented by most popular notions of facilitation.

Shaw (2002) critiques some of the more formulaic interventions of the 'new' OD (for example large group interventions and open space technology) because they share certain assumptions with other traditional ways of thinking. For example, at both a human relating and organising level, they do not sufficiently take account of issues such as power and anxiety that in some ways they seek to contain rather than give expression to. I have experienced this myself in events that have been built around the principle of large group interventions and appreciative inquiry. The facilitators stated that they would allow us to self-organise; to go to the edge of chaos; but the reality felt different. The simple rules seemed over constraining. There was such an emphasis on being appreciative that rawer conversations expressing emotion (frustration and anger mainly) were difficult to have. Dissident and minority voices found it hard to be heard. The methodology became a source of power held by the facilitators.

Stacey (2007) does offer some suggestions akin to simple rules for working with complex responsive processes, suggesting leaders and practitioners refocus their attention on:

- The quality of participation.

- The quality of conversational life.

- The quality of anxiety and how this is lived with.

- The quality of diversity.

- Unpredictability and paradox.

We can see similarity here with some of the thinking I have described before about rules, diversity, conversations, safety and risk.

I cannot deny that this way of working represents a challenge for practitioners and clients who want to see utility and practical implications of any intervention. However, for me, it does describe what goes on in conversations between client and consultants and the potential of these conversations. It also suggests the more honest we can be with our clients about our approach (and I am not always) and about what is going on in the moment, the better for me and them. And it is this type of working that I believe holds up the prospect of real change but not in ways that we can predict. It is also at one level very ordinary – it's all about talking with people.

Postscript and Final Thoughts

I have come to the conclusion that this chapter is a lesson in complexity in action. I did not set out at any point in my life in an act of objective analysis and planned action to write a chapter on complexity as it relates to the field of OD. It is the product of a sequence of unconnected events over a period of time and chance conversations guided by relationship (both of friendship and power), of ego, anxiety, and coincidence.

In fact, my first offering to the editors was for a chapter on data collection and diagnostic tools as I thought the discipline of writing this would be 'good' for me. Then the editor suggested someone else might pick this up as his sense was the area of complexity was more 'me'. I was seduced by his encouragement that this could be a really important chapter central to the book as a whole and that I was the person to write it.

As the deadline for a chapter outline neared, in a panic I downloaded all the stuff I knew about complexity from my reading and working on the MSc at Roffey Park into a chapter summary. I had an idealised notion of what a book chapter might look like and thought it important to write in a clever intellectual way. I got feedback from the editor (in the nicest possible way) that for a field guide it seemed over-theorised and distanced from the reader (I got other feedback but it was this I chose to pay attention to). He was a both a colleague who I respected and, because he was editor, I attributed a special power and weight to his comments.

I wrestled with how to write the chapter. I revisited old papers and books. I re-read Patricia Shaw's book on Changing Conversations and was heavily influenced by it. I wanted this chapter to be conversational and in the experience of writing it rather than outside it. I ran a session on the MSc because a guest speaker pulled out which made me refresh my thinking and confronted me once again with the question voiced by one participant which went something like 'Well that's all well and good but how do I use it with a hard-bitten CEO who is looking for guaranteed results from a change effort?' I listened on the same residential to a client of mine tell a story about the work we had done together and enjoyed some new insights from this. I loved the way in which the story illustrated the theory.

There was no clear plan. I started at different places and with different styles. This end bit I wrote before the main body. At the last moment I contacted Ralph Stacey about one of his models and got some feedback that resulted in me rewriting the section on chaos theory following a bit of a spin where I put the chapter in the 'too difficult tray'. So it replicates in so many ways my thinking and how I do the work I do:

- I show up and use my presence.

- I rarely start out with an end in mind but I would talk with my client about this.

- I start off in all kinds of different places but try and stay in the present.

- I pay attention to how people talk about things.

- I notice patterns.

- I am influenced by power relationships and seek to understand these.

- I knowingly and unknowingly use my own power relationships.

- I try to get to talk to people who don't always get heard to listen to their story.

- My actions can lead to people coming together to talk about stuff that's important to them in a way that is different to how they might normally do this.

- I tune into my own and others' anxieties and fears and move towards rather than away from them.

- I like to break the rules (which is a rule).

- I very rarely start and finish.

- I measure value though the quality of connection and conversation.

- I seek multiple connections.

A Final Plea: Don't Throw the Baby out with the Bath Water

Finally, I do not want to persuade practitioners to give up all their traditional models and ways of thinking about change. Rather I would like to promote in you as a practitioner a greater awareness of at least two things. Firstly, see the value differently in these models. Very often to introduce a model such as Kotter's serves a really useful purpose in that it supports a conversation for people involved in change about what is going on and their anxieties and frustrations around the change process. This is what I think is most useful rather than any action plan that might result from the generation of this data. Second, there are certain changes that are suited to a planned approach and others not. In his model below, Stacey (1995) previously sought to describe these as situations where people are close to agreement and certainty about the proposed change. In these cases, plan the changes. However, if people are far from agreement and certainty about what needs to be done, Stacey recommended we seek patterns. In a final twist of complexity, Stacey[1] has now rejected this model. However, I still find it useful as a way of thinking and using it with your clients may support a different kind of conversation, which embodies the either-and- approach I am advocating.

Figure 5.4   Know when your challenges are in the zone of complexity

References

Berger, P. and Luckman, T., 1979. *The Social Construction of Reality.* Lodnon: Penguin Books.
Burke, W.W., 2007. *Organization Change: Theory and Practice.* 2nd edition. Thousand Oaks, CA: Sage Publications.

---

1   It is only right to say that Stacey has rejected his own model as it suggests managers and practitioners can make rational choices about the tools for particular situation which he now sees as being at odds with the full unpredictability and complexity of organisational life.

Bushe, G.R. and Marshak, R.J., 2009. Revisioning organization development: Diagnostic and dialogic premises and patterns of practice. *Journal of Applied Behavioral Science,* 45(3), pp. 348–68.

Cockman, P., 1998. *Consulting for Real People: A Client-centred Approach for Change Agents and Leaders.* 2nd edition. New York, NY: McGraw-Hill.

Eoyang, G., 1997. *Coping with Chaos: Seven Simple Tools.* Cheyenne, WY: Lagumo Publishing.

Eoyang, G. and Olson, E., 2001. *Facilitating Organization Change: Lessons from Complexity Science.* San Francisco, CA: Jossey-Bass.

Gleick, J., 1997. *Chaos.* London: Vintage.

Holladay, R., 2005. Simple rules and organizational DNA. *The OD Practitioner,* 37(4).

Johnson, B., 1997. *Polarity Management. Identifying and Managing Unsolvable Problems.* 2nd revised edition. Amherst, MA: HRD Press.

Kimball, L., 2008. Practicing OD in complex systems. *The OD Practitioner,* 40.

Kotter, J., 1995. Leading change: Why transformation efforts fail? *Harvard Business Review* (March–April).

O'Connor, J., 1998. *Leading with NLP.* London: Thorsons.

Shaw, P.M., 2002. *Changing Conversations in Organisations. A Complexity Approach to Change.* London: Routledge.

Stacey, R.D., 1995. *Strategic Management and Organisational Dynamics.* 2nd edition. London: Pearson Education.

Stacey, R.D., 2001. *Complex Responsive Processes in Organizations.* London: Routledge.

Stacey, R.D., 2007. *Strategic Management and Organisational Dynamics.* 5th edition. London: Pearson Education.

Stacey, R.D., 2010. *Complexity and Organisational Reality.* 2nd edition. London: Routledge.

Stacey, R.D., 2012. *Tools and Techniques of Leadership and Management Meeting the Challenge of Complexity.* London: Routledge.

6

Underpinning OD Practice with Data: Using Data Wisely

James Traeger

What is Data?

Imagine two OD practitioners sitting on a fence (as OD practitioners generally do), having a conversation, as the wind blows across the wheat field in front of them.

'So how do you collect all the information you need when you are doing your "diagnosis"?'

'You just write lot of notes'.

'But how do you know if your notes are collecting the right things?'

'You just write LOTS of notes! Try and capture it all!'

'But what about the sounds, sights, feelings … how do you capture those? After all, when we are talking about an OD person doing their practice, we are talking about hard and soft measures, about all the shades of mood, relationship, motivation, power relations, really intangible and tricky stuff to track. How do you make sure you are writing the right notes?'

'Well, I suppose you could record it too? You know, with a digital recorder'.

'What about body language …? Nuanced looks? The fact that you notice you are getting a certain story, told in a particular way from the HR Business

Partner, who is sitting next to her internal client, who you suddenly realise she doesn't like very much …?'

'Well, you could video it as well'.

'So what you are talking about, really, when it comes to data collection in OD research, is capturing or collecting EVERYTHING'.

'Yes, I suppose I am'.

'The whole experience. All of it. Because any aspect of the interaction might contain something useful and illuminating with respect to the cultural and organisational change you are there to facilitate?'

'Yes, that's right. You really have to get under the skin of what is going on. Try and record it in every way you can, try and capture every angle of the experience'.

'So wouldn't it just be easier to live it?'

Introduction

This chapter will explore the dilemma that is being discussed by the two practitioners of OD above. If you are wondering what this dialogue is based on, it is, I suppose, an abstraction of many similar conversations that I have had over the years, all of which were circling around the central challenge that these two characters were wrestling with: what constitutes data in OD practice? What are the reasons why it is so problematic? How might we look at data in a way that is useful, and ultimately tame this tiger? How can we make it a tool that helps us in our work, without reducing the world to something mechanical, dry and supposedly objective, when we know in our bones that is a kind of travesty, because OD is about people and people are rarely dry or objective?

The chapter will be conversational. In the course of it, I hope to start a dialogue between us. This is, of course, hard in this medium, but in itself, this should demonstrate what I think the world is made of, and why this data thing is such a trouble to us. My view of the world is dialogic. The truth, such as it is, exists in the spaces between us. So I will aim to ask you some questions as we go. It will also be anecdotal: I will try to depict the dilemmas and choices we OD people face. These will be hyper-real examples, in that, like the discussion above, they will be based on examples I have encountered, but without pretending to be real case studies. They are, in essence, exemplars – stories from a fertile imagination; not true or right, but merely used as tools to develop the discussion. They aim to stimulate your imagination, and provoke your own examples.

Yes – provoke. In being dialogic, and wanting (vainly) to have a discussion with you, it doesn't mean I will always aim to be nice. Some say there is too much niceness in OD – not enough edge to really provoke. What do you think? I hope to build a relationship, but by provoking as well as by building between us. I blame this on my background. I come from Eastern European, Jewish stock. This means that in my culture, what outsiders would see as an argument, I might see as an opportunity to build bonds; even if this means I am shouting at you. I tell you this so you don't misread this data. In Yiddish, there is a verb 'to kvetch'. Broadly it means to niggle, to natter and to bond in the process. It has no direct, simple translation in English. This in itself shows how, when it comes to human experience, the data can be read in so many ways.

This chapter will, broadly, break into three parts, based on three basic questions:

- Why are we in such a mess around this thing called data?

- What are the consequences of this in our world of OD practice?

- How can we hold this data thing better in order to be better at what we do?

In answer to the first question, I will draw on my own experience, that of other colleagues, plus the students I work with, who are engaged in various qualifications (usually at doctoral Level) in Organisation and People Development.

I will also introduce the views of some writers around this work, who have some interesting, important things to say about the nature of our world, when we are engaging in the practice of changing and improving organisations. As I write this, I wonder how you will be with this theory. Will you, the reader see what I discuss here as too theoretical? My anxiety around this is based on my experience, which is that people make some interesting (and some would say, erroneous) distinctions between theory and practice. So, what really is theory? What are we saying the world is made of, when we introduce it as a word (and other related words, like 'academic' and 'intellectual')? Or is it that we are just afraid of a few long words? I will try to keep my count of long words to a minimum. But I would say it is important to think about the ontology (Look! There's one!) of all of this. In other words, what is the world really made of, when we are doing our work as practitioners, and what are the consequences of this for how we measure it, and make sense of what we measure? So, excuse my defensiveness. (Did you notice it?) This too, is something we can measure; this too is data.

Ultimately, however, I do want this all to be useful to you (and of course, 'there's nothing as practical as a good theory', as Peter Drucker allegedly once said). I would like to leave you clearer about some choices you can make. In my view, when we are considering how we measure our world, everything (whether it be about analysing the quality of relationships in a business, assessing the basis of employee engagement, deciding on the sweetness of the smell of a rose, or making up your mind about whether to do another half an hour of emails, or call it a day and spend some time reading your child a bedtime story), everything, in the end, comes down to the choices we make.

The Mess we're in with Data: The Problem with Statistics

THE STRATEGIC OD TEAM HAS AN IMPACT PART 1: COMMISSION SOME (MORE) DATA GATHERING.

Imagine another conversation between our pair of OD practitioners ...

'The Board has instructed us to get some data. They want us to come up with some data that shows what impact we have as a function'.

'So, have you evaluated your work?'

'Yes. We have done lots of evaluations. We're always evaluating what we do, in fact'.

'How do you mean?'

'We have done survey upon survey. Engagement surveys, staff surveys, "top 100 companies" surveys, exit surveys, 360 degrees, 270 degrees, 180 degrees, we're literally going round and round in circles with surveys'.

'So what are they telling you?'

'Well, everything really … and nothing'.

'Say more'.

'They are telling us that we are having an impact. That the organisation likes what we do, basically. It is 'happy' with what we are offering. We're moving in the right direction'.

'So what's the problem?'

'We just don't feel like we are getting any … traction with any of it. It feels a bit like we're in a shop, and basically the customer is coming in and buying, but I don't get any real sense of buy-in. It is a really passive relationship'.

'So you want more engagement, more buy-in?'

'Yes, I mean look: we are a small team with limited resources working with a huge organisation – 15,000 staff across the piece. We know that lots of what we do make sense. We get broad encouragement from the Board. Basically, they want us to "keep calm and carry on", with everything we do, but with fewer resources. You know, the message is: "All's right with the world. Except you've got less to spend". So what I'd like to collect is the data that tells us what we do that really makes a difference. I'd like to know what, in all that we do, has the most impact. Then we could stop doing some of the other things and just do that. That's the data I need'.

'I see …'

Organisations, and the OD practitioners working within them, like those in this dialogue above ('based on true events', as they say in Hollywood), often get hung up on issues of data. This usually means they are searching for the holy grail of 'clear measures of success' of OD practice and intervention. But, in the mind of the main character in this dialogue, as in the minds of so many of us in OD, there is a kind of confusion.

This isn't a confusion that is immediately evident, or indeed based on some fault or lack of intelligence. It is perfectly reasonable to propose what this character is proposing – that it may be possible to isolate the factor in our work that has most benefit, and do more of it. It makes sense. Yet, it is based on a view of the world, a kind of 'scientific materialism' that has been the bane of our lives since and before the much-maligned Taylor (1911), who coined the phrase 'Scientific Management' so many years ago. Taylor, bravely in my view, expected that it was possible in the world of organisations to do what seemed to be possible in the world of machines. Design it right, maintain it well, grease the right parts in the right places, and you would have your perfect business machine (long before IBM dreamed of their version).

But, for the way we live now, this worldview has a fatal flaw (and it may well have done so in Taylor's time too). In seeing the world this way, we are confusing two incompatible paradigms; that of 'things', which follow the neat rules of material science (and even then only up to a point), and that of 'people', who follow different, less predictable and deterministic pathways. I love what the great twentieth-century ecologist, Gregory Bateson, had to say about this.

In Bateson's worldview, the key issue is what distinctions we look for. This is never a neutral thing, but rather part of a 'form', or 'pattern' that we aim to recognise.

> *In a strict sense, therefore, no data are truly 'raw', and every record has been somehow subjected to editing and transformation either by man [sic] or his instruments. (Bateson, 1972: xxvi)*

And we ...

> *have tried to build a bridge to the wrong half of the ancient dichotomy between form and substance. The conservative laws for energy and matter concern substance rather than form. But mental process, ideas, communication, organisation, differentiation, pattern, and so on, are matters of form rather than substance. (Bateson, 1972: xxxii)*

So, what Bateson is saying that is relevant for us as OD practitioners, is this: whilst we may think we can talk the language of 'substance', talking about 'data' and 'measurables' and 'benchmarks', we are actually doing so under false pretences. That is, of course, unless we realise that in using this type of language, we are actually always making some kind of political point (consciously or not) in order to serve an agenda. This is what Bateson famously calls, 'the difference that makes a difference'. What he means by this is that, for our purposes, there are so many ways we can cut the cake of organisational life, but the only cuts that matter are the ones that we choose, for our own reasons, that help us *really eat it*.

So, we are actually always acting in the world of form, of meaning, pattern and relationship, where truths exist 'between us' rather than 'out there'. We may talk about data, but when we do, we are casting a pattern on the world, and making a certain claim for our sense of it, in a dialogue (often with power). We are never talking about something that is really there.

If we suggest the world (of organisations) is really there, we are, as Ben Goldacre would say, committing 'bad science' (Goldacre, 2009). Indeed, Goldacre shows that even the world of science, cannot always remain free from human unpredictability and partiality. As Goldacre himself explains about OD's famous light bulb moment, in Hawthorne, Illinois, in 1923:

> *I will give you the simplified 'myth' version of the findings, as a rare compromise between pedantry and simplicity. When the researchers increased light levels, they found that performance improved. But when they reduced the light levels, performance improved then, too. In fact, they found that no matter what they did, productivity increased anyway. This finding was very important: when you tell workers that they are part of a special study to see what might improve productivity and then you do something ... they improve their productivity. This is a kind of placebo effect, because the placebo is not about the mechanics of a sugar pill, it is about the cultural meaning of an intervention, which includes, amongst other things, your expectations, and the expectations of the people tending to you and measuring you. (Goldacre, 2009: 139)*

Now, this isn't to introduce some kind of magical thinking into our discussion about data; far from it. Most people who crave good science, like Goldacre and Bateson, spend time unmasking practitioners of bad science, not because they are cynical, or that they believe in magic. It is because they have ideals; because they believe something: in a kind of *real mystery* of good science, and how little we truly understand about the wonders of the universe that have unfolded in front of us to date. So when we talk about getting the right data, we are often guilty of using sciency language; language that expresses thinking that is loose, inappropriate and woolly; as woolly as it is to disingenuously suggest that getting stuck into the people side of organisations is about practising 'soft skills'.

What we dismiss as merely the placebo effect may be highly significant in terms of what we do as OD practitioners. Even people practising real science, such as pharmaceutical companies, understand this, so why shouldn't we? There are quite stunning consequences of the placebo effect, when it comes to us in OD making sense of data. As Goldacre explains:

> [Drug Researchers] found that colour [of pills] had an effect on outcome: the pink sugar tablets were better at maintaining concentration than the blue ones. Since colours in themselves have no intrinsic pharmacological properties, the difference in effect could only be due to the cultural meaning of pink and blue; pink is alerting, blue is cool.. Another study suggested that Oxazepam, a drug similar to Valium (which was once unsuccessfully prescribed by our GP for me as a hyperactive child) was more effective at treating anxiety in a green tablet, and more effective for depression when yellow ... and in case you think I'm cherry picking here, a survey of the colour of pills currently on the market found that stimulant medication tends to come in red, orange or yellow tablets, while antidepressants and tranquillisers are generally blue, green or purple. (Goldacre, 2009: 68)

So the world that actually unfolds before is simply too complex and mystifying to suggest that as OD practitioners (dealing with the people side of things, for heaven's sake!) we can simply talk about the world as simple cause and effect chains, where data can be analysed and variables isolated, without this type of language (and the attitude behind it) having some kind of impact. It is all about the conversations we have, and in Goldacre's words, 'the cultural meaning of an intervention'. We are, in the world of form, always engaged in some kind of placebo effect.

In beginning to consider this chapter, I found myself looking around me, at the world in a particular kind of way, wondering what sense I could make of data, as I went about my life. Unconsciously, I was beginning, in Bateson's terms, to practise the art of making a difference. So, one morning, as I toyed with different ways we can cut the cake of the world in front of us, I found myself in the restaurant of an hotel in Rugby, UK, watching the staff serving breakfast. I considered them, in their work, from a Taylorist perspective, wondering on what basis the decision had been made (seemingly right in my view!) to have four of them on duty. It seemed about enough; they could all be attentive enough, without overstaffing.

I then considered the scene from a motivational perspective, wondering (to borrow Herzberg's terms) about the 'hygiene factors', the baseline requirements needed to get effort out of them, such as pay (Herzberg, 1993). Then I thought about the motivational factors that might be needed to eke out that crucial, extra bit of discretionary effort. What data would I collect about this?

Next I considered them from the perspective of Barry Oshry's 'Seeing Systems' (Oshry, 1995), and I wondered how they might configure themselves as 'Tops, Middles, Bottoms and Customers'. I also wondered, borrowing from the perspective of James Scott (1992), what data I could dig out, if I really looked for it, that might demonstrate their 'hidden transcripts' of rebellion. For example, what graffiti might I find on the staff toilet walls?

In all of this self-absorbed stew, which gave me at least 10 different ways that I could cut the data cake, what occurred to me as most fundamental, profound and chastening, was that in all of this looking, they had noticed me noticing them. This seemed to have an impact on them, making them (understandably) self-conscious and even slightly embarrassed. Before I knew it, I had (stupidly, thoughtlessly) made an impact, even a dent, in their world, by turning them into a kind of object in mine. This taught me about data most profoundly.

So, as OD practitioners, we always have an impact, and perhaps it is this impact we most want data (or at least some information) about?

THE STRATEGIC OD TEAM HAS AN IMPACT PART 2: STARTING THE WORK

'You said you wanted this evaluation work to have an impact, differently to what you had done before, with your nice neat surveys that tell you "all's right with the world"'.

'Yes. That's right'.

'So, where does this impact start?'

'I suppose it starts with us'.

'Say more'.

'Well, when I talked before about the customers who we work with, being in a shop, passively buying, it did make me wonder what messages we were giving out, you know, as a team'.

'What messages ...?'

'Yes, I mean, we expect them to engage with us, but how do we engage with them? Do we inadvertently set up that kind of relationship, by how we invite them to engage with us?'

'How would you know that?'

'I think I would ask some of our key customers, I mean people we work with, how are we perceived as a team'.

'And is it 'as a team'?'

'What do you mean?'

'What I mean is; my guess is that you mean different things to different stakeholders. I suspect you are all quite different. You probably aren't seen "as a team", more as individual consultants adding value with your own groups of clients'.

'Yes, apart from with the Board'.

'The Board?'

'Yes, I think they see us as a team, as one unit'.

'How do you know that?'

'Well, no, that's true, our own Director sees us as individuals, but the minutes that come down from the OD Steering Group suggest that we are like a vehicle, a hire car that can be rented from time to time'.

'So, that metaphor says quite a bit about your impact as a team. Is that the sort of "data" that you think might be significant?'

'Yes, I notice the mismatch. The messages that we get from our Director, the individual attention, versus the way the Board seems to "direct" us, point us at a problem and then drive us towards it. I mean, I called you in because they have told us to collect data about the things we are doing that aren't valuable, so we can "just do what we have most impact on", as if we are a kind of service for rent. It's just the wrong metaphor for what we actually do. We can't be broken down that way'.

'So, here you are again, being pointed, driven, broken down ...'

'Yes, and actually what we should be doing is working to change their mindset – as one team, as an influential entity. I mean, what we need to do is have a bit more of an impact on them'.

'So, again, the data seems to shift. Now we are talking about data as metaphors'.

'What metaphor would you like to be in the eyes of the Board?'

'That's a good question. I think that's one for us to discuss as a team ...'

So, the trouble with data, from an OD perspective, and in fact from the perspective of a scientific approach to anything, is that it is always partial. It is never truly meaningless, or at least, it has the meaning that people ascribe to it, usually as part of some kind of dialogue. This suggests that we are never neutral observers, bias-free and in some way immune and objective. We always have a bias. That is why our emphasis, as OD practitioners, is often towards ourselves. By recognising, working with and making choices about our own impact and perspective, in our own domain, we can have a greater impact on the world. This includes making choices about what constitutes 'data' in our work. If we recognise this is a choice, then we make it with some integrity.

I had a good example of that in my own work, when I was regularly confronted by bad science and woolly thinking, often (I have to admit) my own. For many years, a key focus of my work was with organisations, around gender, culture and change. The prevailing mood of this work, the background against which my colleagues and I were working, was one where a fundamental belief prevailed. This belief, held by most people as axiomatic, holds that men and women are fundamentally different creatures, or, what Deborah Cameron, Professor of Language and Communication at Oxford University, calls the 'Myth of Mars and Venus'.

> *Most research studies investigating the behaviour of men and women are designed around the question: 'is there a difference' – and the presumption is usually that there will be. If a study finds a significant difference between male and female subjects (in other words, a result which statistical tests show could not have been produced by chance), that is considered to be a 'positive' finding, and has a good chance of being published in a scientific journal. A study which finds no significant differences is less likely to be published. This means that some negative findings are never even submitted for publication. (Cameron, 2007: 17)*

What Professor Cameron is saying here is that people are always skewing the data, usually because they have important beliefs and attitudes that they want to protect, even in so-called scientific journals and work. This selective presentation of bias as facts, even in so-called 'scientific' environments, wasn't just evident in the world around me. It took me a while to grasp this, but I too was its instrument. In my own frustration, and my wish to make a difference, I too was skewing the facts. This would get me into trouble.

Once, I was working with a group of HR Business Partners (mostly women) on a development programme for a bank. In the evening we were eating together and, over dinner, I got into a discussion, which became an argument, about gender culture. I took the line, supported by my endless facts (because I had *studied* these things, of course), that the situation for women in the workplace hadn't really shifted very much. My argument was (just as Deborah Cameron's is) that the Myth of Mars and Venus is just that – a myth, and that men and women aren't fundamentally different. I argued that this is a value-laden (and often unconscious) choice which most people make mainly in order to reinforce a sense of fundamental difference between genders. One unfortunate side-effect of this is that most organisations are fundamentally male domains, in which women are likely to be marginalised. This is why most big organisations are still fundamentally unfriendly towards women, and that women have to behave (and be) like men in order to get on. Now it may have been one glass of wine too many, or perhaps it was just a kind of demon that got inside my head, but I was full of data to support my argument.

For example, according to McKinsey's (2007) 'Women Matter' survey:

- Women make up 55 per cent of university graduates in Europe, but their employment rate though is 21 per cent less than that of men. The average wage gap between men and women is as high as 15 per cent. There are also marked differences in the levels of responsibility.

- Women are particularly under-represented in management and decision-making roles. In Europe, women represent only 11 per cent of the membership of the governing bodies of listed companies.

And so on. The data (I would have argued, and *did* argue) is literally endless.

The more I argued for this data, the more resistant my audience became. Their view was that, in their own organisation at least (a big, traditional high-street bank, which, in my view had shown very little evidence of de-gendered enlightenment), things were very favourable, that women and men were 'just different' and that they, as young women, had plenty of opportunities for advancement. They became quite angry, and I learned later, they complained about this rather sexist facilitator on their HR Business Partner programme. I was not asked to work with them again.

This may strike you as highly ironic. It did me. Actually at the time, I was very hurt and very angry, but over the years since, I have become much more philosophical. Of course, you could put their reaction down to what psychologists call 'cognitive dissonance' – that miraculous, wonderfully human ability to be highly selective about the data we choose in our own lives, in order to convince ourselves that all's well with the world. This loveable capacity, it is argued, acts like a natural painkiller, helping us to feel better about whatever situation we find ourselves in. Perhaps I was just offering them 'too much truth', to paraphrase T.S. Eliot?

Or could it be that at some level, I had missed something very important about so-called objective data. What I learned is that it is never, ever, devoid of a human context, and this was one context in which I had disastrously (perhaps drunkenly) misspoken. Indeed, from their perspective, perhaps they had seen this as some overweening teacher-man holding forth to them as women, implying that their lack of awareness of their own plight was something approaching stupidity. Perhaps that was indeed somewhat sexist whatever the 'facts'? What I missed was the opportunity for relationship. Whatever data we select, and however we use it, we need to consider, first and foremost, the social flow, the form of relationships we are actually in.

So the 'a-ha' here for me, isn't in whether something is true or not, but in how we use what we know, or what we select to know, to have an impact towards an agenda which is more or less explicit, but at least owned up to in our own hearts. For example I am committed to well-being in my work, not because I can produce objective data for it, but because I believe in it, for myself, and for those around me. I was (and still am) keen on greater gender equality, not because it is about 'truths in the world' (I now realise), but because it is about key distinctions (or 'differences' to use Bateson's terms), that I would like to change. However, they can only be shifted through the relationships that I make with those around me, in some kind of mutual dialogue. It's the opportunity for that mutuality that I completely missed in this particular example.

Data can (and will) be produced either way, for or against *any* argument. In the words of the Philosopher of Science Julian Baggini, this is because of what is called the 'under-determination of theory by evidence':

> *In plain English that means that the facts never provide enough evidence to conclusively prove one theory and one theory only. There is always a gap – the possibility that an alternative theory is true. That is why courts insist on proof beyond 'reasonable doubt'. Proof beyond all doubt is impossible. (Baggini, 2010: 182)*

So, there are still people who firmly believe that the world is flat and have enough data (in their view) to prove it. It is my duty to recognise my own bias, to be prepared to use it, yes, but to see it for what it is. In this way, I have an agenda, and can never pretend that I am neutral, or that what I choose to see as facts, are facts in the immutable sense of that word. I own up to my bias; proudly, but honestly. This is the foremost duty of an OD practitioner.

It doesn't stop there, however. The purpose of my bias, my use of my data, is to create a relationship. Again, this isn't true; it is what I believe in. So the mistake I made with the women from the bank was to suggest that my agenda was better than theirs, irrespective of the 'facts', in their world, that this wasn't actually the case. In doing so, I forced a breakdown in the relationship, and they gave me a good kicking. I think I deserved it.

Once dialogue is in place, the data becomes useful, as a tool to build what an organisation is (in my view, I hasten to add) – a set of relationships, flying, more or less, in formation.

THE STRATEGIC OD TEAM HAS AN IMPACT PART 3: FINDING DATA THAT WORKS

'Thanks for coming in. I am really excited to tell you about some things that have happened as a result of our earlier conversations'.

'Great to be here – do tell me what's been going on?'

'Well, after our last conversation, I went to our Director and talked with him about the Board's request to find the right data. You know – the kind of metaphors that we are using to describe what we do'.

'Yes I remember. What happened?'

'He was quite good actually. He said he also felt frustrated about the way the OD function was "ghettoised" as he put it'.

'Another interesting metaphor. What do you think he meant?'

'I think he meant that we are, using the metaphor from last time, like a hire car, useful to get from A to B. It's as if A to B are already fixed, known destinations, but if we work to our full potential, then we should be punching at a higher weight, getting involved in planning the overall journey. Sorry for the mixed metaphors, I'm just really excited!'

'No it's great. Carry on!'

'So, we kicked it around for a bit and he asked me what I thought OD was really for, and I said it should be about the health and well-being of an organisation. If nothing else, we should be exemplars, role models and coaches of health and well-being. We should be like doctors; healers of the organisation. As a team, that really resonated with us all when we discussed it'.

'That's really good. That resonates with me too'.

'This is great – but I am still a bit troubled that the Director gives out such a double message'.

'Why does that trouble you?'

'It's as if he says one thing to me, and then another to the Board that he is a part of. Well I don't know what he says, but then these papers come down that he's signed up to'.

'What do you think he's doing when he's signing up to these papers?'

'I suppose he is playing a role, being part of the political machine'.

'So how could you help him? I mean, he sounds like a leader playing his part in the turf wars of a Board. How could he be supported?'

'I am not sure how we can help him'.

'What I mean is, if he is part of this political machine, and he says something else to you, in private as it were, how can you help strengthen his arm from an OD point of view?'

'Feed him, I suppose, with what he needs to help us make it happen'.

'Exactly. So, what strikes me is this is probably what he was saying through that original request about "wanting data about the impact of the OD function" …'

'In other words, it wasn't really about 'data' at all. Or at least, it was about a certain type of data that supported a certain agenda for change'.

'Yes. Change that you believe in, like the health and well-being in and of this organisation'.

'It seems to fit, because together we decided to ask about that and to focus on that. It's really interesting, I don't know if it was there already, but we certainly saw it when we started looking, right across all the surveys, employee engagement polls etc. There was this really interesting pattern, a trend about people (especially younger people) using certain words, like "health and well-being", "meaning", "purpose". So we decided to focus on that'.

'That really fits. There's real congruence there. It's like all the information came alive when you started looking at it in a certain way'.

'Yes. When we decided on this well-being angle, suddenly we knew what 'data' we were looking for. But – and here's the good part – we decided that what we wanted to do was look at our own health and well-being, first, as a team. So we had our own session and lots of really interesting things came out'.

'Like what?'

'We had a good conversation – stormy at times, but good – about how hard we work and whether we thought that what we were all doing was fair. One issue that came up was between those who worked full-time and those on flexi-time. Anyway, we made an agreement to change things around a bit'.

'Brave move to look inwards first, rather than see it as everyone else's issue'.

'Yes, and our Director was involved in the session too. He is now suggesting that we turn what we did for ourselves into a workshop. He's also going to facilitate the Board in this session'.

'It sounds like an idea whose time has come'.

'So, it gives us a good focus as a team, which is what we were really looking for when we first talked. But instead of going and doing more meaningless surveys, we now have the direction we were looking for'.

'And in terms of having something useful for the Board?'

'Yes, well the "data" around well-being in the organisation – the stuff we've already gathered – is useful in the session, as part of a sell. It just gets the session going. It's as if the numbers make people sit up and listen, because they look like numbers, but what really matters is that they are just a tool really, a political tool, an entry ticket to a conversation about well-being that we really want to have'.

Holding Data Better: 'From ... To'

So, if this story is anything to go by, there may be hope. Once the OD practitioner understands the distinction between the worlds of things (where the traditional, sciency meaning of data seems to fit), and that of people (who work according to irrational, unpredictable and complex rules), and works effectively between them, it is more than possible to demonstrate success in OD practice. Indeed, in my view, there are some relatively straightforward distinctions to make that are of practical benefit when the data is mentioned in the OD context.

I make these distinctions in a list below, not exhaustive in itself. These aren't hard and fast rules but are offered by way of enabling you to consider your own practice. I consider these as 'from … to' distinctions, as in, if we shift our emphasis *from* one side of this conundrum *to* the other, it may prove useful in our work. Try them on for size, as it were, and see if they are of benefit, and then perhaps add some more of your own.

ONE: FROM 'DATA' TO 'CAPTA'

This first distinction, from 'data' to 'capta', is made in order to be honest about the nature of the (peopled) world that we, as OD practitioners, are working with. It recognises that whilst the word 'data' suggests that certain distinctions are naturally 'out there' and waiting to be 'found' by the researcher, this new word, 'capta', honestly recognises the importance of the researcher's viewpoint. The world isn't a blank slate, but a place where our value-laden looking can be owned up to, whilst maintaining the rigour of scientific inquiry. So whilst 'data' comes from the Latin root 'dare' meaning 'to give', 'capta' comes from 'capere' meaning 'to take'. It therefore recognises that the distinctions we make in (or take from) the world do actually matter.

It strikes me that in shifting our discussions from 'data' towards 'capta', we are making a value-based honesty-shift in our inquiries as OD practitioners. It seems the biggest disadvantage of this may be the word 'capta' itself, which is more obscure than good, old-fashioned 'data'. But maybe not that obscure. Indeed, even mainstream scientific researchers are more frequently using it as a term. For example, the archaeologist, Christopher Chippindale says:

> Is the customary word 'data' a good name for archaeological records and facts? 'Data' means the things that are 'given', but archaeological observations and facts are never given at all. Rather, they are captured by the researcher, who seeks to grasp from the material record the essentials of some complex and little-known phenomenon, often remote in time and usually ambiguous in material expression. We should prefer to use the better word 'capta', the things that have been captured, and to realize that this word captures the essence of what we do. (Chippindale, 2000: 605)

My friend and colleague, Chris Seeley, made a beautiful, diagrammatic distinction between data and capta in her PhD thesis (Seeley, 2007), and I offer you it to you below, as I think it further clarifies the way in which moving from 'data' to 'capta' represents an honourable shift in our work as OD practitioners. At the core is the recognition that what really turns 'data' into 'capta' for us is the meaning that we are trying to take, on the organisation's behalf. We can derive useful knowledge for the organisation based on that 'taken' meaning, and not on some universal, abstract 'given' truth to us by a value-neutral world.

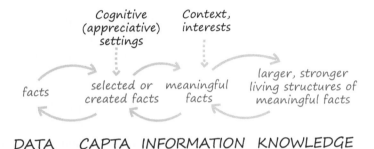

Figure 6.1   **Chris Seeley's distinction between data and capta**

So, if you can shift your discussions with clients away from 'data' and towards 'capta', this might help shift the conversation towards some clearer, more honest thinking.

TWO: FROM 'DATA ANALYSIS' TO 'PATTERN SPOTTING'

In our OD work, how do we do our diagnosis? What are the capacities that we bring to make sense of the capta, or, to use Chris Seeley's representation above, how do we turn our capta into useful knowledge? Traditionally, the language of 'data analysis' had been used. I would argue that it might be more useful to talk in terms of 'pattern spotting'.

The term data analysis implies a heavily conceptual, sense-making bias, and we can challenge this by suggesting that people, and OD practitioners especially, must use wider capacities of sense-making in order to capture the full range of human experience in an organisation. Indeed, Heron and Reason (1997) talk about 'wider ways of knowing', a hierarchy of human sense-making, containing at least four distinctions:

- Practical knowing – 'how to do things'.

- Conceptual knowing – 'thinking about things' (where narrow 'data analysis' coheres).

- Presentational knowing – visioning, imagining, dreaming about things.

- Experiential knowing – feeling, embodying things.

In Heron and Reason's worldview, the basis of knowing anything is experiential, i.e. in the moment, in the body. Most customer-aligned organisations know this implicitly, which is why they talk about understanding the 'customer experience'.

So, we talk about pattern spotting as encompassing (but being more than just about) a conceptual sense-making. As an OD practitioner (as in the story above), I am often helping organisations make sense of their 'capta' through a good metaphor, narrative or vision-piece. On this basis, good OD work is about helping refine and develop *all* the levels of Heron and Reason's cosmology, developing people's experience, their metaphors, pictures and dreams, their sharpness of thinking *and* their practical doing. It is in our ability to spot patterns between these layers where we do our best work.

Once, I was doing a piece of work with a local authority, which involved (amongst other things) improving the quality of school catering facilities. The Senior Managers had all sorts of refined spreadsheets of performance and value. The Catering Assistants (it was 'Dinner Ladies' when I was at school), had one simple, practical measure of quality – how much waste was in the bin at the end of the lunch service. This was their own personal, highly-valued class of 'capta'. One pattern we uncovered and helped to codify was their very practical measure juxtaposed against the Senior Managers' much more conceptual measures. This led to a generative conversation about how quality was measured in the service; that spoke of the need for better coordination. In this case, this was where our value lay as OD consultants.

Had we ignored this pattern and merely focused on arid data analysis, we might have missed this vital opportunity for connection and relationship building.

Yuri Slezkine, Professor of History at University of California, Berkeley, makes a simple distinction between two types of human tribes, the fixed, village-dwelling 'Apollonians' and the shape-shifting, storytelling 'Mercurians'. Slezkine asserts that all through the ages, human societies across the world have lived according to this pattern, where fixed communities have relied upon mobile, transient tribes of strangers to come by from time to time, to sharpen their knives, to tell stories, to perform circuses and 'make meaning' as outsiders often do best, as if from the margins. Examples he discusses include the Parsis in India, the Chinese diaspora, the Armenians in Asia, and (from my own background), the Jews in Europe. He calls these 'Mercurians', or 'Service Nomads'.

> *All these groups were non-primary producers specializing in the delivery of goods and services to the surrounding agricultural or pastoral populations. Their principle resources base was human, not natural, and their expertise was in 'foreign' affairs. They were the descendants – or predecessors – of Hermes (Mercury), the god of all those who did not herd animals, till the soil, or live by the sword; the patron of rule breakers, border crossers, and go-betweens; the protector of people who lived by their wit, craft, and art. (Slezkine 2006: 7–8)*

My view is that we, as OD practitioners, are continuing this trend, living by our wit, craft and art, being the 'Mercurians' of the organisation, transient visitors to the various settled 'villages' (Operations, Finance, Customer Services etc....), helping to make meaning, spot patterns, sharpen knives, perform circuses, read palms, cross borders and act as go-betweens, before ultimately moving on.

From this point of view, it helps to think of our role as being wider, more imaginal and transpersonal, and less about narrow data analysis. After all, shouldn't there be a bit of magic to our work?

THREE: FROM 'ORGANISATIONAL IMPROVEMENT' TO 'ORGANISATIONAL HEALTH'

I want to lay my cards clearly on the table here. I believe that OD should do more than help organisations make money, or become more efficient (a very machine-like metaphor). I think that the century-or-so's history of OD suggests that people like us actually join the Mercurian tribe because we believe it is possible to perform some kind of win-win. If organisations become better places for their people, they will ultimately be more effective in their purpose, whatever that may be. This means that, perhaps, we need to come clean and focus on what our work should really be about, and, therefore, our work with 'data' (or 'capta') should reflect that.

So, if our work is value-laden, then in owning up to what we believe in, we should return to the core emphasis of OD, which is organisational health – making organisations places that are fit for people to dwell in and thrive.

If we make the distinction at the level of 'capta' between less and more well-being (rather than less and more improvement), then we are ceasing to regard the machine metaphor as worthwhile and starting to live as if organisations are organic homes for hearts and bodies as well as minds. This, in the end, could be the stand that makes the crucial difference for our world.

Conclusion: OD Practitioners as Story-makers

Whatever you think of what I have proposed here, there is one thing I hope you might find to be self-evident – that my incitements around data are motivated by a yearning for honesty. I want OD practitioners to come clean in our use of words like 'data'; to be bold and truthful about what we seek and what we find.

The wind blew and the wheat shook. The OD practitioners climbed down off the fence and started to walk. One turns to the other ...

'Thank you'.

'For what?'

'For helping me see what matters'.

'How did I do that?'

'You asked the difficult question'.

'Which question?'

'You asked me what matters'.

'Which is?'

'Not what can be counted, but what has meaning'.

'Does this help you?'

'Yes, because there's so much that can be counted, and actually only a few things that have meaning. Take this wheat field. There's so much you can say about it. But what matters to me is the quality of the bread that is made. And that isn't something you can find out by anything you can see in front of us that you can count'.

Let me conclude with another admission: I will often use terms like 'data', 'analysis' and 'improvement' myself. I will often use these distinctions as my ticket to ride. It is by using language like this that we achieve credibility and buy-in for our work, especially with the Apollonians who guard the village gates. But being a good storyteller means that I must know when to shape-shift, and start to challenge the status quo by using different distinctions, such as 'capta', 'pattern spotting' and 'organisational health'. Knowing when to switch keys is of course not an easy trick to learn, but it is possible.

The best practitioners in our field, people I admire, do it all the time.

References

Baggini, J., 2010. *The Pig that Wants to be Eaten: And Ninety-nine Other Thought Experiments.* London: Granta Books.

Bateson, G., 1972. *Steps to an Ecology of Mind: Collected Essays in Anthropology, Psychiatry, Evolution and Epistemology.* Chicago, IL: University of Chicago Press.

Cameron, D., 2007. *The Myth of Mars and Venus: Do Men and Women Really Speak Different Languages?* Oxford: Oxford University Press.

Chippindale, C., 2000. Capta and data: On the true nature of archaeological information. *American Antiquity*, 65(4), 605–12.

Goldacre, B., 2009. *Bad Science.* London: Harper Perrennial.

Heron, J. and Reason, P., 1997. A participatory inquiry paradigm. *Qualitative Inquiry*, 3(3), 274–94.

Herzberg, F., 1993. *The Motivation to Work.* New Brunswick, NJ: Transaction Publishers.

McKinsey and Company, 2007. *Women Matter – Gender Diversity A Corporate Performance Driver*. [Online]. Available at: http://bit.ly/9Ia1vn

Oshry, B., 1995. *Seeing Systems: Unlocking the Mysteries of Organizational Life*. San Francisco, CA: Berrett-Koehler.

Seeley, C., 2007. *Wild Margins: Playing at Work and Life*. Unpublished PhD thesis, University of Bath. [Online]. Available at: http://www.ashridge.org.uk/Website/Content.nsf/wFARACAR/(2007)+Chris+Seeley+-+Wild+margins+playing+at+work+and+life?opendocument [accessed: 3 April 2012].

Scott, J., 1992. *Domination and the Arts of Resistance: Hidden Transcripts*. New Haven, CT: Yale University Press.

Slezkine, Y., 2006. *The Jewish Century*. Princeton, NJ: Princeton University Press.

Taylor, F.W., 1911. *The Principles of Scientific Management*. Paperback edition (2003). Mineola, NY: Dover Publications.

7

Working with Groups in Organisations: 'Could you Come and Do Something with my Team?'

Penny Lock

Introduction

This chapter looks at groups in organisations through the lens of an Organisation Development (OD) practitioner and considers how they might field the typical request shown in the title. The request itself may seem simple enough, but how do you respond in a way that best furthers the goals of the group and the organisation of which it is a part?

The key questions addressed here are:

- How do you approach working with groups with an OD mindset?

- How do you ready yourself for the unpredictable issues that can emerge when you work directly with a group?

Group or Team?

In this chapter I use the terms fairly interchangeably, but a sense of the difference is useful under some circumstances with clients. Teams typically are defined as groups:

- Containing two or more people who interact, whether in person or virtually.

- That are seen to do work that is relevant to the organisation.

- That have a clear boundary about who is in the team and who isn't.

- That work interdependently; that is, members need each other to achieve the objective of the team.

- That hold themselves and are held by others to be mutually accountable for their outcomes.

Many groups in organisations don't have these features, but are called teams. Many teams that do have these features operate in such different environments and to such different ends that they share less in common than some groups. So, how far do you need to consider this distinction when working with clients? On occasions you can take yourself and your client down a rabbit hole if you get too hung up on whether or not a group is a team. Sometimes the discussion is useful as part of your preparatory work because it can guide your understanding of how closely the individuals in the group need to work and how interdependent they are.

To equip yourself to work with groups, it is useful to know something of the research in this area. When I'm thinking about the task of groups in organisations and how effectively they are operating, I go to the literature on teams, some of which is quite new and really helpful. This perspective underpins the first part of this chapter, which is about making sense of what a team needs and preparing to work with them. When I am focusing on understanding what goes on when I'm working directly with a group, I tend to go to the literature on groups, some of which is quite old – and equally helpful. This comes into the second part of this chapter. If your frame of reference is limited to what happens within a group without attention to what the purpose of that group is in an organisation, you aren't operating from an OD mindset. If you don't have some understanding of the processes and patterns that occur in groups, you reduce your capacity to engage effectively with them.

AN EFFECTIVE TEAM?

If teams are critical to organisational success and hence a pivotal focus for OD, we need some idea of what makes a team effective, not least because it helps us understand whether the work that we do with them can make any difference to the organisation. An effective team is one:

- Where what the team does – what it produces, the services it offers or the decisions it makes – either meets or exceeds the standards of its clients.

- Where how the team works – the processes it uses to do its work – enhances the capacity of team members to work together interdependently in the future.

- Where the experience of working in the team makes a positive contribution to the learning and well-being of team members (Hackman and Wageman, 2005).

This is useful because it keeps you focused on what the team is contributing to the organisational system while reminding you that teams comprise individuals whose well-being is important. It also keeps in view that we learn all the time through working together, and we take those insights into teamworking with us through our working lives.

The first part of this chapter offers some ways of finding out what the team or group really needs and identifying what you are going to do or not do. Direct work with a team may not be the best response; however it is a common outcome, so the second part of the chapter looks at some key ideas that equip you to work with the emergent issues in a group.

Much of the work that you do with a group will be as a facilitator or as a team coach. This chapter doesn't go into the tools and techniques that you might use in those types of work, useful though these are, of course. It does point out where to find useful resources in this area. Careful investigation of the team's needs, good planning – along with ways of coping with the processes that you can't plan for – provide a solid foundation for work with teams on which tools are a later embellishment.

'You Want Me to Do ... What?': What Teams Request and Why

There are as many possible reasons behind the request to 'do something with my team' as there are teams. I looked back over ten years' worth of client approaches to see what patterns, if any, lie behind the requests made to my company. These are of course influenced by the kind of work that we do and are perceived as doing. I am an external consultant, so the pattern may well have been different had I been internal and I'm sure would have been strongly influenced by the industry and culture of the employing organisation.

With these provisos in mind, however, I suspect that the list below is not atypical of requests made to many OD practitioners and gives a field-based flavour of the issues that teamwork generates for team members, leaders and stakeholders.

First, what prompts someone to request help? This is a summary of what led clients to get in touch and is in no particular order.

Table 7.1   What led to a request for help with a team?

- There is a new leader.
- Industry-wide or organisational change
- Team newly formed or pre-existing teams merged.
- Team is unhappy. Examples include the team wanting to influence the leader but finding it hard to do so, therefore hoping that the consultant will either create the space for them to do so ... or voice the concerns on their behalf.
- Leader is discontented. This is often where the leader feels team members are not taking sufficient responsibility or the team is underperforming.
- Stakeholders are discontented. This is often the next management layer up, another team or department or highlighted by poor external/staff survey feedback.
- Team has new remit within the organisation. For example, the HR department adopting a business partner model.
- Ongoing team performance review
- Good practice in board development
- Need neutral help with cross-functional or cross-organisational project team or steering group.
- The organisation expects us to get together as a team.
- 'We've put this date in the diary and need someone to facilitate'

Table 7.2 looks at the type of work clients have proposed. This is loosely structured around my framework for team coaching which is:

- what the team is there to do;

- how well is it doing it, and in whose eyes;

- relationship with stakeholders;

- internal team working; and

- ongoing team learning.

Table 7.2   Purpose of work clients proposed

What?

- Develop, re-align or re-affirm team purpose.
- Develop a shared vision.
- Develop a mission.
- Develop a strategy/strategic objectives.
- Align team or personal objectives more closely with the strategy or with each other.
- Develop or harmonise the forward plan.
- Develop a team scorecard.

How?

- Review progress against the above.
- Review team performance.

Stakeholders

- Identify stakeholders.
- How can the team increase their engagement with them?
- How can the team change its relationship with them?
- How does the team increase its visibility and reputation with stakeholders?
- How does the team communicate better with them?
- How does the team increase its influence with them?

Internal teamworking

- Sort out roles and responsibilities.
- Identify/leverage skills within the team and gaps.
- Discuss mutual needs and expectations.
- Get to know each other.
- Build team cohesion.
- Improve level of trust.
- 'Team build'.
- Build motivation/commitment.
- Incorporate new members.

- Profile the team, e.g. MBTI.
- Assess team aptitude or readiness e.g. for change, for risk.
- Improve team processes, including.
- Communications.
- Meetings.
- Decision making.
- Stress management.
- Challenge.

Learning

- Review.
- Celebrate success/plan for the future.
- Identify learning, e.g. at close of project or initiative.

'AND MY RESPONSE IS?' SHAPING YOUR INQUIRY

I have a mental framework that guides my initial response and the proposal I develop. I don't use a checklist as such, but my practice was shaped early on by Edgar Schein's *Process Consultation* (1999) and Peter Block's work *Flawless Consulting* (1981) that is described in more detail in Chapter 11. These gave me a schema for preparing for client meetings that is a helpful basis for contracting with groups and for reflecting on what happened.

Sometimes the request comes from someone junior phoning because a group wants a facilitator at short notice on a particular day and the opportunity to get beyond the immediate request and into a more development conversation about the context to the team is limited. More usually, clients want to engage in the kind of discussion outlined in the diagram below because it will help them review their thinking and decide if they want to work with you and what that work should be. What I ask varies, but in some form or other I cover the areas below. Often I'll get part of the picture during an initial contracting conversation and more when I explore the team with the members themselves.

As I go through the conversations with and about the team, I note my reactions, feelings and observations, in a similar way to that described in Chapter 3. After the conversations, I notice what alignment there is between these and the information I'm getting from the questions on the following pages.

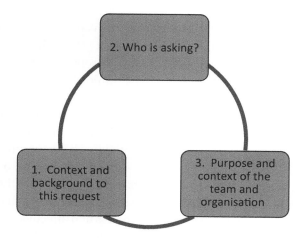

Figure 7.1   Areas of enquiry

What I'm doing is drawing out the team's account of itself and building a story or narrative around where it is and what it may need. If you use the language of diagnosis, you are coming from a mindset that there is a reality out there to be uncovered which is at odds with the way I understand organisations and how we given shape to them by virtue of the way you think of them. I prefer to build this narrative through and with the team.

One: Context and Background to This Request

This is the more immediate line of questioning upon which to build the initial scope of work.

WHAT ARE THEY TRYING TO ACHIEVE THROUGH THE WORK THEY ARE REQUESTING OF ME?

Form follows function. I'm listening here for the outcomes a client wants, how fixed their ideas are and the consistency between their desired outcomes and the kind of work they are proposing.

There is a strong tendency for a client to request an intervention such as an away day or a team build directly and to see such an event as an end in itself. If you don't inquire further, you miss a key opportunity for OD.

Not only are team members often weary of away days – as an oil engineer said to me recently: 'we don't want another offsite jolly where we spend a day building towers out of matchsticks' – but the probability that the work will improve the effectiveness of the team can be diminished.

Though there is good evidence for the relationship between team leadership and team training with how a team performs (Kozlowski and Ilgen, 2006), only relatively recently could we say with any certainty that team building has any positive impact. This is in part due to the difficulty of sorting out what team building means, along with the problem of tracking the effects of the intervention through to the team's performance. A recent study has shown that team building does improve team outcomes, particularly process and affective outcomes (Klein et al., 2009). All components of team building studied – role clarification, goal setting, interpersonal relationships and problem solving – have a positive effect, but the largest benefit comes from goal setting and role clarification. These effects are strongest in larger teams, perhaps because these tend to be in a more negative state or have more ambiguity about goals to start with. If you can get behind the generic request for a team build therefore and find out what is really needed, you can better tailor the content of an offsite event to the specific situation of the team and have some confidence it will impact performance.

You may however need to dissuade the team from an event altogether and suggest an alternative approach to meet their outcomes, such as timely coaching from – or for – the leader.

WHY ME? WHAT WAS THEIR ROUTE TO ME?

This helps me know who has recommended me and what expectations this may have raised. It helps me to assess whether I am the right person.

WHAT DOES THE GROUP SAY? DOES THE GROUP EVEN KNOW?

A request often comes from an individual, but if my client is a group, I want to know their view. I will negotiate to communicate with the team wherever possible, as this makes it much more likely that the work will make a difference. There is also less resistance from a group or team if they have had a hand in shaping the work.

Common pitfalls if you don't do this are that the team doesn't know that the work is being proposed and become resistant because they are feeling 'done unto'. Or, you may find that the view of the person calling you in is at real odds with what the team thinks needs doing. My worst experience of this has been facilitating a meeting where the leader had already set the agenda around highly transactional issues of rotas and working patterns, only to find that the real issue in the team was the leader himself.

HOW BIG?

I've worked with groups who describe themselves as a team with over fifty members, and leadership teams as small as five. Size matters in terms of what you do and whether you need co-facilitators with you. For work with larger groups with more than around 18 people see Chapter 8.

WHO IS IN THE TEAM?

This is an obvious question in terms of logistics, but it is also a really illuminating question. An effective team knows who is in it and who isn't. When there is uncertainty, it can give you a clue as to where work might be needed. Not infrequently I've noted hesitancy in a leader about who is in their team. Sometimes that hesitancy indicates boundary issues with other parts of the organisation. On one occasion I was coaching a team when an unexpected and uninvited person turned up who felt she was part of the team although the leader and other members didn't! This led to a productive discussion about the unique purpose of the team, its boundaries and how well it was engaging with staff in the organisation if its members themselves weren't clear about membership.

WHY NOW?

This helps to further contextualise and set a timeframe for the work. If the work is around setting strategy or objectives, for example, where does this sit with the business cycle? If it is about devising a plan to increase employee engagement, is the start of a period of redundancies the best time to do it? Recent research on team effectiveness emphasises the importance of timing. We are invited in to a team at a particular point, but need to remember that the tasks required of a team vary over time, the team's ability to do those tasks develops with experience and through working together, and the team itself will go through different stages of development.

CHARACTERISE THIS TEAM – WHAT'S IT LIKE?

This open questioning tends to produce rich information that often resonates more when you share it with a team than the more factual information you get from other questions. In one group for example, the leader was described as being like a water boatman, able to skim over choppy waters. His leadership and ability to stay afloat during a difficult period of transition strongly contributed to group pride and belief in their efficacy. Pride and sense of efficacy both correlate with team performance (Kozlowski and Ilgen, 2006).

WHAT OTHER WORK HAVE THEY DONE/ARE THEY DOING TO ACHIEVE THIS GOAL? WHAT'S GONE WELL/LESS WELL?

This gives a sense both of how the work requested is placed in terms of importance, what it is contributing to and how it is likely to be received by the team.

WHAT MIGHT DERAIL THIS WORK?

This question can give a great indication of team and organisational climate and guide how you handle further inquiry and the events themselves.

Two: Who's Asking?

WHO AM I TALKING TO?

Every point in our contact can provide useful data and of course become part of the intervention. It speaks volumes about a team if the leader is ringing you direct and therefore wants personal contact with you and to test out your relationship. Contrast this with the scenario where the task has been taken on by another team member or an administrator or secretary.

You don't want to leap to conclusions, but with the former I would hypothesise that work with the group is important to the leader; with the latter I would be wondering whether the leader has (possibly appropriately) delegated the task of finding some help to a more able team member or sees finding a consultant as mundane or at worst, work with the team as not too important. Sometimes, when the call is of the 'we've fixed a date and need a facilitator' type, someone quite junior will be working through a list of people and the expectation may be of someone to operate largely as an extra pair of hands rather than as a partner.

As Chapter 11 illustrates, contracting is crucial. If the work turns out to be team development or coaching then time to plan and agree the work with the whole team is needed. Even with a one-off facilitation that you agree to do at short notice; you need to gain as much information about the team and their expectations of you as possible. This is going to be much clearer if the person calling is a member of the team or the leader of it.

WHAT AUTHORITY DO THEY HAVE?

If they lead the team, even though they are willingly requesting help, they may nevertheless feel threatened by someone else engaging with their team. If I can build a good relationship from the outset, it will help me understand their investment in the team, what the success of the proposed work means to them and how we handle our respective roles with the group. It is particularly important for me to be clear whether they or the group is my client. How much freedom do I have? How are they, as leader, going to react if this reveals problems with their leadership?

Can this person help me to get into the group? Can we agree the content of the work or the design of an event together? Can they sign off the logistical and financial aspects?

Team leadership is a key potential lever for improving team effectiveness (Kozlowski and Ilgen, 2006). How will the team leader react if it emerges that the focus of work should be on how the team is being led, or that greater benefit could be achieved by the leader coaching the team themselves?

Three: Purpose and Context of the Team and Organisation

WHICH INDUSTRY OR SECTOR IS IT IN?

A basic question, but in the complex systems within which each organisation works, the industry in which they operate will influence the culture and ethos of a team. It is very different working with a team in the oil industry than a team in the prison service.

How might the nature of their business affect what plays out in the team? For example a leadership team of scientists who are used to operating autonomously in their professional roles may take a long time to operate as a team in their leadership task.

What is happening in their industry? Consider the impact on groups in media of the investigation into phone hacking or groups in the oil and gas industry after the Macondo oil spill.

WHAT IS THIS TEAM FOR?

To assess the element of team effectiveness that relates to outperforming against the expectations of its stakeholders, a team needs to be clear about its purpose. Sometimes you get an unclear account of the purpose of the team, or differing versions of the purpose from different team members. Recently a team leader struggled to give me the name of his team as its purpose had become confused with other teams with which it overlapped. Members of a cohesive team will give similar accounts of what the team is for.

WHERE DOES THE TEAM SIT IN THE ORGANISATION?

Organisational context, where the team sits in the organisation, how much the team's output is valued and how well resourced a team is all directly influence team effectiveness. Teams are shaped by their context. For top management teams their immediate context and the priorities that follow from that are likely to be closely aligned to the organisational context. A surgical team also operates within an organisation but is more likely to be shaped by the immediate context of operating on patients and the concerns of having a clean theatre and smooth workflow. The surgeons will find it very easy to describe their individual performance but may be more resistant to the idea that their effectiveness as a team can also be viewed in terms of their contribution to the hospital's ratings.

Groups that comprise people from different functions or different organisations will have some means of reporting back to their areas, but the individuals may have different levels of authority and autonomy. This can present difficulties during an event if some are able to make decisions and others not.

HOW DOES THE OUTPUT OF THE GROUP CONTRIBUTE TO THE ORGANISATION'S PURPOSE?

How well can the group articulate this? How clear is their line of sight between what they do and the purpose of the organisation? Research on engagement indicates that the closer the fit between an individual's contribution, how obviously valued it is by the organisation and how well it fits with the organisation's objectives, the greater that individual's buy-in to the organisation (Gifford et al., 2010).

Notice how team members describe the ways in which they are effective. Do they talk about the outcomes the team achieves or do they talk about the success of their part of the team? In a newly formed board I worked with recently, one member drifted into describing their role on the board in terms of their own function: 'I am responsible for finance and bring related issues to the board's attention' rather than seeing themselves as a director with a shared corporate responsibility along with their fellow board members. Do team members naturally articulate their success in a way that links with organisational performance and purpose? Do they know what constitutes success in the eyes of their stakeholders since this is a key measure of team effectiveness?

WHAT PROCESSES HELP AND HINDER THIS TEAM?

This prompts a discussion of issues that are often problematic for a team such as decision-making, meetings, individual versus team rewards, how the team develops and retrieves the knowledge it needs to function, and individual and team performance review.

WHAT IS IMPORTANT FOR ME TO KNOW ABOUT THIS TEAM'S HISTORY?

We think of the culture of an organisation as being shaped by the experiences it has gone through, the battles, mergers, successes etc. (Schein, 2010) and similarly the history of a team is really helpful in shaping what you do.

Teams have life cycles. At the start of the team's life, just as when any group forms, the first matter is for them to get to know each other and the task they are there to do. In setting out an approach to team coaching by leaders, Hackman and Wageman (2005) describe the value of enabling team members to get to know each other and to understand the task required early in the life cycle of a team. In the midpoint of the team's life cycle there is value in examining the strategies by which the team is achieving its task. At the end of a task cycle, the team can be coached in terms of what it has learned. It may not be easy to determine where a team is in its life cycle and members come and go, but the simple logic of acquainting team members with each other and what is expected of them before expecting them to review how they best achieve a task makes good common sense.

Distillation

It is tempting to think of a sequence: information gathering – design – intervention. What actually happens is that information gathering affects the team. You are shining a light on things that may not have been noticed. It is a form of intervention and you continue to build the story about the team through the interventions that you do. There is often a point however, when you need to distil the information you have to date, alongside your impressions and feelings and use this to propose next steps. It helps to follow closely the principles of contracting described in Chapter 11. Keep the end in mind – it is very easy to deliver the intervention a client has asked for and default on the outcomes the team needs.

Edgar Schein's first principle of process consultation is 'Always try to be helpful' (Schein, 1999). Being helpful means bringing all you can in terms of understanding teams as part of organisational systems and knowing what can help team effectiveness. It sometimes means saying no or arguing hard that the group will be better served by focusing on getting more resources or re-appraising the alignment of its goals with those of the organisation than by looking at their interpersonal relationships.

Challenge yourself on how what you are suggesting is likely to make the team more effective. Taking the approach of Hackman and Wageman (2005) mentioned earlier, is it likely to improve the team's performance against what its stakeholders need? Is sorting team processes going to facilitate interdependent working? Is this work going to improve the lot of the team members? Never lose sight of the system the team is working in and plan your intervention or design your event to keep highlighting this.

Be compassionate – clients take a huge risk in exposing their work to us. Be transparent about the story you are building of the team and why you propose what you do. I find it helpful to do this in writing sometimes, in a brief document relaying back to a client what they have requested, their context and drivers, who the team consists of and what it does and what I therefore propose. This gives them a chance to add or amend and keeps us on the same page. With a group I'll make explicit the picture of the team we are working on so that we can continue to refine it together. If this involves me in feeding back the result of my work so far, I'll do this in an interactive way so that we continue to create the story together.

Preparing for the Unpredictable

Since so much work that you do will be face to face with a group, this final section looks at how you prepare for this and particularly at some of the hidden processes that occur when groups of people get together. It looks at approaches that make sense of the apparently unpredictable and what this means for what you do.

Whether your first encounter with a group is to work with them to analyse their situation or to work with them on their issues, you will have some idea as to how you are going to structure the event. This could be anything from a highly structured piece of facilitation with timings set out on an agenda sent to the group beforehand to a free-flowing conversation. It will depend on them and you and on what you are trying to achieve. Whatever the format of the event, you want group members to feel as open and comfortable as possible, so even if you are very comfortable without structure, think about what will help them engage best.

ON TOOLS AND TECHNIQUES

Most people working with groups in organisations use some tools or exercises. Notable exceptions include Gestalt practitioners and people using conversation and story drawing on complexity theories. For the rest, it is helpful to have a clutch of key techniques that you feel comfortable with – icebreakers, generating ground rules, contracting for outcomes, a means of generating ideas, a way of prioritising those ideas, a technique for enabling honest and constructive feedback between members and an approach to action planning. A useful compilation is a book by Ingrid Bens (2000). To this basic set you add more specific interventions, for example, if you do a lot of work on strategy.

Review each of the ones you use to see whether they support or detract from an OD mindset. Can you adjust them to enhance this? Peter Hawkins's recent book *Leadership Team Coaching* underlines this, with useful exercises such as contracting at a group event for what the system needs from them, not just what they need (Hawkins, 2011).

There is a tension between using something you are on top of that is just right for what you are trying to achieve with a group, and extending your practice by trying something new. Some of my worst facilitations have occurred when I've been dead set on using a particular technique and I've focused on that rather than on what the group needs. Large companies often have their own approaches to review and action planning. If they do and I don't know how they run, I'll step back and let someone from the company facilitate that part of a session. Tools and techniques can help you feel prepared and can facilitate discussion, but they are always a means to an end, not the end in itself.

BENEATH THE SURFACE – PROCESSES IN GROUPS

Knowing the context of the group, its contribution to the organisation, something about the people in it, having a reasonable sense of what you are going to do and that this has been clearly contracted with the group enables you to work with some confidence: some. As we have said throughout this book, organisations aren't rational. Neither are groups. Understanding some fundamental ideas about groups helps make sense of apparently unaccountable moments in groups, such as when they seem determined not to focus on the task in hand, hang on to ideas that seem to make no sense, blame other individuals or teams, won't get tangible or take responsibility, seem in thrall to their leader or start to pick on one member. This is known as working at the process level with groups, compared with when we talk of how you structure a day or break into small groups, which is the level of procedure. These ideas on process help you as facilitator make sense of unexpected feelings you experience during or after working with a group.

Unpredictability is part of the nature of groups. It is what makes working with groups fascinating and frightening. Here are some of the key frameworks that have made it possible for me to experience the fascination more often than the fear and hence work more productively. I choose these because they link back to elements of what makes a group effective in its system – the importance of processes that enhance members' ability to work interdependently and in a way that improves their well-being and the need for a group to achieve the task required of it.

Member Needs: What's in It for Me?

An account for how groups develop comes from the work of Will Schutz, whose work on FIRO (Fundamental Interpersonal Relationship Orientation) is widely known as an individual psychometric (Schutz, 1958). Schutz observed stages in a group which he saw as reflective of the different ways in which individuals get their needs for relationships met. Working with small teams of US Navy personnel and then with air traffic controllers, Schutz developed a system which could predict who you could put together in a team to support successful work, even under the highly stressful situations of his original subjects. He suggests that we all have needs for relationships in the same way as we have a need for food and drink. As with food or drink, our needs in relationships differ. Some of us get a lot of satisfaction from being with others, some of us are just as happy alone or with a small or select group of others. Schutz identified three types of need shared by everyone, albeit in different degrees: inclusion, control and openness. Applied to a whole this model provides a good explanation for the climate of a group.

Inclusion: In or Out?

When a group first gets together, the need to be met is that of inclusion. Think about when you first join a group, or go into a working party or project team. People are quite polite, ask questions of each other but usually at quite a superficial level. The underlying concern is to work out who is there and whether you fit in. Am I in a group that I want to be in? Do they want to be with me? How quickly do you move to make others feel comfortable? How much do you wish people would do the same for you? Members of a group that hasn't sorted out inclusion issues may feel very disconnected from each other, have people coming in late or not paying attention.

Control: Who's in Charge?

Once a group has sorted out who is who, you may see more confrontational behaviour – disagreement over ideas for example – that are indicative of the need for control. There may be some challenge of the leader – uncomfortable if you are the new facilitator or set advisor. Sub-groups may form; some individuals may be more forceful in getting things done their way. This is the phase when control needs are being worked through – who will be the most influential? Who needs structure and who prefers ambiguity? A group with control issues may show excessive need for rules, outright resistance to or struggle with leadership.

Openness: Trust and Mutual Regard

Typically when a group matures, members are better able to work through conflict and have a greater understanding of each other. Communication is more open and members appear comfortable with each other, often deeper relationships, genuine friendships develop. This is indicative of the need for affection and openness. People seem to know where they stand and how to get the best out of each other. If this remains problematic, relationships may not be close enough to enable individuals to really grapple with complex issues, lack of trust and rivalrous behaviour.

Implications

Understanding the differing needs of individuals and the differing phases of a group guides how you work with a group and how you design an event. Early on, providing opportunity for group members to get to know each other sufficiently well – connection before content – enables the need for inclusion to be met. Acknowledging the range of needs we have in relation to control is important in guiding how much structure and ambiguity you encourage in the way the group works and in allowing those who want to lead to come forward. The degree of interdependence that team members need when working with each other provides a steer for how much openness they may need and therefore guides the degree of interpersonal feedback you may build in to an event.

Anxiety

Anxiety is pervasive in groups, arising from such issues as the need to perform, the nature of the work itself, the wish to outperform others, the threat of redundancy, the stress of delivery or fear of a manager. It is a major factor in determining the nature of a group. Menzies-Lyth, whose work on social defences is a cornerstone of Group Relations, wrote:

> In all situations where I have worked, anxiety has been a central issue: how anxiety, its experience and expression and the related defences, adaptations and sublimations are a major factor in determining personal and institutional behaviour. (Menzies-Lyth, 1988: viii)

Defences

To avoid experiencing the unpleasant feeling of anxiety, groups develop defence mechanisms. It is probably more helpful to be able to recognise that some sort of defence is kicking in than to identify accurately what it is.

Defensive behaviour can be demonstrated in a wide range of ways, through a group rejecting what you say, becoming over-intellectual or excessively trivial in what they discuss, even by people leaving or arriving late.

From the psychodynamic literature on groups, the most significant defences in organisational life are splitting and projection. Some people find certain thoughts and ideas impossible to bear, such as guilt over behaving in a way that clashes with their values, or acknowledging that they did some work badly. They separate off or 'split' these disagreeable feelings and project them on to the outside world. Rather than acknowledge that I was incompetent, I project my incompetence onto members of another team. Once I project feelings onto others, it becomes easy for me to despise them rather than grapple with those thoughts about myself. I therefore retain an acceptable view of myself and that is, frankly, more comfortable. Signs that this is happening include a lot of 'us and them' language or a tendency to see things in black and white terms, seeing people as 'goodies or baddies'.

In organisational life we may also project our good parts on to others to protect them from the bad aspects of ourselves and then we lose our sense of them as part of our identity. For example, we put a leader on a pedestal or hero-worship someone, thus giving away part of our personal power and reducing the scope for shared leadership that is more likely to support challenge and the complex decision-making that is healthy in contemporary organisations.

The Group Off-task

A group cannot be effective if it doesn't achieve the task the organisation or wider stakeholders need it to. The ability of group members to do the task can be blocked by the relief from anxiety that belonging and being led in a particular way can give. This happens without the group members themselves being aware of it. There is a strong possibility that some of the groups you are called to work with are groups who aren't performing as well as they might. Some of these will be groups who aren't doing enough of what the organisation needs them do and spend their time engaged in something tangential to their real purpose. The thinking that is most helpful in these circumstances comes from Bion (1961).

Bion observed groups behaving as if certain basic assumptions were true and agreed by all. These are not conscious assumptions but you can infer them from the way the group is behaving. Only one of these basic assumptions will be in play at a given time, but a group can stay in basic assumption mode for seconds or years. The three modes described by Bion are Dependency, Pairing and Fight-Flight.

In dependency mode, the group operates as if one of the members, usually the leader, can meet all its needs. Thus, other members contribute little and behave in an immature way. There is a sense of almost magical power emanating from the leader. In such a group, the members have split off their own capacities and projected them on to the leader, thus limiting the resources and energy that they can contribute to the group.

In pairing mode, the group shares an unconscious belief that two members will or have joined together to produce a wonderful solution, a sort of messiah who will solve all problems and save the group. In such a group there will be a sense of hopefulness and expectation that can only be maintained as long as the messiah remains 'unborn'; that is doesn't actually emerge to lead the group.

In fight-flight mode the group operates as if it has met either to fight something or to run away. These goals of battle or escape become more important than doing any effective work. The leader here has a particular role to play in leading the group against the enemy, but they will be ignored once the danger is past. Here, anxiety has been split off and projected on to the enemy.

Here is an example of a group in basic assumption mode. Two organisations were merging and several project groups were established to handle the transition. This organisational change gave rise to a lot of anxiety and uncertainty, for example over what jobs would be lost and where people might be physically located. Each project group comprised representatives from both organisations and their overall aim was to recommend to the Project Board how systems like finance, supplies and human resources could best function when the two organisations merged, as well as to introduce people from the different organisations to each other. This mixing of people from the two organisations was a deliberate attempt to break down barriers, enable them to get to know each other and reduce a sense of paranoia about the other.

Some of the project groups were able to develop proposals for the Project Board to consider – they stayed 'on-task'. Some experienced significant conflict between representatives of the different organisations, but nevertheless delivered. One group however, seemed to become totally paralysed and produced nothing.

When I went to a meeting of this group, I found that the representatives of one of the organisations had dropped out altogether. The remaining members seemed to be in fight-flight mode. They told me that the ideal system for their function was their organisation's system as it was currently working, and could point to all the flaws and inefficiencies of the system used by the other organisation. They had not however formulated any report for the Project Board that would enable even such a one-sided recommendation to be considered. They were way 'off-task'. In their view, not only was their system superior in every way, but in the event of jobs being lost, these would (regrettably) have to be from those employed in the other organisation, since they were clearly inefficient, lazy, didn't deliver and by dropping out of this group had demonstrated they couldn't cope with change and should leave or be sacked.

In contrast to this kind of situation, a group on-task is one where objectives are tackled and there is growth and development for the members. It is a group that is in touch with reality and operates as a system open to the organisational and client environment around it. A basic assumption group is marked by stagnation and regression. To move forward, the group needs to get back in touch with reality and recognise that the qualities it is attributing to members or outsiders are actually parts of itself.

Implications

Building on the work of Edgar Schein, it is useful to think of what a group does and what you therefore pay attention to at three levels. What the group does, its task, is the obvious level. For the groups in the example above, the task was to work out ways of merging different systems. The second level is how the group works, the procedure level. This includes how and where you meet, how you structure an event, for example with small group work or exercises. The level discussed in this section is the third, deeper level, known in facilitation as the level of process, which includes group dynamics, issues of power and of course anxiety. It is largely invisible, compared to the obvious elements at the procedure level, but nevertheless hits you full on in some circumstances. Working at this level in a group can be the most difficult part of facilitation and usually the least sanctioned in everyday conversation. It is often the level at which real shifts take place that enables a group to perform better.

Competence at working with process hinges on being able to notice that something is going on below the surface. This can be hard when your attention is also on running a plenary feedback session or introducing an exercise. It requires you to be fully in touch with what is happening in the group, in you and to be able to stand back and take in the whole picture at the same time. I liken it to being on a beach and looking at everything around you: the people, boats, rocks, cliffs etc. If you then half-close your eyes, you see the same scene but differently. There is less detail on the individual people or boats, but now you really notice the shimmering of the water and where that pattern of shimmers is disrupted.

Having taken in that pattern, you can start to make sense of it. How would you describe the disruption? It could be something like 'reading between the lines of the way this group talks, they repeatedly blame their competitors, but make no attempt to analyse their own failings' or 'no one in this group is challenging what the leader says'. Apply what you know about this group, at this time, in this context. Why might they be anxious? What are they not saying or tackling?

Having noticed process issues, the way to help a group is to bring the issue – or your impression of the issue – to the group's attention. This is often the 'naming the elephant in the room' comment. Develop your ability to name your feelings and observations on what is happening in the group in a way that steers clear of assumption or blame. Helping the group acknowledge its patterns of behaviour and the anxiety behind them paves the way for the group re-engaging with reality and the task the organisation needs it to achieve.

The more you know about yourself, your own default settings and biases, the better able you are to identify that behaviour in a group may relate to anxiety. In all facilitation, your own feelings are a key aid to working out what is going on. If you are feeling bored each time a group member speaks, it is likely that others are too. If you experience an unexpected feeling that you can't immediately locate the cause of, for example suddenly feeling disproportionately tired, then it is possible that unconscious processes are playing in. Anyone working with a group has moments of total bewilderment if not panic, none more so than when unconscious process is to the fore just because it is, well, unconscious and murky. When this happens, a group needs you to work with it, not buckle under the stress. One of the best pieces of advice I repeat to myself when it all seems to be going wrong and I'm sliding into self-doubt and self-blame is 'you can't afford the luxury of thinking it's you when you are in the group' (Shohet, 2011). Work to contain the anxiety for yourself and the client group while you are with them; analyse the issue and your own performance in supervision afterwards.

Conclusion

This chapter has looked at ways of equipping yourself to work with groups from an OD mindset. From research on team performance through to frameworks on groups there are a lot of resources to draw on. You will be most useful when you hold the organisation purpose in mind as you contract with a group, and when you become comfortable with your own style so that you can really attend to the group when you are with them. Learn as much as you can about yourself, so that you can rely on yourself and your perception. Find among all the literature that is out there the ideas that support and challenge the facilitator that you are. Contract to get feedback on how you are doing and be rigorous in reflecting on your experience. Above all, continue to resource yourself with great supervision.

References

Bens, I. 2000. *Facilitating with Ease.* San Francisco, CA: Jossey-Bass.

Bion, W.R. 1961. *Experiences in Groups and Other Papers.* London. Tavistock Publications Limited.

Block, P. 1981. *Flawless Consulting: a Guide to Getting your Expertise Used.* 2nd edition. San Francisco, CA: Jossey-Bass/Pfeiffer.

Gifford, J., Finney, L., Hennessey, J. and Varney, S. 2010. *The Human Voice of Employee Engagement: What Lies beneath the Surveys.* Horsham: Roffey Park Institute.

Hackman, J.R. and Wageman, R. 2005. A theory of team coaching. *Academy of Management Review,* 30, 269–87.

Hawkins, P. 2011. *Leadership Team Coaching.* London: Kogan Paul.

Klein, C., Diaz Granados, D., Salas, E., Le, H., Burke, C.S., Lyons R. and Goodwin, G.F. 2009. Does team building work? *Small Group Research,* 40, 181.

Kozlowski, S.W.J. and Ilgen, D.R. 2006. Enhancing the effectiveness of work groups and teams. *Psychological Science in the Public Interest,* 7(3), 77–124.

Menzies-Lyth, I. 1988. *Containing Anxiety in Institutions.* London. Free Association Press.

Schein, E.H. 1999. *Process Consultation Revisited.* Reading, MA: Addison-Wesley.

Schein, E.H. 2010. *Organizational Culture and Leadership.* 4th edition. San Francisco, CA: Jossey-Bass.

Schutz, W. 1958. *FIRO: A Three Dimensional Theory of Interpersonal Behaviour.* WSA/Holt Rheinhard and Winston.

Shohet, R. 2011. Personal communication during a supervision.

8

Large Group Interventions: A Potent Alchemy

Sue Belgrave

Introduction

A tale of 1,000 bean bags and more than 100 great ideas.

Walk with me into a room too big to be called a room; let's call it a 'stadium-sized space' and watch – more than 1,000 people seated on bean bags are drawing their view of what is best about their organisation on small pieces of white paper. Fifteen minutes later those drawings are being collected and will be assembled into a collage representing 'Our organisation'. Fifteen minutes after that the bean bags have been dragged by their owners into new positions causing the technical team to hold their breath; no one has ever had so many bean bags (filled with polystyrene balls) in one space and there is a genuine fear that the static electricity created by dragging the bean bags from place to place will adversely affect the technology! Everyone is listening to the lead facilitator introduce an Open Space designed to address the question 'What do we need to do now to take our company to the next level?' About half an hour later more than 63 topics have been accumulated. People move (dragging their bean bags behind them) to locations marked by bus stop-type signs on wheels – easy to find and easy to trundle around in search of more space if the group grows. And then the conversations begin. 'What can we do about the shift patterns?', 'How can we keep people engaged?', 'More effective communication?' and the list goes on. Some groups are large, some small; all are connected and full of lively debate.

In a variation designed specifically to fit the event, a decision-making team is located on a podium ready to assess proposals and in the moment, decide which ideas should be taken forward and which should be put on hold.

Brown bag lunches are delivered and after lunch a second round of conversation begins; this round, if I am honest, perhaps a tad less energetic than the first as people start to feel the impact of the previous night's celebration and the bean bags ever versatile become useful for another, less dynamic, purpose.

As the space closes the reaction around the circle is consistent; 'we set the agenda', 'we talked about what we wanted to talk about', 'we made connections with people we didn't know', 'we came up with some great ideas that we can act on'. So the largest Open Space I have ever been involved in came to a close; the room emptied, polystyrene balls covered the floor like melting snow flakes, but the energy of what had happened stayed with the participants for months to come.

Just one example from more than 15 years' experience of a way of working which has entranced me from my very first event; an event which the leader of the design team (and my mentor) was unable to attend at the very last minute. I remember being gently told to 'trust the process'. I did so then with much trepidation. Now I trust the process with delight and anticipation, curious to see what will emerge from the potent alchemy which is the world of Large Group Interventions (LGIs).

History

The ways of working which are now referred to collectively as LGIs, grew in the 1990s in the USA and the UK as a response to the combined challenges of creating change quickly and finding solutions to complex problems which required involvement from a broad spectrum of people. Across the USA and in Europe people were experimenting with new ways of working and their experiments were bearing fruit.

In the 1990s two wise women in the field of Organisation Development (OD), Betty Alban and Barbara Bunker identified that what seemed like a random set of new approaches to change, actually shared a number of common principles. This was captured in their book *Large Group Interventions* (Bunker and Alban, 1997) after more than five years of conversation with practitioners who were using these new methodologies to create rapid change for their clients. In 1996 I spoke at the OD Network conference in Dallas with Julie Beedon from VISTA Consulting telling the story of how The Body Shop (always an early adopter) had used an LGI to facilitate a global franchisee conference. LGI came very naturally to The Body Shop where Anita Roddick had built a business designed to deliver both social change and profit through the ethical sourcing and sale of skin and hair care products.

The principles which these methodologies share derive from thinking which emerged in the 1950s and 1960s and became embodied in methodologies created by individuals. Amongst others Merrelyn and Fred Emery created The Search Conference, Marvin Weisbord and Sandra Janoff Future Search, Rob Jacobs and Kathy Dannemiller Real Time Strategic Change, Dick and Emily Axelrod The Conference Model, Harrison Owen Open Space Technology, and slightly later David Cooperrider and Jane Magruder Watkins created Appreciative Inquiry. The methodologies reflected the diverse experience of their creators and tended to have different functions. Of the methodologies named above Future Search, Real Time Strategic Change and The Search Conference are designed for creating a future vision and The Conference Model is for work redesign, Open Space for participative working, Appreciative Inquiry is both an insightful way of looking at the world and a change methodology. With the exception of Open Space which shares the principles but follows a different path, there are more similarities than differences between the methodologies and exploring them in detail you will see shared commitments to:

- A clear purpose.

- Having the whole system (or representatives of the whole system) in the room.

- A positive future focus.

- Self-managed collaborative processes designed to enable all voices to be heard.

- Work in real time on real issues.

- Reality being the key driver.

- The creation of a shared database.

- Equal commitment to design and logistics.

- The building of community.

LGIs regularly and reliably:

- Increase engagement and motivation for change.

- Encourage diversity of thinking.

- Stimulate creativity and innovation.

- Support equality of opportunity.

- Deliver action (e.g. reduce costs, solve problems).

- Build community.

More detail about the methodologies can be found either in *Large Group Interventions* (Bunker and Alban, 1997) or *The Change Handbook* (Holman, Devane and Cady, 2007).

Unsurprisingly the LGI principles referred to above echo the broader values underpinning the field of OD, which include:

- Open methods of conflict resolution rather than suppression and compromise.

- Development of organic rather than mechanical systems.

- An understanding that the main building blocks of any organisation are people and groups.

- People are essentially good.

- Congruence between individual and organisational goals.

- Individuals are in process rather than fixed.

- Acceptance and utilisation of individual differences rather than resistance and fear.

- Emphasis on collaboration rather than competition.

- Seeing the whole system.

Looking at the list of what LGIs can deliver and comparing it to the challenges that organisations face today it becomes clear why an LGI is potentially such a useful tool for the OD practitioner; in my experience successful delivery of an LGI is dependent on understanding and adhering to design principles broadly shared by all methodologies.

Design Principles

In the 1990s practitioners of LGIs tended to be trained in and to favour specific methodologies; my story is that I was trained in both Future Search and Open Space by their creators. In my role teaching about LGIs now I am frequently asked how to choose which approach to use. The answer is annoyingly for those who ask the question 'it depends'. The world has changed since the methodologies were first conceived and the way they are being used is also changing. There was a time when practitioners would have run a Real Time Strategic Change or a Future Search or a Search Conference in their entirety which might have required 3–5 days out of the office. That was difficult to achieve in the 1990s; now it is almost impossible. What this means now is that practitioners are less likely to have specific training and more likely to cherry pick from the methodologies to create something that will fit into the time they have available. The upside is creativity, flexibility and innovation in the work; the downside can be less-than-successful outcomes – if the practitioner does not clearly understand the underlying design principles. The design principles are as applicable when working with 30 or 300 or 1,300 people and offer a helpful lens through which to plan any large meeting. Clear understanding of the principles will allow an experienced practitioner to cherry pick wisely. It is rather like cooking; if you choose to make a white sauce using the roux method (melt the butter, cook the flour in the butter add the liquid slowly) and you do not cook the flour thoroughly, the result will be a lumpy white sauce. You will have a sauce but it will not be the best sauce it could be and it may be remembered for its lumps rather than for its overall deliciousness. If you stick to the recipe when you are learning to make the basic sauce you can then with confidence add new ingredients to suit the occasion in the future.

Design Team

The first task of the design team (a multidisciplinary group who gather data, plan the event and deliver on the day) is to 'nail the purpose'. A robust purpose sufficiently motivating and relevant to justify the cost and effort of the event has to be identified and agreed with key stakeholders at the very outset. While this can be a time-consuming process it offers the OD practitioner the invaluable opportunity to have dialogue in the critical areas of mission, strategy and leadership. Once 'nailed' the purpose becomes the star to sail the ship by; the destination on the road map.

The second task is to ask 'Is the organisation willing to act on/support outcomes from the event?' If there is no willingness then truly it is a mistake to begin, because to awaken the possibility of inclusion and then to ignore the voices which speak up is worse than to do nothing. It is true that there will be value in the conversations which take place; it is also true that people will remember that nothing happened as a result.

It is also perfectly possible to say that the purpose is the conversation (as in Open Space) and what emerges, emerges. The reputational danger is if there is an expectation created that the outputs of the day will be acted upon and then nothing happens.

Architecture of an LGI

Typical elements of the design with suitable activity listed alongside might be:

- Connection – shared timeline (taken from Future Search).

- Context Setting – CEO briefing.

- Data gathering – Group Mind Map (taken from Future Search).

- Sense-making – Appreciative Interviews (taken from Appreciative Inquiry).

- Visioning – Collage.

- Action planning – Stop Start Go.

- Reflection/Evaluation – electronic voting pads.

Each phase needs its own purpose and the flow of divergent and convergent thinking, both within specific activities and throughout the day, needs to be managed. More information about designing LGIs can be found in *Meetings by*

Design (VISTA Consulting Team, 2002) or in any of the books relating to specific methodologies referenced at the end of this chapter.

Self-managed Processes

Self-management is the only way large groups can work collaboratively. All activities need to be explained in a carefully worded worksheet made available on tables; to facilitate the work three table roles are employed:

- A facilitator whose responsibility is simply to ensure that everyone's voice is heard.

- A note-taker who takes notes using the words of participants where possible.

- A time-keeper who keeps track of time.

These roles are self-selecting and need to rotate for different activities; avoid having trained facilitators imposed on the tables as their 'expert' presence can paradoxically limit conversation.

Post Event

The follow-through phase can be an elephant trap for all those involved in LGI. So much energy is invested in the design and in the event itself that it is very easy to lose impetus in the follow-through; potentially one reason why the methodologies have not become more widely adopted. Change will happen through conversation on the day and in the world of measurable outcomes that may or may not be enough. An LGI is both an end in itself and a beginning; encouragement, formalised or otherwise, will be needed if momentum is to be maintained. Begin with the end in mind; early on identify a member of the design team to coordinate the follow-up communication and activity.

Logistics

Logistics or the practicalities of the event require as much preparation as the design process. Efficient organisation at every stage of the process will help to create confidence in anxious participants.

WHO NEEDS TO BE THERE?

The agreed purpose will help determine who needs to be there. Ideally the whole system or representatives of the whole system, including customer or partnering organisations need to be in the room and there are also ways of working with discrete elements of the system. Attention to detail is important, for example the way in which people are invited to the event is significant. A personal invitation says something very different to a mass email.

WHERE?

The venue needs to be big enough to hold all those who will be attending in one room and to hold them in that space comfortably for the whole day. Dispersal into breakout rooms breaks the bonds of nascent community. Natural lighting makes a substantial difference, and pay attention to the acoustics and to the floor. A noisy hard wooden ballroom floor will make for a noisy day. Carpet on the other hand deadens sound and makes it vital to have a sound engineer on site. People will be seated cabaret style on tables, big enough to accommodate eight people, and not so big that you can't speak to each other across the table. Think about access for people with disabilities and about any special provisions needed for those with hearing loss, visual impairment or any other disabilities.

The location of all facilities needs to be considered. Tea, coffee and water need to be available all day; brown bag lunches work well; quick, flexible and inexpensive.

A Word or Three about Anxiety

Bringing large numbers of people together for an LGI will create anxiety in the organisation; the design has to provide a container for that anxiety or the event will fail. Anxieties relate to power and the loss of control often expressed as 'this won't work; they won't be able to do that; you don't understand our organisation'. Are the senior team and the facilitators prepared to let go of their traditional roles (aka power) to allow a more inclusive approach to emerge?

For participants the questions will be a mixture of the practical ('Will there be lunch?', 'Who will I be sitting with?') with the more fundamental ('How will it all work?', 'Amongst so many voices will my voice be heard?' and 'Will it make any difference?'). Paying attention to participant concerns is an important discipline; if you can't answer them there is still work to do.

The practical concerns will be taken care of through the meticulous planning of the logistics; the more fundamental concerns through the design and the way of working.

The role of the key facilitators (ideally members of the design team) presents challenges to experienced facilitators, because in this way of working their role is simple; guiding participants through the process by reading the worksheets and doing that seemingly mythical thing of 'holding the space'. Facilitators need to let go of their desire to help, to intervene and to control, they need to trust the process and allow participants to make their own sense of the activity in which they are engaged. It can be a hard practice to learn. Whole books have been written on the topic of 'holding the space'; put very simply what you are doing as a facilitator is conveying a sense of confidence in the design, commitment to the process and holding anxiety.

Some senior people fear chaos; the fear of a large group of people who are in some way uncontrolled or out of control. In fact to enable large groups to be effective in LGIs rather higher levels of control than might be initially apparent have to be exerted but control is applied through the design and the application of key principles, rather than through the individual positional power of senior people.

If you think of the iceberg model and its levels of content, procedure and process, there is little control over the content or the process; people will have the conversations they need to have in the way they need to have them. The procedure, which is in effect the container for the event, is another matter entirely. The procedure is tightly controlled and informed by principle at every level. The procedure includes table roles, worksheets, the rules of Open Space, the guidelines for Group Mind Mapping. If the procedure is not followed then anxiety will not be held and the outcome will be at risk.

If, for example, the table scribes use their own words rather than those of their colleagues on the table, individuals will feel their voice is not being heard. If expert facilitators are used on the tables, the conversation will lose its richness. In Open Space if the topics do not originate from the group in the moment, then the magic, creativity, energy and commitment is lost. Be aware senior people and facilitators will try to make changes like this because of their own anxiety! The principles and ways of working need learning; just like any skill there's a process of learning; in the beginning you follow the steps slavishly; as your understanding of the principles grows you learn where you can flex and where not to flex.

Earlier in this chapter I outlined what LGI can deliver; the devil being in the detail it is important to consider exactly how and why LGIs deliver such remarkable results.

Encourage Diversity of Thinking

Recent work by Roffey Park in partnership with KPMG identified that the pool from which top teams in the FTSE 100 companies are drawn is not deep. The top teams in many organisations consist only of white middle-class men who think in the same ways, because their upbringing and experience is the same. That presents an organisational risk. Diversity does exist in organisations but often at levels seldom accessed by top teams.

By requiring that a cross-section of people is involved both in the design and during the event and by using the table roles, LGIs ensure that a uniquely wide range of voices is heard. Using a maximum mix (max mix) combination, alternated with a functional approach to the table seating plans ensures that participants work both with people they do not usually encounter, and with those who they may already know.

Stimulate Creativity and Innovation

LGIs stimulate creativity and innovation by allowing people to see things differently and to work in new ways.

How exactly? Sending out key reports in advance as pre-work makes sure that if information is available about the topic it is equally available to everyone. Beginning with a divergent data-gathering activity, for example a Group Mind Map allows a range of richly divergent perspectives to be shared, thereby creating a new picture of the world of the organisation.

Group Mind Mapping (incidentally a good divergent stand-alone activity from Weisbord and Janoff's (1995) Future Search methodology) in which people contribute ideas on a massive paper, has a clear set of rules to facilitate participation:

- Whoever names the issue says where it goes.

- All ideas are valid.

- Opposing trends are OK.

- Brainstorm not discussion.

- Give concrete examples where possible.

In the process of creating the mind map participants see things differently, trust that their individual voice will be heard and as a result feelings of empowerment and possibility begin to emerge.

In many designs participants are asked to engage in creative visioning using collage, song writing or play-acting activities which go beyond the usual logical/linguistic workplace preferences. The best include some of poetry/music/theatre and art. The voice of a poet and I am thinking of Levi Tafari opening an event in Liverpool, can cut to the emotion of a purpose like a razor.

In the planning stage all of this is almost universally greeted with derision and exasperation and equally on the day universally enjoyed. I can think of many occasions when senior people have said 'people in my organisation won't do that' or 'it won't work here'. That has never been my experience; in fact the experience is more usually that people want more time for that activity and if you have allowed time for three or four groups to perform then eight or twelve will often want to take the stage! So why is that? It is because the design is carefully crafted to bring people to the point when they are ready to participate in a more creative way. Their voices have been heard; they have had some control over what they do. Creativity is natural to us; it's just that organisational life squeezes it out and most of the time allows it no space to breathe. If you are looking for further validation then notice that the LGI process maps neatly onto Maslow's individualised hierarchy of needs (Maslow, 1954), meeting needs at Levels 3 (love and belonging) and 4 (self-esteem and confidence) with the result that activity at Level 5 (creativity and self-actualisation) becomes a possibility.

Be aware sometimes people taking part in an LGI may have fun.

Support Equality of Opportunity

There will always be people in organisations who have no difficulty in making their voices heard and there are many more whose voices are never heard because they need time to think before they speak, because their views are controversial, because they do not feel confident that their ideas are valued or because cultural mores hold them back.

The validity of *all* voices infuses LGI thinking with a focus on ensuring that the maximum number of diverse voices is heard. The table dynamic is important; exercises are designed so that there is a period of personal reflection to allow people to order their thoughts, followed by sharing in pairs before having a group conversation. The most important points from the table discussion are then agreed and then shared with the wider room; individual, small group, table group, whole room ensuring that individual voices truly are not lost and that the community benefits from the 'wisdom of the crowd'.

The role of the table facilitator is specifically designed to ensure that everyone's voice is heard. Table roles rotate so that in terms of the organisational hierarchy the most powerful people do not always have the metaphorical pen.

In Group Mind Mapping the most powerful and principled guideline is 'whoever names the issue says where it goes'. When applying that principle, two things invariably happen (which mirror exactly what often happens in organisational life to those who have quieter voices); other participants rephrase the idea and suggest options for connection to the contributor. Result; the quieter voice is not heard. Skilful and strong facilitation at this point ensures that whoever names the issue is able to say where it goes. Once the principle is established, a rising tide of confidence is created as those whose ideas are usually trampled upon or seized by others, realise that this is different and that not only will their unique voice be heard, but their thoughts will be recorded in the way *they* want them to be recorded on the shared mind map. That is a very powerful statement of equality.

Increase Motivation and Engagement

As companies fight to reduce costs, increase productivity and at the same time retain good employees, employee engagement has become a very important topic of conversation. Surveys like the UK *Sunday Times* 'Best Companies to Work For' have become very influential and much research energy has gone into understanding what contributes to employee engagement. Marcus Buckingham (Buckingham and Clifton, 2001) has not been alone in identifying that a sense of alignment between personal and organisational values is important; people are looking for a sense of meaning in their work. Feeling that your voice is heard, that you know where you fit in and that you have a clear line of sight between what you do and the broader mission and purpose of your organisation also really matters.

LGIs, while not conceived specifically to deliver engagement, do just that. The designs are created around enabling the voices of all participants to be heard whether in a Group Mind Map as described above or working in a team to create a vision for the future. At the more flexible end of the LGI spectrum, Open Space Technology regularly delivers increased levels of motivation. This is because participants are trusted to set their own agenda in support of the principle that given the freedom to choose people will choose to engage in meaningful, rather than dilatory dialogue. This is a manifestation of McGregor's (1960) Theory Y (people want to be the best they can be) rather than Theory X (people will do as little as they can get away with).

Deliver Action

LGI thinking started at a time when many change initiatives were hitting the buffers; one wave of change hardly implemented at the bottom of the organisation before the top started on the next one. The early questions were around how to do change faster; the answer came in the words of Marvin Weisbord 'people support what they help to create'.

If you enable people to participate early in creating change they will support it and as a result the whole phase of trying to get buy-in becomes irrelevant.

Most (Open Space being an honourable exception) of the methodologies build towards some kind of action planning. This is action planning with a difference; created from a shared place of understanding of the context in which the organisation is operating and with a shared commitment to success. Most designs work to create future visions which build on the best of what is and most end with a sense of ... if that is what we want the future to be what I/we have to do differently is .... It isn't rocket science and it's an indicator of how, in the last 10 years this thinking has become so much more mainstream that as I write these words it all seems very obvious. Why wouldn't you do this?

And yet I still have the frequent experience of introducing LGIs to organisations whose initial reaction is 'our employees will never do this etc., etc'. and then when they do it they are astonished by the energy, the motivation, the commitment and the creativity of the people who work for them. LGI, unlike many workplace practices which succeed in reducing people to sober monochrome, releases the capacity to be glorious technicolour.

But 'ah' the naysayers continue even after the explosion of technicolour activity 'it's easy to create a bubble of energy on the day but how much actually changes as result?'

LGIs can kick-start action and can deliver sustainable change; the methodologies would not have survived if they did not. There is a saying 'you can never step into the same river twice'; the world of the organisation is changed by the conversations that take place in the event. Begin with the end in mind and ensure that the purpose goes beyond the event with processes in place to secure sustainable delivery.

Build Community

The big one comes last!

It is October 2011. I am sitting in a room crowded with 60 young people, participants on the Young Foundation Uprising programme, listening to a young man talking about a project he wants to start. 'Imagine a community', he says, 'where people know each other, where they talk to each other as they go about their business, where people feel safe and that they belong; imagine if that was our community in London now'.

The room fell silent realising just how far we are from a sense of community in many areas of the UK today and how much of a sense of loss people experience as a result.

Riots traumatised some UK cities in the summer of 2011. Rioters destroyed businesses in their own backyard in a deeply troubling demonstration of how little stake they had in those communities. People like Siva Kandiah who ran a corner shop in Hackney, woke up to find the business into which he had poured 11 years of his life, in ruins.

That was one side of the riots, the other is what happened next; by 8am the next morning 'riot clean up' was trending on Twitter with more than 60,000 followers. People were appearing with their brooms on the streets of

Clapham and over in Hackney, East London funds were already being raised from around the world to rebuild Siva Kandiah's business, which reopened just three weeks later.

Community is very important to us; fundamentally important. We are social animals better together than apart. When people talk about why they go to work the sense of belonging, of companionship is often what they talk about. In the absence of a geographical community the work place is often the only community they have, and yet how often do those workplaces ever have a sense of community?

Some workplaces have a really strong sense of community; in my working life I have had the privilege of working in places where there was a sense that people looked out for each other, that they listened to each other, that they held shared values and they enjoyed relationships that went beyond the transactional.

Many workplaces are not however, like that, not by design but just in the midst of a complex fast-changing pressurised world where it's easier to get sign-off for expensive IT hardware than for developing our human software. Somehow community just gets squeezed out. People feel isolated, confused, disconnected, demotivated and not at all inclined to go the extra mile. We know this is all on the increase because there has never been more interest in employee engagement surveys. Tighter budgets, more uncertainty, a need for more flexibility and innovation require employees to be more engaged and studies show that they are not.

So how do LGIs create a feeling of community?

By having everyone in the same room, it's an easy start. By helping people see their similarities and their differences, by enabling people to talk to each other in a way that ensures all voices are heard. By giving people a shared emotional experience of connection creating a memory which in the months to come people can come back to and say 'Do you remember when we were all at that event and we had that amazing conversation?'

Communities need stories good and bad, and they can be created in an LGI. We yearn for connection; it is no accident that when we celebrate, we celebrate by joining with others not by going on solitary retreat; truly there is delight in connection. I listened recently to a quirky programme on BBC

Radio 4; the presenter is engaged in making random connections with people around the world via the Internet. So what? So what I heard was the individual sheer delight of those who picked up their phone in the moment of connection. Imagine that sheer delight multiplied 100 or 200 or 300 or 1,000 fold; the delight of 1,000 people in one room making connections, finding solutions working together. Sheer delight – so why would we not create more opportunities to experience that sheer delight of connection?

Conclusion

In conclusion, I am curious. If LGIs can deliver all of the above – why is their use not more widespread?

Based on my experience I am aware of two reasons, and there are probably more; perceived cost and complexity which leads to anxiety as outlined above and a reported 'we have done that and it didn't work'. The first relates to clarity of purpose and design conversations, the second to what I referred to earlier as 'cherry picking'.

If I ask, 'what exactly did you do?' the response is often, 'we did a bit of Open Space', or, 'we got everyone together and they brainstormed using flip charts and then we heard back from all the groups'. (In the early 90s the concept of table conversations with flip charts and groups reporting back was genuinely novel. It is no longer novel, and in fact overdone, it can become almost as tedious as wall-to-wall PowerPoint.) What is happening is cherry picking without clear understanding of the principles. People are drawn to the individual activities, to the procedures if you like, but these are operated incompletely because there is no commitment to underlying principles and therefore the results fall short of expectation.

Open Space is particularly attractive because on the surface it seems easy; get everyone together and have a whole lot of conversations going on at the same time. It's not unusual for people to say, 'we decided what the topics will be and then let them choose which conversations they wanted to join'. That is not it at all; the key is that the participants decide the agenda and the organisation trusts individuals to have the conversations they need to have. Another example might be 'Prouds and Sorries' from Future Search, an activity designed to follow a Group Mind Map and precede visioning activity, to allow people to share what they are proud of and what they are sorry about in relation to a specified issue. It can be a very emotional conversation, raw and healing at the same time, and it needs to be contained. Taken in isolation it can leave people feeling vulnerable and exposed.

Authentically working with the LGI methodologies is challenging and can require a step-change in working philosophy, a move towards those OD values of optimism, democracy and humanism. If people can find the courage to take that step they will be rewarded. And a bit of Open Space is better than no Open Space at all, but this is a field book for practitioners and I want to be clear where best practice lies.

And for those of us who practise according to the principles, I think perhaps we may have fallen short in the key area of evaluation which also contributes to the comment 'it didn't work'. Well, perhaps it did work, but we were not assiduous enough after the event in collecting the data, gathering the stories to strengthen our case.

Finally, where next? In the last 25 years people in organisations faced with increasingly complex challenges and a requirement to do more with less, have moved towards more participative ways of working. Coaching as a management style has become widespread; workplace consultation is not uncommon, action learning sets are more widely used; effective team work is a prized competence. A coaching style of management encourages increased participation of one employee; LGI can encourage participation of 1,000 employees. LGI, arguably the ultimate form of participative working, should have a bright future, but as outlined above there are obstacles in the way. A real hope is that LGI thinking and principles will become much more mainstream-applied to enable communities in and out of work to meet the challenges of the future. LGI principles allow space for both the individual and the collective voice to be heard and for people to make connections which reflect their humanity and the best of what is. They enable collaborative working to be an experience not a theoretical construct. They offer vital opportunities for organisations with a predominantly western individualistic mindset to enjoy a way of working closer to the mindset dominant in some of the vibrant emerging economies of Asia.

As complexity increases, resources diminish, capacity to work collaboratively is going to be at a premium and maybe we can even learn to do all of this virtually around the globe connecting with the energy of social networks.

At times of increasing uncertainty people need more connection not less, and LGIs offer the possibility that the connection can becomes transformational – a potent alchemy indeed.

Case Study – Making it Different

A one-day event for 150 people (two levels of management plus other key stakeholders) which took place at the end of a senior leadership development programme in an organisation which had faced substantial reduction in head count as part of UK government spending cuts.

PURPOSE

- To bring together people who had been involved in the leadership programme with others who had not.

- To find a new way of having senior team meetings.

- To celebrate collective creativity.

- To begin to work out how to 'Make it Different' for their customers in the new financial climate.

The event was designed over a period of six months with a design team who had no prior experience of LGIs. We had four half-day design meetings with other ad hoc meetings of subgroups responsible for logistics/facilitation. All activities, with the exception of the Open Space, were facilitated by the design team.

OUTLINE DESIGN FOR THE DAY (09:30 TO 16:00)

1. Welcome by members of design team.

2. Timeline – When did I join the organisation and why? (from Future Search).

   Seventy foot horizontal timeline with participants writing the answer to 'Why did I join the organisation?' on paper gingerbread men and attaching them to the timeline at the year they joined.

3.   Introduction to the day by the design team.

4.   Activity One – Sharing stories of the challenges of the last year. Structured activity using worksheet and table roles sharing stories of loss and frustration alongside stories of possibility.

5.   Overview of the way ahead from CEO.

6.   Activity Two – Q and A based on LGI principles (from Real Time Strategic Change).

      Coffee break.

7.   CEO responses using Mastermind format.

8.   Activity Three – Create a guide to innovation (using Appreciative Inquiry).

      •   Appreciative interviews to understand more about the conditions in which innovation is possible.

      •   Sense-making of themes from interviews.

      •   Creation of guide to innovation using collage.

      •   Display guides in gallery.

9.   Lunch.

10.   Open Space – (from Open Space Technology).

      'What can this team do to support Making it Different?'.

      Two sessions of 45 minutes each.

      Close.

11.   Ask for volunteers to run next event.

12.   Close and Evaluation.

References

Bunker, B. and Alban, B.1997. *Large Group Interventions*. San Francisco, CA: Jossey-Bass.

Holman, P., Devane, T. and Cady, S. 2007. *The Change Handbook*. San Francisco, CA: Berrett-Koehler.

Maslow, A. 1954. *Motivation and Personality*. New York, NY: Harper.

McGregor, D.1960. *The Human Side of Enterprise*. New York, NY: McGraw Hill.

VISTA Consulting Team. 2002. *Meetings by Design*. Bromsgrove: VISTA Consulting Team Ltd.

Weisbord, M. and Janoff, S. 1995. *Future Search*. San Francisco, CA: Berrett-Koehler.

9

Culture and OD: Appreciating the 'Unseen Hand' Governing Behaviour in Organisations

Paul Brewerton and Grahame Smith

For many of us, understanding culture in organisations is akin to resolving a difficult riddle or puzzle. So in writing this chapter we were reminded of a childhood riddle, which goes like this:

> Question: 'The more you have of it, the less you see. What is it?'

> Answer: 'Darkness'.

Introduction

Substitute 'culture' for 'darkness' and the riddle works almost as well, except that culture affects the *way* we see, as well as *what*, and *how much*, we see. The longer organisational members are exposed to their culture, the less they *see* it with real clarity. Culture is rooted in our profound psychological need to be with other human beings, or to belong to groups – equally people do not want to be excluded from groups. This can mean people are compelled to accept cultural norms, aligning the way they behave so that they become accepted and valued members of their group. So when groups (of any size) form, culture is not consciously created: there is no need, because it emerges as a kind of by-product of normal human interaction within groups. To belong to groups we have to become less selfish and demanding in order to enable others' needs, along with our own, to be satisfied. And an acceptable way to behave emerges – in other words we develop a culture. Achieving this sense of belonging is a powerful motivating force for humans, and we will put up with much in return.

The way we behave, respond, feel and think, even the meaning of words are all governed in some way by culture. Paradoxically we are surrounded by the artefacts of organisational culture, yet we can remain unconscious about the influence of culture on our decisions, responses and actions. So if we want to think about organisations, never mind change them, we face a significant challenge if we try to do so without taking account of culture.

The potential prize is great, as is what is at stake, namely sustainability, the conditions for success and ultimately high performance. Whether you are a student of organisations, an HR or Organisation Development (OD) practitioner, a strategic leader or organisational founder, at least taking account of culture makes good sense. Although 'taking account of culture' does not mean having to embark on a massive organisation-wide 'culture change' programme. In our view the expression 'culture change' is unhelpful, because it implies that one might be about to address the wrong goal. It assumes that culture is a 'thing' in its own right, like organisational infrastructure. The right goal is surely about some kind of 'organisational change'.

More about this later, but in our (the authors') working definition, culture is about the shared assumptions within an organisation and the shared meaning its members derive about their organisation. Whatever is 'contained' in 'shared assumption' and in 'shared meaning' is what might enable or block our attempts to change the organisation. If the organisation changes, sustainably and helpfully, that might or might not reflect in a change in the culture. In which case, it is best to focus on organisational change not 'culture change'.

'Working with culture' might not involve doing anything extra or in addition, just doing so a little differently. It does, however, mean that whatever your start point in working with organisations, deepening your awareness of the culture that has already emerged will almost certainly save you embarrassment, time and money. Indeed, it can be an enlightening, provocative and beneficial experience for everyone involved.

Through our work as OD practitioners, or if you prefer through the experiences we have 'borrowed' from our clients, we have become increasingly aware of the importance of considering organisational culture no matter the starting point our clients choose for us. Very few clients have, at the outset, even mentioned culture, never mind declared they were keen to, 'Do something about the culture in this organisation!' It'd be more accurate to write that, at the mere mention of the word, most clients have physically recoiled, their body language displaying a mixture of suspicion, fear and futility. Almost none have narrowed their eyes, revealed a steely glint and nodded sagely in anticipation of finally getting to grips with the root causes of issues in their organisations. Cultures, in all organisations, emerge as a result of a combination of factors (values and beliefs, influential people, external pressures and so on) and, for us over time, culture has emerged as a consistently under-acknowledged factor – a reason why the initiatives we have led or facilitated have either succeeded or failed. Indeed, looking to our own businesses, we now appreciate the influence culture has had on business performance. How in some cases the culture has almost overpowered us. How it has subverted our business plans and made it impossible to deliver on our aims. At others times the culture has been the reason why we have had the feeling of a metaphorical 'wind at our backs'.

In this chapter you should expect from us at least the following:

- Our position on organisational culture and OD.

- Some perspectives from our work in the field.

- A definition (or two) that both illuminates culture and has practical value.

- Some background theory.

- A framework for getting to grips with culture.

Our chapter begins by explaining our position on culture and OD and includes some 'perspectives from the field' about culture. We then introduce our 'guide to' or 'framework for practice' in the field, which offers a method for working with culture, including a range of definitions and an introduction to the background theory. Whether you plan to study culture or actually intervene in organisations this framework might be helpful. At the end of the chapter we have added a short list of personal lessons learned from our practice so far, which we hope will have both a preventative and provocative value for you.

Our Position

Before going any further, here is our position on both OD and organisational culture. Put crudely, if you intend to practice in OD, then you will 'come up against organisational culture'. Your only choice is whether to do so consciously or not.

Our working definition of OD reads:

> *How an organisation develops and implements strategy with the full involvement/engagement of its people.*

From this definition we can see that OD is about the way members behave now (and will behave in future) within their organisations. This means that OD and culture occupy, more or less, the same 'space' because culture is fundamental to the way members of groups behave. Since culture is concerned with the shared assumptions in organisations, those operating at the unconscious level, a set of unspoken rules governing the way members act, could that also mean culture is a reliable predictor of organisational performance? Studies about the link between culture and performance identify clear correlation, without establishing a causal relationship. And yet the evidence of the importance of culture in creating the conditions for success is significant. Examples are many but Weber and Camerer (2003) argue that the 'majority of corporate mergers fail' in some part due to 'cultural conflicts' that take hold during the merger process, unseen by protagonists and so ignored until too late.

Organisational culture is about the deeper-lying levels of awareness, assumption and belief that usually go unnoticed by busy, talented and hard-pressed people working in all sorts of organisations. The link between culture and performance might not be simple, but studies carried out by Kotter and Heskett (1992); by Marcoulides and Heck (1993); and by Denison (1990) (to name only a few) have made the case for culture and its role in leadership and performance. They revealed that organisations with strong, highly rated or more positive cultures consistently outperformed their peers. And some of the greatest writers and leaders in the field of OD agree about the significant role culture plays:

> *If you haven't touched culture, you haven't done anything. (Warner Burke)*

> *It (culture) is deeply connected to the organisation's goals and means. (Edgar Schein)*

Accepting that OD is concerned with a very broad range of initiatives and approaches, no matter where and how you plan to intervene, aligning those actions with the culture is essential. But that doesn't necessarily mean having a separate process which first addresses organisational culture. Thus we are describing an integrated approach to culture and OD.

In summary, organisational culture and OD are highly interdependent. Understanding culture can help us understand and then explain what is really going on and why some leaders and organisations are successful and some are not. Whether you are taking a diagnostic role, or designing and delivering an intervention, organisational culture will play a vital part so thinking about and adapting your approach, in the light of what you learn about culture, is potentially wise.

How we Wrote this Chapter

In starting to write this chapter together, we chose a series of conversations as our preferred method of working. We felt this would be a great way to share experiences since we have such different backgrounds and practice, and each time we met, we concentrated only on having a great conversation. We had no structure in mind, and simply 'held' the subject matter between us, all the while allowing the working relationship to develop. Frankly, we at times felt guilty about the small number of words we had to show for the hours we had spent together. On reflection, we were probably more concerned with finding ways to be together, than we were about how to productively tackle such a vast subject matter. It now seems somewhat ironic that we were on one level so consciously aware of the subject of 'culture', yet we remained completely unconscious about the degree to which we needed to first find our culture *before* we could start to perform together.

To try to summarise the culture that emerged around us is quite difficult. But storytelling is a big part of it, as is looking for the meaning in those stories. In fact when we were asked, by our editorial colleagues, to summarise our culture, we simply wrote a story of what had happened. And we think this helps to illustrate exactly how difficult it can be to describe one's own culture – one's simplistic response (to the challenge) can be to act it out!

In these conversations we noticed some recurring themes which we want to share with you briefly here as they go some way to explain our 'position' on culture.

Culture Emerges

We notice, not least from our experiences of writing together, that cultures emerge and that the expression 'creating a culture' is somewhat inaccurate.

Even if people start out with the intention, say at the formation of a new group or team, of building a specific type of 'culture', in reality the culture will emerge over time in response to a wide range of factors both within and outside the organisation. That is not to say it is impossible to influence or shape culture. Rather it is an acknowledgement that a complex system exists and that unintended, as well as intended, consequences result from the kind of interactions that take place in organisations.

In the language of 'systems thinking', organisational culture can be described to have 'emergence', because it is a naturally occurring, complex system. Culture is novel and radical, has uniqueness and is characteristic of a specific organisation. Organisational culture is coherent and to a degree self-maintaining, resisting some changes and enabling others. Culture evolves and responds to internal and external pressures and stimuli, and can be perceived to have changed.

So in working with culture we should ask:

a)   What culture has emerged?

b)   Is it the culture we need now, and will need in the future, if the organisation is to fulfil its purpose?

c)   How do we work out where to start?

The 'Conversation' is the Real Prize

Although organisational culture is a complex area to work with, don't let that mislead you into the assumption that only a complex approach will work. Our practice has taught us that the 'conversation' your intervention leads to is often the real prize. A helpful question to keep at the front of your mind when working with people in organisations is, 'What would be a really great conversation to have right now?' And there are some superb frameworks and models to help you process both the mundane and the messy stuff about culture – one such is Johnson and Scholes (1993) model Cultural Webs.

But do remember to discard the model, framework or tool, once it has served its purpose.

Don't Shoot the Messenger

As external consultants we may often 'speak difficult truths to power' (sic), because it is, at best, our role to do so. If these views prove unpopular or politically unsustainable, then it is relatively easy to remove an external consultant from the organisation and subsequently it might become easy to dismiss the message too. The organisational equilibrium will soon return and in this way, such 'challenging' or even 'unwelcome' messages pose little threat to the external consultant or to the organisation.

In working on culture, even in trying to understand or map it meaningfully, it is not just possible but likely that uncomfortable truths will be revealed – it is a good indicator that you are working at the right level. Not unreasonably many of the strengths found in organisations can have a corresponding weakness and, sometimes, a 'shadow side'. For example, if an organisation were to value 'focus on results' a little too highly, that might come into conflict with 'integrity'. In the financial services sector where a highly competitive market has driven the need to act quickly in order to capture market share, coupled with focus on achieving sales results this has, in fairly recent times, in some organisations revealed a 'shadow side' in the form of mis-selling.

Mature, well-developed organisations seem to be able to face such difficult conversations with courage, humility and gratitude. They take on board the unpalatable truths and work hard to explore the 'shadow side' in order to rebalance their culture.

However, an internal consultant might face rather different best and worst case outcomes. They might consider the risks of exploring the darker aspects of organisational culture to be too great. Instead they might be tempted to focus only on the positive, avoiding or skirting around anything riskier or dark. In such a scenario, they might be tempted to simply deliver the intervention and walk away rather than really challenging organisational members.

Deeper Personal Preparation as Facilitators

Culture is a complex, ambiguous and uncertain field within OD. If your work as a facilitator is successful, you will be taking the group through some emotional highs and lows. Some of what they have to confront will be individually and collectively difficult.

You must have real 'presence' – the ability to be still yet forcefully connected. A state of high awareness is needed, noticing subtle distinctions, appreciating both what is said and not said, and you must retain an ability to pay attention to what is going on around you, while noticing what is happening within you. The judgements about whether to intervene or not, in the moment, will require clarity about the process and desired outcomes, as well as great sensitivity and emotional intelligence.

Give yourself some reflective space. Organise your own thoughts about culture. Think about the cultures you belong to now and have belonged to in the past. Identify what you might have acquired from working with this culture. And how might your own expectations and experiences affect your role with the group you are supporting? As a facilitator prepare for a role that could require you to be agile too. One moment you could find yourself reassuring the team, the next asking them to account for a tricky inconsistency.

Introducing a 'Framework for Practice'

In the next part of this chapter we plan to introduce a 'guide to' or 'framework for practice' for working with culture. This framework is expressed as a series of key questions. Indeed if you are a successful consultant, working in any field, you are probably already using a framework like this one. And that is because culture is so fundamental to OD.

1. What is the culture?

2. How do I know I need to consider culture?

3. Where do I start?

4. What will my role be and how will I go about contracting with others?

5. What is my picture for success?

6. What diagnostic and research approaches will I use?

7. How do I overcome 'business as usual'?

8. Can I really change a culture?

In answering the first question we have begun by defining organisational culture and where it becomes relevant we have also included some background theory.

One: What is the Culture?

To answer this question, we're probably best starting with a definition or two. You'll notice that some of these quotes date back a few years. Maybe we shouldn't be surprised because at the heart of organisational culture is something profound and unchanging, untouched by the ebb and flow of fashionable management theory. So we've found that these definitions of culture haven't changed much and that they remain just as current and relevant as when they were first put forward.

Management theorists Joanne Martin and Caren Siehl (1983) referred to culture as 'Glue that holds together an organization through shared patterns of meaning'. Behavioural researchers Robert Cooke and Denise Rousseau (1988) described culture as 'Shared beliefs and values guiding the thinking and behavioural style of members'. Sociologist Geert Hofstede, in his tour de force research into national cultural differences at IBM (1991) said that 'shared perceptions of daily practices should be considered to be the core of an organisation's culture'.

So what do these definitions have in common? There seem to be two elements common to all three: that culture is somehow 'shared', so it is a group-level phenomenon. And that culture is about 'meaning', be that beliefs, values or perceptions, so it is concerned with what groups understand their organisation to signify, represent and *mean*.

Ed Schein has been using a similar definition of culture for many years and this goes one stage further, by describing the mechanics and practical relevance of culture. He wrote that culture was:

> *A pattern of shared basic assumptions that was learned by a group as it solved its problems of external adaptation and internal integration, that has worked well enough to be considered valid and, therefore, to be taught to new members as the correct way you perceive, think, and feel in relation to those problems. (Schein, 2004)*

We also find Dan Denison's (1990) model of culture helpful in that it challenges us to think about the complexities and dynamics of culture. Interestingly, Denison's own academic leanings stem from sociology, anthropology *and* psychology, and his definition does tend to integrate many of the ideas from these alternative academic perspectives. Denison puts forward the idea that culture results from the interaction of competing tensions that exist within every organisation. Firstly the tension between the need for Adaptability (change, learning and customer focus) and the need for Consistency (core values, agreement and integration). And secondly, the tension between Mission (top-led strategic goals, vision and intent) and Involvement (empowerment of individuals and teams).

Denison is particularly interested in how culture drives organisational performance and he echoes the view of many other researchers that an effective culture depends on the internal and external needs of the organisation at any given point in time. For example, an organisation undergoing great change and uncertainty may require more Adaptability and a greater focus on Mission, but this may alter as the organisation becomes more stable, with a heightened need for Involvement of employees in developing and embedding consistent, predictable values.

Returning to Ed Schein's account of culture, we can get a read on why it can be so challenging to get to the heart of what makes organisations tick and what can enable or block our attempts to improve them. Schein talks about culture existing at three levels.

The first and most accessible of these levels involves artefacts (the tangible stuff in organisations we can touch, smell, hear, see, such as uniforms, logos, the way car parking is organised, how the cafeteria works, etc.).

Secondly, Schein talks about values (the things that the organisation publicly says that it values, such as 'customer first' or 'our people are our greatest asset'). Note though that these are 'espoused' values, they aren't necessarily driving how the organisation really functions.

Finally, Schein delves into what he calls the fundamental assumptions that provide the shared meaning in organisations. These assumptions are implicit organisational beliefs about how the world works, the nature of justice, time, truth, relationships and emotion – the whole raft of human experience. And the *implicit* nature of these beliefs is crucial: the fact that they are buried and therefore barely, if at all, visible either to outsiders or even organisational members, makes them difficult to name and doubly difficult to challenge. Examples could be 'the world is fair' or 'people need to compete to perform', or 'love has no place here'. But these sound rather like organisational values at Schein's second level of analysis. The difference is that the belief level represents what is *really* valued by the organisation. Not what the organisation says is valued, but what its people truly believe in and therefore what it *means* to be a member of the organisation.

Let's take a moment to reflect on the significance of what we are saying here. It seems that organisations over time become their own societies. These societies possess their own belief systems. These beliefs are internalised by employees and so govern all activity within the organisation. These beliefs go unnamed (and may even be taboo in some cultures) and unchallenged unless exposed and held up to scrutiny. But to scrutinise can appear as heresy and may be treated with disdain, disbelief and denial, so reinforcing and protecting the belief system held dear by its members. When the belief system is serving the greater good of the organisation in terms of it achieving its strategy and objectives, to challenge it is less of an imperative. But when the organisation changes strategy and its hidden beliefs are out of alignment with the required change, we could be in big trouble if we leave the beliefs untouched.

Two: How Do I Know I Need to Consider Culture?

So how do we know as OD professionals whether we need to consider culture as a Very Important Issue (VII) within our client organisation? Well here is a short, non-exhaustive, checklist of clues that might tell you that culture is, or may shortly become, a VII in any organisation:

- Employees agree that things need to change but no one seems to be doing things differently.

- Everyone is excited by the new strategy but no one seems able to bring it to life.

- The organisation has seen a tailing off in performance in the past few years but no one can quite put their finger on why.

- There is a lot of 'rose-tinted' talk about how things used to be.

- The organisation has core values or brand values that are 'off limits' and cannot be challenged.

- There is a significant shift in the external environment (economic, social, regulatory, technological, etc.), which will require a fundamental change in the way things are done.

- There is a new senior leadership team or a stable and successful team has endured changes in membership.

- The organisation is new, as in a start-up situation, or there has been consolidation between two or more organisations, as in a merger or restructure.

- The organisation has had significant success in the past but remains unsure as to quite how this success has come about, as it prepares to expand its operations internationally.

Of course, there are many other signs to look for when considering whether culture is an area that requires further exploration, but it is important to ask whether any organisational change will create a conflict or inconsistency with an organisation's underlying values and assumptions. This is likely to require examination of the extent of the need for change, how far this is misaligned with the organisation's underlying assumptions and then how to go about developing new ones that people will accept.

Three: What Will My Role Be and How Will I Go About Contracting With Others?

Key to the contracting process is making clear your own role in this culture change, as much for your own as your client's benefit. Understanding the potential impact of the role you choose is mostly a matter of asking yourself appropriate questions. It is good to be clear in your own mind about the following questions, but it might not be necessary to publish the answers you derive. Here are a few examples, but this is by no means an exhaustive list:

- Are you an external consultant or are you a part of the organisation?

- With whom do you need to contract?

- Are you a facilitator, an OD specialist or business leader?

- What is your most natural contribution in this context?

- What do you bring as an individual in terms of skills, strengths, assumptions and experience?

- How might any of these affect your ability to observe the culture?

And of course, you won't be able to complete the contracting stage without a clear and agreed outcome or set of outcomes.

Four: What is My Picture of Success?

Have you ever noticed that if you want to make progress quickly the best thing to do ... is to STOP? By the way, we particularly like the acronym that this creates: Step back, Think, Organise, Proceed.

The thing you need most, before you do anything about culture, is a crystal-clear picture of the performance outcome(s) the organisation needs to achieve. Culture and performance are interdependent, but culture serves performance in that it creates the 'space', the conditions, for performance to be good or bad.

Language is important too – ensure organisational aims are expressed in the language of performance. For example, 'We want customer satisfaction to increase to 98 per cent by the time customers receive their service' versus 'We want our culture to be about fantastic customer service'. Both may seem to be about culture, but in the first example the language ensures culture is meaningfully aligned with the purpose of the organisation.

In the practical world, we will more often be confronted by the issues people want to face, the problems they are having, or we might find ourselves involved in initiatives that aren't quite 'setting the world ablaze'. And that could be the impetus for wanting to 'do something about culture'.

Your role will be to ask what the organisation would rather have. You need to shift thinking from issue, task and action and refocus minds on performance goals and desired future states. These outcomes, goals or aims will give you (and the organisation) a valid starting point and a benchmark for subsequent decision making. And this will allow you to make progress much more rapidly and effectively.

You can provide a really effective challenge by asking about the 'destination' the organisation wants to reach. In other words, success becomes a place, rather than a target or even a set of objectives. The types of questions you could ask are like those you might use in a strategy session:

- Why do we exist as a team or organisation?

- What does our work mean? (to each of our communities).

- What are our ambitions and aspirations?

- What are we capable of now and in the future?

- How best can we fulfil our purpose?

- Where do we need to move to?

- How will we recognise we have arrived there?

- How would we describe the 'dimensions' of the destination?

Using what you learn, especially about meaning, you can develop your 'Gold Medal' view (a reference to the Team GB Olympic Cycling Team – one single laser-like goal that everyone understands).

You might also have the resources to develop a rich picture of your chosen destination, together with a contrasting doomsday scenario to remind yourselves of the dissatisfactions that have caused you to want to move. If you have one, this could be your 'Burning Platform'.

Above all, we need the picture of success to create or help to create engagement for all sorts of people in the organisation. The more your picture incorporates their perspectives at the outset, the more powerful it will become later on in the execution phase. You should see greater ownership and better alignment with the culture apparent even in the language members use.

Five: What Diagnostic and Research Approaches Will I Use?

Thinking clearly about the approach to diagnosis and mapping culture you will use, will create a solid foundation for your work with organisational culture. But you might want to be wary about becoming over-zealous about the elegance of your diagnostic framework, as the following quotations illustrate:

> *Remember that all models are wrong; the practical question is how wrong do they have to be to not be useful. (George Box, University of Wisconsin)*

> *No one ever got a fat pig by weighing it. (Andrew Templeman, Cabinet Office)*

In responding to these challenges, the key practical decision is to select the diagnostic framework you will use to understand and map culture. By 'diagnostic framework' we would include everything from mass employee surveys to conceptual models such as Schein's 'onion skin' model of culture described earlier in this chapter, which could be very helpful with a focus group or perhaps a depth interview. It might be tempting to immediately grasp for a survey tool, in order to amass plenty of hard data with which to support your conclusions (and guesses), and which will lead to surefooted interventions later on.

By very definition, what you are seeking to understand is well hidden, residing more in the unconscious of the organisation and its members. In order to evaluate culture, you need to tease out significant 'disconnects' and conflicts between espoused values and behaviour in action. And, though not impossible, it is unlikely that any survey tool will penetrate to the right level of awareness and give you the information you need. That is, of course, not to say there is no role for well-designed questionnaires. Just not as a first step.

As pragmatists ourselves, we also note that it is often much easier to have a structured conversation with relevant individuals and groups within the organisation, around your chosen model. The resource implications are lesser and one can achieve a great deal of shift in as little as a few hours. An attractive by-product is the degree of engagement and energy this approach creates within the organisation for participants. And it can either lead to further conversations across and up and down the organisation, or it can direct you to produce a more accurate and relevant questionnaire.

Important though diagnostic frameworks and models are, we should also recognise that, at some point that you will determine, it will become equally important to discard your initial diagnostic model. This is because culture is emergent and dynamic and it will shift over time, requiring different methods to assess and explore it as time goes on. In thinking about how to evaluate the model you choose, ideally the model you select will help you:

- Create a map of the territory.

- Provide a common language and enhance understanding.

- Offer the opportunity for 'safe' challenge.

- Provide a way of measuring progress.

- Enable concealed truths to be revealed or exposed.

- Make sense of what goes on around here.

Frameworks can be either qualitative, quantitative or a combination of both. A qualitative model such as Cultural Webs (developed by Johnson and Scholes (1993)) can be used with large and small groups alike. It is easy to introduce and people find it highly practical and relevant to work with, both as an analytical tool as well as for modelling the future culture. It also simplifies decisions about the individual change initiatives the organisation will need in order to achieve its ambitions and create the culture the organisation will need in the future.

How will you make the choice of framework? The next few points will help you appreciate the consequences of using it:

- How far do you want to push the organisation outside its comfort zone to create change?

- How far do you *need* to push it?

- How deep do you need to go to understand what makes the organisation tick?

- Do you need to get down to the level of basic assumptions to see what is holding back/holding down the organisation?

And of course keep in mind what is at stake, so that your intervention delivers sufficient value for the investment (time, money, effort and concentration, personal risk etc).

In summary remember to:

Select > Apply > Discard

And don't become a slave to the model. Your model or framework will serve its purpose, but you'll need to change it as time goes on.

Six: How Do I Overcome 'Business as Usual'?

If, in working with culture, you have followed this 'framework for practice' this far, you will probably have now helped the organisation to paint a 'picture of success' involving a range of influencers, so that the future picture looks compelling and credible and will have currency in the organisation. You have moved on to establish the 'as is' picture of the organisation's current culture, using a model selected in partnership with the organisation. This process, again involving a range of stakeholders, has provided some clarity on the 'gaps' between the aspirational future state for the organisation and its current reality. And this in turn provides an indicative 'route map' for what may need to change in the organisation.

So far, so good. But what might prove most difficult is in engaging the wider organisation to ensure that the intended culture can now emerge and become the predominant culture. Working with culture can benefit from some of the latest and some of the longest-lasting thinking from management science, psychology and neuroscience in our summary below of 'things to remember' when embarking on culture change.

Firstly, there is now a view that any change, not least a significant cultural shift within an organisation, is picked up in the same part of the brain that experiences discomfort and pain. Humans are creatures of habit and so, as Schwartz and Rock (2006) point out, *change is pain*, or at least it is when experienced by humans. Part of this relates to the perception of 'social threat' (undermining our predictable picture of the world) and the similarity between the way that our brains handle social threats and physical threats. Essentially, our brain doesn't really discriminate between the two. So as David Rock (2009) describes it, when we experience any change or possible change to our sense of Status, Certainty, Autonomy, Relatedness or Fairness (Rock proposes the acronym SCARF here), we experience physical discomfort and we might well enter 'fight or flight' mode, getting ready for a fight, or getting ready to run.

As OD practitioners, we would do well to acknowledge this as it suggests that any change put forward by the organisation, however positive and well intentioned, might have the unintended consequence of scaring the living bejeebers out of most employees. So how to get round this very old, very real human response to change? Get people involved and get them figuring out their own versions of the new picture of success, and their role in bringing this to life! The latest research in neuroscience shows us that involving people and giving them space to have their own 'light bulb moments' is necessary for them to truly buy into change and make it part of their own belief system. We should see this as particularly important when considering deep-level cultural change.

It's important that we recognise that change means disruption to the status quo. And equally important to point out that change means everyone. From top to bottom, if change is to work, everyone needs to be involved and needs to 'get it' and show it. And as we know, those at the top have a disproportionate influence on others' attitudes and behaviour – if they challenge evidence of the old culture and champion the new, organisational change has a chance of succeeding. If senior organisational members believe that change means everyone else but them, culture shift will stutter and stumble and may well peter out.

The OD practitioner's level of awareness in observing emerging change is key. An effective practitioner at this stage will move to the 'balcony view' to check on progress, providing a different perspective on what is happening, checking how people are feeling, providing feedback, and enabling individuals and teams to do this for themselves.

The notion of 'Social Identity Theory' is worth a few words here. A couple of social psychology researchers in the 1970s and 1980s put forward the idea that people tend to associate themselves with particularly relevant social groups in order to feel happy, safe and secure. This happens in all aspects of life including the workplace. In practice, it means that we try and make ourselves feel good by promoting the positive aspects of groups we are part of while at the same time minimising the negative aspects. To do this, people have a natural tendency to find fault with 'out-groups' (those outside our social group) as a way of building our positive view of the 'in-group' (our group).

We can see the importance of this during mergers or acquisitions, or any organisational change which disrupts groups: we gain a sense of safety by sticking with our in-group and by criticising everyone else. How then to harness this important social phenomenon while working on culture? Two important actions are to: create a common enemy (ideally outside the organisation, so binding people together within it); and create a compelling picture of the future that people want to be part of and which will be good for their sense of self-esteem.

Just as important as recognising how we experience, and resist, change, is the notion of habit formation. Recent research (summarised by Daniel Coyle (2009) in *The Talent Code*) suggests that we need to repeat new thinking and new behaviour a number of times before it becomes habit. The minimum number of repetitions required is three, any fewer than this and the behaviour or thought has no chance of sticking. And far more than three is desirable.

From an OD perspective, we need to remain alert to the likelihood of old ways of behaving creeping back in if we don't keep at it by encouraging and reinforcing the new. As creatures of habit, it clearly takes a while for humans to build up enough of a new neural pathway before it becomes the preferred modus operandi. This is why changing organisational levers such as reward and HR systems, organisation structures and so on, is so important when trying to create impetus for organisational change.

Building on this idea, the 'Formula for Change' (created by Richard Beckhard and Gleicher, refined by Kathie Dannemiller and sometimes called Gleicher's Formula – Dannemiller and Jacobs (1992)) highlights the change factors necessary to overcome resistance and achieve change or shift, namely *Vision* (or picture of success), *Dissatisfaction* (or burning platform), and *First* concrete steps that can be taken towards the vision, so the formula looks like this:

$$V \times D \times F > \text{Resistance}$$

Each change factor has a multiplying role, so any low or zero values will reduce the force required to overcome R (resistance) to an insufficient level and change will not happen or be sustained. The 'D' of the Change Equation also supports William Bridges's (1991) view in *Managing Transitions*, that it is much more important when creating the conditions for change, to sell the problem than to sell the solution, in order that people grasp the need for change.

Finally, consideration needs to be given as to how you will measure progress against the picture of success or vision for the organisation. Will you use the same diagnostic framework that you started with, or will this need to shift as the intervention continues? How will you communicate first successes to the organisation, and using which forums and communication channels? How quickly should you try and assess progress? Answers to these questions will depend on the depth and scale of the change needed.

Seven: Can You Really Change a Culture?

After really considering ours and our clients' experiences, our answer is a 'conditional yes'. As we explained much earlier in this chapter, we do not really believe in 'culture change' – and we do not believe this is merely a semantic issue – as this is in our view means working with the wrong goal in mind. However, we are convinced about achieving 'organisational change' through 'working with culture'.

With a couple of caveats about knowing what success looks like first, and understanding how you will model and measure it and so on, it is possible to get off to a start, quite rapidly, and without much in the way of resources. And we would encourage anyone to try.

The insight we have gleaned here is about avoiding a Newtonian worldview when thinking about or working with organisational culture. Taking a classic change management approach we might reasonably turn to Lewin's model, as it frames the process of change extremely neatly:

Unfreeze > Change > Freeze

However, since we have defined culture as having emergent (rather than steady state) properties, doesn't our thinking about change as it relates to culture need a little 'updating'? If the culture isn't 'frozen' in the first place, then we cannot make it thaw, and how would we freeze it, even if that were an advisable course of action?

Culture is about people, and people can and do change. Although at this point we note that 'parachuting in' a new senior executive or an external expert, doesn't necessarily lead to measurable changes in organisational culture – especially where strong cultures exist. Why is that? Well, at a basic level, people cannot remain healthy when they do not share values, beliefs, behaviours and so on with their peer group. Being required to hold two radically different mental 'positions' at the same time (cognitive dissonance) causes people to experience 'pain' and discomfort. This might happen when an individual has a different set of values, principles and beliefs from those held and demonstrated by their colleagues. Thus they either leave, if they can, before their mission is accomplished, or they adapt to become more like their peers and more accepted within their group. And yet, ironically, this kind of difference is so often a powerful source of creativity. Thus a strong, mature culture is effectively protected from outside pollutants. Only when the number of 'paratroopers' reaches 'critical mass' does the culture of such organisations begin to transform.

Culture is dynamic, even though it might appear not to change much. This is because culture is about the way the people in the organisation handle external adaptation and internal integration, necessarily in response to changes in their environment. Changing culture is not change as one experiences it in approaches like Business Process Reengineering. It will almost certainly require more complex and sustained intervention before a new 'way of doing things around here' emerges.

This question is also about influencing versus controlling a system. Robert Merton in his paper on the *Unanticipated Consequences of Purposive Social Action* (1936) delivers a stark warning about the belief that humans can control the world around them. When we intervene in such a complex system as culture, we will have influence rather than control.

Think of culture as being like an ecosystem – there are checks and balances at work and complex interdependencies, which occasionally produce unintended consequences. What would be the cultural impact of reducing the number of parking places available in the employee car park? Would people begin car sharing, leaving the car at home and using public transport? Or simply start arriving earlier in order to grab a space, with latecomers filling up all visitors' spaces despite clear demarcation, as one of our clients learned to their chagrin? Of course, positive unintended consequences may also arise too from experimentation. For example when Tim Berners-Lee developed the World Wide Web to improve the publishing of physics papers at CERN, he probably didn't envisage the web as we know it today.

Having exposed these points, that is not the same as saying, 'Forget everything you know about change and change management'. In fact when we work with organisations, we *rely* on great models and frameworks like Lewin's model, and Gleicher's Change Equation, because they serve to expand and extend our thinking, giving us the opportunity and the means to think divergently and creatively about a very complex social construct – organisational culture.

Deciding to intervene in culture is all about addressing stimulating and exciting challenges like these:

- How do you sustain and embed organisational change in ways that take proper account of the culture and ensure that the organisation begins to learn?

- The new culture can't 'take' without changing the levers and reinforcers in the culture: structure, people management systems, reward systems, leadership behaviour, symbols, and processes.

- What are the appropriate ways to measure progress and development in culture?

- How do we help managers surface the shadow side and harness any positive benefits and unintended consequences?

- How will organisational members develop their 'reflective ability' and use it to remain aware of how culture is progressing?

- How does the organisation learn to have more difficult moments and conversations about culture and its impact on organisational performance?

- What is needed in order that habituation is successful and there is no return to 'business as before'?

Conclusion

Working on organisational culture is for us a continuous learning experience, but by way of a conclusion we want to reflect on some of the personal lessons we have learned. Some are about challenges we consistently face, and some are the superb things we have seen our clients achieve.

The first is that since culture is so strongly linked with leadership and performance, then surely effective organisational cultures make everyone's work meaningful. We saw one client demonstrate this brilliantly when they gave an appreciative presentation to a hard-pressed finance team. The outcome of this simple act was to directly connect every individual with the mission of the unit and the company, in an entirely different way. They created new meaning from what had previously been seen as an extremely challenging, year-long 'battle' against virtually impossible deadlines and minimal resources. In doing so, they acknowledged their organisational culture had positive strengths as well as some unintended consequences. Their solution was to demonstrate how the team's collective strength (a capacity for sustained hard work) had enabled organisational success and, at the same time, speak to their wider team as a well-aligned group of leaders, who were capable of appreciating and responding positively to the team's emotional needs.

- Engaging with organisational culture provides a chance to work at the deepest levels of meaning in organisations, it exposes beliefs and motives that might have remained hidden.

- The awareness gained by individuals through the use of culture models in their own organisations can bring new meaning to their working lives simply by making sense of what is going on around them.

- When organisations engage with their culture, powerful and meaningful conversations are possible – indeed likely.

- The components needed are: awareness, breadth of diagnostics, listening, questioning, willingness to provoke and techniques for using all the above skilfully.

- As a leader, be humble: recognise changes in the external environment and in your competitors and be prepared to flex accordingly.

- To create an effective culture, it is essential to effectively manage competing tensions between, on the one hand, Mission/Direction and Involvement and, on the other hand, those of Adaptability and Consistency.

- Underlying cultural characteristics can be hard to articulate: help by using symbols, metaphors, other methods of expressing deeply held views.

- Staying aware throughout the change process is key – the organisation needs to retain a 10,000 ft view to avoid 'business as usual' re-emerging.

- Change is uncomfortable and will be experienced as such: prepare people for this reality and then allow them to experience that journey.

- Whatever model or framework for exploring/describing culture you pick, it will be useful to discard it at some point: don't become a slave to your model, stay aware.

We hope you will soon add to the above from your own experiences of working within, through and around organisational culture.

References

Bridges, W. (1991). *Managing Transitions: Making the Most of Change*. New York, NY: Harper Collins.

Cooke, R.A. and Rousseau, D.M. (1988). Behavioural norms and expectations: A quantitative approach to the assessment of organizational culture. *Group and Organization Studies*, 13, 3, 245–73.

Coyle, D. (2009). *The Talent Code*. New York, NY: Random House.

Dannemiller, K.D. and Jacobs, R.W. (1992). Changing the way organizations change: A revolution of common sense. *The Journal Of Applied Behavioral Science*, 28(4), 480–98.

Denison, D.R. (1990). *Corporate Culture and Organizational Effectiveness*. New York, NY: John Wiley & Sons.

Hofstede, G. (1991). *Cultures and Organizations: Software of the Mind*. Maidenhead: McGraw-Hill.

Johnson, G. and Scholes, K. (1993). *Exploring Corporate Strategy*. London: Prentice-Hall.

Kotter, J.P. and Heskett, J.L. (1992). *Corporate Culture and Performance*. New York, NY: Free Press.

Marcoulides, G.A. and Heck, R.H. (1993). Organizational culture and performance: Proposing and testing a model. *Organization Science*, 4, 209–25.

Martin, J. and Siehl, C. (1983). Organizational culture and counterculture: an uneasy symbiosis. *Organizational Dynamics*, 12, 2, 52–64.

Merton, R. (1936). Unanticipated consequences of purposive social action. *American Sociological Review*, 1, 6, 894–904.

Rock, D. (2009). *Your Brain at Work*. New York, NY: Harper Collins.

Schein, E.H. (2004). *Organizational Culture and Leadership: A Dynamic View*. San Francisco, CA: Jossey-Bass.

Schwartz, J. and Rock, D. (2006). The neuroscience of leadership. *Strategy and Business*, 43, 1–10.

Tajfel, H. (1978) (ed.). *Differentiation between Social Groups*. London: Academic Press.

Weber, R.A. and Camerer, C.F. (2003). Cultural conflict and merger failure: an experimental approach. *Management Science*, 49, 4, 400–415.

10

Planning and Managing Complex Change: Where OD Meets Project Management

Niki Dalton

Introduction

Before we begin, let us remind ourselves of the working definition of Organisation Development (OD) from Chapter 1:

> *How an organisation develops and implements strategy with the full involvement/engagement of its people.*

The purpose of this chapter is to help the OD practitioner to understand complex changes in organisations, to evaluate the change required and which approach(es) are best suited and most likely to deliver the desired outcome. Most specifically, it will help the practitioner to have confidence in proposing and justifying the use of OD principles where appropriate.

Change in organisations is inherently difficult to implement. People are complex, fickle, often irrational and, some believe, inherently resistant to change, more of which later. Whatever the truth, the days of a 'command and control' style of leadership where the principal employee behaviour is compliance are long gone in most business arenas. As Hiatt and Creasey observe in their tutorial 'The Definition and History of Change Management', after 25 years of business improvement initiatives, a new set of values and belief systems has been impressed on employees which include empowerment, accountability and continuous improvement. As a result employees play a key role in any change programme and that can manifest itself in a positive or negative light.

So understanding the 'what' and 'why' of the proposed change as well as the benefit to the organisation and individuals within it, is the essential starting point.

Complex Change Programmes

First we must define complex change programmes. For this we will consider three dimensions:

- How an organisation recognises the need to change.

- What types of change result.

- The impact of the change relative to the size of the organisation.

Firstly, let's deal with how an organisation recognises the need for change. Sometimes external pressures force the need for change on an organisation. These pressures may come from: competitors; customers; shareholders/'the city'; auditors or government legislation. Pressure may also come from employees by way of direct feedback (e.g. negative employee engagement scores) or as a consequence of their actions (e.g. high turnover). In other instances change may result from research conducted internally or through consultancy (e.g. into new technologies). Finally it can result from real foresight on the part of leadership, perhaps seeing a trend that others have not. See below for an overview of typical triggers.

It is worth noting that how the organisation recognises the need for change will impact on the manner in which change is approached and communicated. Where the future has been envisioned by leadership, there will be a natural air of enthusiasm and excitement. This contrasts strongly with enforced change which may be met with reticence or resignation on the part of leadership. This will be perceived by employees however hard leadership try to mask it.

Typical Triggers for Change

COST REDUCTION

Whilst cost reduction programmes may have once been viewed as one-off actions in times of difficulty, they are now a consistent feature of most business environments as companies strive to stay competitive. Frequently this is achieved through a combination of salary bill reduction and reduced operating costs in areas such as technology and facilities. Typical 'change programmes' include business process re-engineering, shared services or outsourcing and technology implementation, as discussed below.

TECHNOLOGY ADVANCES

Organisations have been challenged by wave upon wave of opportunity through the rapid pace of technology advancement. From the introduction of computers into the workplace through the introduction of networks, the Internet, Enterprise Resource Planning (ERP) systems like SAP, mobile devices and now social networking, the pace has been relentless. Technology can provide growth and opportunity but can also be the main enabler of cost reduction.

LEGISLATIVE CHANGES

Changes to legislation might affect an organisation in small administrative ways or rock the entire business premise in a dramatic manner. The organisational response to such changes may manifest itself in many ways.

DIVERSIFICATION AND NEW MARKET OPPORTUNITIES

New market opportunities may be driven by geographical expansion, new products or services or new customer bases.

RAPID ORGANIC BUSINESS GROWTH

Many successful organisations see exponential growth in their core markets. This has been seen in technology innovators such as Google and Facebook.

MERGERS AND ACQUISITIONS

Organisations often grow through merger or acquisition. The extent of the 'change programme' will depend on the desired level of integration with the original organisation. For example, if an acquiring organisation wishes to keep the acquired organisation as a distinct entity within its group, the change programme will be much smaller than if the acquired organisation is to be totally subsumed into existing operations.

BUSINESS SALE OR OUTSOURCING

Organisations may need to focus their business through the sale or outsourcing of non-core business operations. Typically, companies look to sell non-core, market-facing operations and outsource internal support functions, although exceptions do occur.

DIVESTMENT OF A BUSINESS OR PARTS THEREOF

This typically occurs when a specific business is no longer required or successful or has been overtaken by alternative routes to market (e.g. shop or bank branch closures due to the rise of Internet shopping and online banking).

The triggers above can manifest themselves in many different areas of organisational change, such as:

- Organisation redesign, including structure change and leadership change.

- Redefinition of roles/jobs.

- Redundancy.

- Recruitment and/or retraining.

New HR strategy may also be employed, particularly for new organisational structures such as shared services or new business units. This may include new policies and processes for development, reward, recognition, career management, performance management and more.

The size of the impact can vary widely. However, for the purposes of this chapter we will consider programmes with significant change characterised by impact on some or all of the following:

- A large number of employees (let's say in the hundreds or thousands).

- The location of some or all of those employees.

- A change to jobs requiring rehiring or retraining.

So, having looked at the types of changes that an organisation may be undertaking and their possible organisational impacts, we can consider the typical approaches to planning and managing the change.

Programme and Project Management

The terms 'Programme Management' and 'Project Management' are usually differentiated only by scale and complexity, so for the purposes of this discussion we shall consider them to be one and the same.

Project management has been practised since the dawn of civilisation. In modern terms, it has its origins in civil construction, engineering and military activity with Henry Gantt and Henri Fayol generally considered the forefathers (Stevens, 2002; Witzel, 2003). Both were students of Frederick Winslow Taylor's theories of scientific management, now commonly referred to as Taylorism. Taylor's objective was to improve economic efficiency, especially labour productivity. As a result, project management was born with an inherent task focus, finite time horizons and clearly defined end products. Within project management, people were typically only considered as instruments in achieving the specific desired outcomes.

Since those early days, a variety of theories, models and practices have been developed which aim to address different industry needs and contexts. Some are billed as generic project management methodologies, such as PRINCE2 and PMBOK.[1] Others specifically address process improvement, such as Six Sigma, Lean and CMMI (Capability Maturity Model Integration) and finally, there are those that came from the 'quality revolution', such as Total Quality Management (TQM). Having evolved from many of these approaches, PRINCE2 has become increasingly popular and is now a de facto standard for project management for the UK government and is widely used in the private sector and in Western Europe and Australia.

For the purposes of this discussion, PRINCE2 will be used to illustrate best practice in modern project management. Released in 1996 and updated in 2009, PRINCE2 stands for *Projects IN Controlled Environments* and is a generic project management methodology. According to the UK government's

---

1   In the US the Project Management Institute's (PMI) PMBOK is the dominant methodology, which refers to their publication A Guide to the Project Management Body of Knowledge (2000 Edition). For a comparison of the two methodologies see Rankins.

PRINCE2 introduction, it is a process-based methodology and states that a project should have:

- An organised and controlled start (i.e. organise and plan things properly before leaping in).

- An organised and controlled middle (i.e. when the project has started, make sure it continues to be organised and controlled).

- An organised and controlled end (i.e. when you've got what you want and the project has finished, tidy up the loose ends).

It consists of seven principles and seven themes which come into play through seven processes (see Table 10.1 below).

Table 10.1   PRINCE2 principles, themes and processes

Principles	Themes	Processes
Ensure continued business justification	Business case	Starting up a project
Learn from experience	Organisation	Initiating a project
Use defined roles and responsibilities	Quality	Directing a project
Manage by stages	Plans	Controlling a stage
Manage by exception	Risk	Managing stage boundaries
Focus on products	Change	Managing product delivery
Tailor to suit the project environment	Progress	Closing a project

Source: The National Archives. PRINCE2.

Within the types of change being considered, project management is typically deployed through a dedicated project team. The leaders of the business may be involved directly in managing the project, or as key sponsors and stakeholders sitting on the 'Project Board' or 'Steering Committee'. The rest of the organisation may be given updates through communications, and may even be involved in certain activities, but often in an isolated and disjointed way (e.g. initial 'current state' interviews and then user testing).

For people involved in the project, professional project management using a methodology such as PRINCE2 generally feels quite comfortable. There is a project plan, assigned roles and activities, and regular status checks through reporting and meetings, allowing everyone to feel their contributions are worthwhile, and progress is being made.

For those outside the project team, however, the approach can lead to people feeling that an alien being is growing and developing of its own accord, with little reference to day-to-day business, and threatening to deposit a bombshell when it finally matures!

The strengths of PRINCE2 and other process-based methodologies are that they provide a structured approach to managing projects, within a clearly defined framework. They include procedures to coordinate people and activities, including design and supervision of the project. They also cover what to do if adjustments are needed should the project not develop as planned. They enable efficient use of resources and describe all management roles and responsibilities. As they are widely recognised and understood, they also provide a common language for participants, and are adaptable to many different types of project, particularly under the guidance of a skilled practitioner.

That said the influence of the Information Technology industry is clearly evident in PRINCE2 and other process-based methodologies. As a result these methodologies have not really escaped their engineering roots. Perhaps their greatest weakness is evident in the PRINCE2 name – *Projects IN Controlled Environments*. I have yet to encounter a business change, involving large numbers of people that could ever be described as a 'controlled environment'!

Whilst technology implementation is frequently a significant part of a business change programme, it is rare that some behaviour change is not also required if true business benefits are to be achieved. PRINCE2 and related methodologies do not provide a framework for a full appreciation of this.

So, to sum up, project management is vital to achieving certain tasks and producing defined products in an efficient manner. However, it tends to be dominated by a task focus ('is the product being built?' as opposed to 'will the product be adopted, be used properly and deliver the desired results?'). In instances where a team of people is brought together to produce an isolated product it is an excellent approach (as in its roots of construction and engineering). However, very few change programmes are independent of the organisation and its employees. Hardly any involve no behaviour change on the part of existing employees, and even those that do (e.g. new market entry with a new independent business unit), will still need to consider the desired behaviours of new employees.

However, my intention is not to damn project management outright, merely to comment that whilst it has its place it is generally not enough on its own. So is 'change management' the answer?

Change Management

The term 'change management' has long been confused and misunderstood by many in business. Indeed for some, the phrase itself is an oxymoron – to 'manage' change, particularly where people are involved, might at best be considered an optimistic endeavour. However, within the business context, this is exactly what companies seek to do.

The birth of change management came from the convergence of project management approaches, as discussed in the previous section, with psychologists' views on addressing the human side of change. Historically, those adopting traditional project management approaches tended to ignore change management ideas, treating people as mere resources to deliver the project, or just another piece of the solution. They only focused on people when resistance became apparent, or when serious implementation problems arose. Even then, the approach was often to isolate and eliminate such issues or at best to attempt a quick fix to the 'people problem' (Hiatt and Creasey).

By contrast, psychologists started to research the field of human reaction to change back in the 1980s by William Bridges's seminal work *Transitions: Making Sense of Life's Changes* (1980). This ultimately led onto studies in workplace change management. Recognising the problems being encountered by traditional project management approaches, a number of early practitioners saw the need to blend the engineers' and psychologists' approaches to create a structured change process (Conner, 1993; LeMarsh, 1995; Kotter, 1996). From this, a strong practice has developed, balancing the performance, strategic and physical requirements of change programmes, with a consideration for the culture, values, history and capacity for change of the stakeholders (i.e. employees, customers, suppliers and investors). The intention is to create programmes with a greater chance of long-term success.

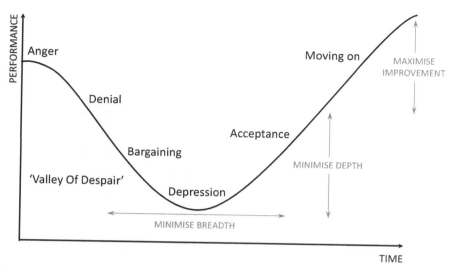

Figure 10.1   The change curve
Source: Elisabeth Kübler-Ross, 1969.

There are many change management methodologies, many of which can be explored through Cameron and Green's (2004) book *Making Sense of Change Management*. As yet no one methodology has surfaced as a standard but most consider change as a 'journey' where the people affected need to be 'ready, willing and able' to adopt the future state or way of working. Two models are typically used to illustrate the journey people go through when experiencing change (see Figures 10.1 and 10.2). The first is the so-called 'change curve' and is based on a model originally developed in the 1960s by Elisabeth Kübler-Ross to explain the grieving process (Kübler-Ross, 1969). It shows how, typically, people have a negative response on first hearing about a change which will have an impact on them. This results in a drop in performance, which is often referred to as the 'Valley of Despair'. Over time, most people accept the change, which results in their performance returning to, or exceeding, previous levels. Good change management programmes minimise the depth and length of the 'Valley of Despair' and contribute to maximising the long-term improvement in performance.

The second model, developed by Daryl Conner (2011), is commonly referred to as the 'commitment curve'. This illustrates the stages through which change management endeavours to take people, in order to ensure that they do recover or exceed their performance levels (see Figure 10.2). Also shown on

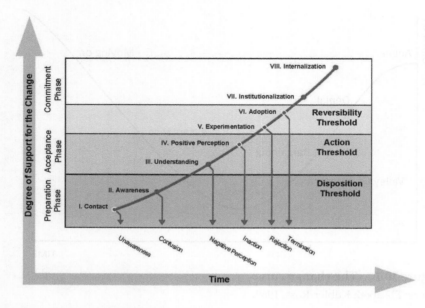

Figure 10.2   The commitment curve
Source: Daryl Conner, 2011.

the diagram is an alternative negative response that may result if the change management initiative is unsuccessful.

Fundamentally, all change management tools and techniques seek to address the following issues:

- Communications. Do people understand why the change is necessary, what it will entail and how they will be affected?

- Leadership. Do people trust the reasons for the change and see the new behaviours role-modelled by those they respect?

- Organisation. Are the teams structured appropriately for the new ways of working and do they have the right roles/jobs?

- Training. Are people able to perform new tasks with new tools as required?

- Performance, reward and recognition. Will people be appropriately rewarded and recognised for the right way of working in the future?

Will old ways of working be discouraged through the reward and recognition structure?

- Career management. Can people see a future for themselves and can new talent be attracted?

- Exit management. Will exiting employees be treated in line with local employee legislation, and with dignity and respect?

When applied appropriately, change management can be enormously powerful. It has the potential to make the difference between the success and failure of projects as identified by John Kotter (1995). It addresses the human elements of change which are absent in project management methodologies. Good change management also anticipates the needs of the people involved before a project is derailed. By ensuring that as many affected people as possible have the understanding, capability and motivation to adopt the new behaviours and ways of working required, it facilitates a far greater chance of success.

However, more often than not, change management is delivered through an additional team within an overall project. This limits the influence that the change management work can have in a number of ways.

Firstly, messages must be delivered and reinforced by leadership in order to be effective. If the change management team has limited influence on leadership, this does not occur and/or can lead to conflicting messages being delivered. Secondly, the change feels like it is being 'done to' the organisation when the messages or interventions constantly come from a separate team within the project. This makes it much harder to gain the buy-in required. Finally, budget constraints often mean the work of a change management team is pared down to basic communications and training with all else being disregarded. This risks the power of the approach being utterly undermined.

Even where there is a significant investment in change management, and it is clearly sponsored by leadership, the irrationality of human behaviour often governs people's responses as noted by the McKinsey & Company paper 'The Inconvenient Truth about Change Management' (Keller and Aiken, 2008). Therefore, trying to ensure people are ready, willing and able to adopt the change within a structured timeframe can be exceedingly difficult, especially as regards the 'willing' dimension. There are no guarantees, no matter how much effort is made.

As we have seen, change management succeeds in addressing many of the shortfalls of project management. However, when we go back to the prevailing nature of change in organisations, it still has limitations. Even if people are ready, willing and able to adopt an initial change, what happens when another opportunity or pressure arises? Working within fixed parameters and forcing change upon an organisation is just too restrictive and slow in today's ever-changing business environment. Organisations need to remain nimble and flexible so that they can react quickly to opportunities and changing circumstances. Perhaps much of the answer lies in enabling organisations to determine the right changes at the right time, and giving them the space to make that happen, rather than binding them up in ever-larger projects with their attendant management constraints?

How is an OD Approach Different?

OD starts from a very different premise. Project and change management approaches tend to assume that change is planned, meaning it is based on moving from one state to another in a stable and predictable manner. By comparison, an OD approach accepts the reality of emergent change, which is fluid, continuous and demands the ability to be flexible, responsive and adaptive. It works with the organisation to facilitate the creation of a 'future state' vision and the key change requirements.

In an OD approach, change requirements are given the space to grow organically, and the end state is not tightly defined. This means it can be adapted as more is learned and as other opportunities or pressures surface. Timelines tend to be quoted as targets, and whilst there is a commitment to them, there is also an understanding that they will adapt to the changing business landscape.

From the outset it is important to involve as many people as possible in defining the change required, and in determining the approach that should be taken to achieve that change. As discussed in the introduction, change programmes arise in a number of ways. Defining the challenge or opportunity clearly, and determining the change required, is also achieved in a variety of ways. To illustrate the difference between a more traditional change management approach and an OD approach, let's look at an example. At the traditional end of the spectrum, we find practitioners gathering information from the organisation and simply retiring to the proverbial darkened room to emerge some weeks later with the answer. Typically, a large project team is then assembled to implement the proposed solution.

For example, an HR function might need to adapt its operating model to changing business needs. The traditional approach could involve the use of an external consultancy working in secret with the senior leadership to design the required operating model – most likely involving some form of shared services or outsourcing. Change management principles would then suggest that a 'Case for Change' be articulated and shared with the organisation. This would then become the rationale for a programme which has essentially already been defined and agreed at the highest level.

At the other end of the spectrum there is the OD approach. An OD approach to the same scenario was used at one of the world's leading brewers, SABMiller. It involved a small number of external OD consultants working with the organisation's HR leadership team through a facilitated exploration of the current challenges in HR and the possible solutions. The consultants' role was not to present or develop a solution, but to facilitate a discovery and learning process, using their perspectives and opinions to create constructive challenge. This resulted in an overall framework for the future HR operating model, which was taken forward by SABMiller into a set of facilitated workshops with each of the regions and key markets, to determine the appropriate application of the new operating model and develop an implementation plan.

The difference between these two approaches may be subtle, but fundamentally it is about how the problem and the possible solution have been identified, and how they are owned. The OD approach typically requires more communication and facilitation up-front, unlike the traditional approach, which involves more up-front diagnosis and analysis, and a less inclusive approach to solution planning. Many would argue that the OD approach takes much longer, and in some instances this may be true. However, time invested up-front will ensure that changes are owned locally, tackled with commitment and generally implemented with greater enthusiasm. As somebody once said, 'change takes time – you can pay up-front or later, but either way you will definitely pay'.

How is OD Execution Different?

The key difference in execution manifests itself through the size and responsibilities of the 'project team'. In order to execute large and complex change programmes, traditionally a project team is assembled. If change management principles have been considered, this team will combine employees with expertise in the area (and who are likely to be impacted by the change), with specialists with experience of implementing such projects elsewhere. The balance between these two will depend on the nature of the change, the budget and the ability of the organisation to free up employees with appropriate skills from their day-to-day responsibilities. Some team members may combine their project role with their day-to-day job responsibilities but this generally proves extremely difficult, so most resource tends to be dedicated full-time to the project. Where a change management approach is being adopted, it is usually delivered by a dedicated team within the overall project team. However, as noted earlier, experience suggests that such teams can struggle to have the necessary impact and influence.

The OD approach feels very different. Typically it involves meetings and facilitated workshops, where work is done with people in the organisation, in the context of their existing roles, in order to determine what and how they will change. The 'project team', if it exists at all, is small, and focuses on supporting the organisation through planning and facilitating those workshops, and providing frameworks, guidance and constructive challenge. For organisations that have already developed an OD and change capability, people's roles will inherently include some capacity for involvement in change programmes. Whether explicit or implicit, roles in such organisations will have a proportion of objectives focused on improvement or development, as opposed to fixed operational goals. This balance of objectives will also exist in much lower levels in the organisational hierarchy. However, even organisations without this approach can adopt various strategies to achieve the same effect during a large change programme. For example, an organisation might employ temporary staff to backfill existing roles, allowing them the opportunity to be actively involved in defining, shaping and implementing the changes required.

How is OD Evaluation Different?

In a typical project management approach, evaluation is addressed in two phases:

1.   Evaluation of project progress (i.e. 'Are we on time and on budget?').

2.   Evaluation of the benefits delivered once the programme has been implemented (i.e. 'How is it delivering against the original business case?').

The first phase is relatively easy to manage using standard project management methodology, such as PRINCE2, yet in the longer term it is not particularly valuable. A project may be delivered on time and on budget but unless it actually delivers the targeted business benefits, it has been worthless.

The challenge with complex change programmes is that they do not operate in isolation, and as discussed earlier, they are subject to considerable variations in business conditions throughout their life cycle. As a result, the business case is notoriously difficult to define and monitor. Many organisations look to a balanced scorecard approach over a number of years post-implementation, often addressing cost, efficiency, employee and customer satisfaction measures. However, attributing such improvements in these measures purely to the change programme is almost impossible. The best most organisations can hope for is to record a general upward trend after the programme has been implemented. Another limitation is that benefits are rarely instant due to the time it takes for the required behaviour change to take place. This further challenges how much improvement over time is actually attributable to the programme over time.

Measuring the directly attributable impact of improvements delivered by change management interventions is just as difficult. The Chartered Institute of Personnel & Development (CIPD) continued the research into the measurement of human capital started by a government task force in 2003 and concluded that 'there is no single measure or set of measures that can uniformly provide a value for human capital' (CIPD Factsheets – Human Capital, 2011). Therefore if the value of human capital cannot be directly measured then change management interventions affecting human capital certainly cannot.

So what does that mean for OD? Maybe OD has the opportunity fundamentally to shift the focus. Instead of viewing change programmes as isolated interventions, and measuring their impact as such, perhaps we should be working with the established metrics of the overall business, and encouraging a constant organisational evolution made up of organically driven changes of varying size and impact.

A great illustration of this can be seen by contrasting two different company approaches to changing their operating models. A luxury retailer, who had been methodically transforming its operating model through OD, decided to pilot a new approach in one of their main city areas. The solution was determined through a series of facilitated workshops and the resulting recommendation was a change in people, organisation and ways of working. (Ways of working included when and how often the cross-functional leads would meet, the measures they would track to prove business benefit and how they engaged with partners and employees.) No process or technology changes were made. Within two months the pilot area was trending above company average on key business performance metrics.

By contrast, the existing management of a specialist, engineering contractor embarked upon the restructuring of the company at the behest of the parent organisation, who had acquired the group some years earlier. This was driven by a desire to mirror the structures employed in other companies held by the parent, and to better service principal clients, who were large international organisations operating from a number of discrete, remote geographical locations.

They moved from a geographic model with end-to-end responsibility for sales, project management and manufacturing to a functional model with separate global client service and manufacturing teams. However, problems arose due to the specialist nature of the business where there was an ongoing and detailed dialogue between the parties during the design and manufacturing of a bespoke product.

Table 10.2   Summary of differences between traditional project management/change management and an OD approach

Area	Traditional Project Management and Change Management approach	OD approach
Type of change.	Planned.	Emergent with some planned elements.
End state.	Defined up front.	Goals are clearly communicated. The actual end state may be targeted but remains flexible to adapt as required.
Timelines.	Planned and essentially fixed.	Targeted and generally committed to but some flexibility to adapt is retained.
Definition of change requirements.	Assessed and stated (often by external consultants with minimal interaction with the organisation).	Often defined through a facilitated exploration and debate. Grow organically as more is learned and other opportunities/pressures surface.
Implementation team.	Structured project team.	Existing employees with roles designed/backfilled to allow capacity.
Evaluation.	Project plan, budget and business case.	Ongoing business metrics.

The new operating model had been planned in great detail, but when launched it caused significant disruption internally, principally due to the removal of absolute responsibility of the local regional entity to deliver the product. As a result every division within what was previously a highly profitable group became loss making within a period of 12 months. This period also saw the rise of significant employee disenchantment and turnover.

For a detailed discussion of evaluation refer to Chapter 12, 'Measuring and Evaluating OD'.

So, whilst the differences between an OD approach and traditional project and change management approaches may be subtle, they are significant and can have a profound effect on the business outcomes. See Table 10.2 on the previous page.

Applying OD to Complex Change Programmes

I asked Denise Smith, the Group Head of Organisation Development at SABMiller how they utilise OD in the context of the complex change programmes. She explained, 'The context for OD work and the associated change agenda is high-leverage strategic priorities, directly related to specific aspirations contained in our business strategy'.

As part of a review of OD capability in the organisation, a sample of business leaders in SABMiller Europe were asked for their views on the value of OD, in the context of a significant change agenda. The outcome of this review confirmed the belief that OD is key to accelerating both the execution and anchoring of major change projects and the realisation of their benefits. Leaders specifically cited the contribution of OD through the following comments:

- 'Ensuring we see the big picture and cover all the bases'.

- 'Asking the right questions about what changes mean for the whole organisation, not just the bit we control'.

- 'Helping the business frame the core business problems'.

- 'It is critical that there is effective collaboration between strategy owner and those implementing'.

- 'We need a process that helps us "join the dots" – and help keep a focus on the big picture'.

- 'We need to use deliberate interventions to help us go faster'.

- 'When we get it right we get a step change in performance beyond good project execution'.

Whilst OD is clearly applicable to complex whole-organisation programmes, there are some important considerations that an OD approach needs to take into account:

- The link between strategy and OD.

- Commercial sensitivity.

- Legislative requirements for employee consultation.

- Ensuring efficient and effective implementation.

The Link Between Strategy and OD

Complex change programmes can produce a step change in organisational capability and typically involve strategic decisions, so understanding the link between OD and strategy is vital. OD does not replace strategy, and whilst determining the future strategy of an organisation certainly benefits from input from those within and outside the organisation, something as significant as a merger or an acquisition will never be the result of an employee competition or ideas forum!

Strategy is set by business leaders (with internal and external inputs as required) and OD's role is to define the organisational capabilities required to deliver that strategy, assess current capabilities and support the business in making required changes, ensuring the appropriate involvement and engagement of people. For example, once the global HR operating model and associated key roles were designed at SABMiller, the HR leadership recognised that certain skills, required for the redefined business partner roles, would be scarce. To validate this, SABMiller developed competency standards for the business partner roles and assessed skills against these in a number of key markets. A global development centre was then launched to ensure skill gaps were filled.

Commercial Sensitivity and Legislative Requirements for Employee Consultation

Many of these large, complex change programmes are commercially sensitive and, in many countries, subject to employee consultation. This means careful consideration must be given as to how openly the organisation can engage with its people around major challenges, opportunities and potential solutions (see Table 10.3 below). However, it does not mean that all employee involvement and engagement must be avoided.

Once commercial sensitivity has been considered, the starting point for a contemporary OD approach is to determine how best to articulate the challenge/opportunity, and then to involve and engage as many people as possible in determining the solution and implementing it. Instead of thinking, 'Who is affected and how will we communicate to and support them?' the OD approach is to think, 'Who is affected and how will we involve them from the beginning?'

The added bonus is that approaching change programmes in this way will also address most of the needs for employee consultation by default. In my

Table 10.3   Applicability of commercial sensitivity and employee legislation

Change programme	Engagement delayed by commercial sensitivity?	Engagement must align with employee collective consultation requirements?
Merger	Yes	Yes
Acquisition	Yes	Yes
Divestment	Yes	Yes
Geographic expansion	Sometimes	Not usually
Market expansion	Sometimes	Not usually
Organic business growth	Sometimes	Not usually
Cost reduction through redundancy	Sometimes	Yes
Shared services/offshoring	Not usually	Yes
Outsourcing	Not usually	Yes

experience many organisations are nervous about consulting and involving their employees, believing people to be inherently resistant to change. However, people are typically resistant to a loss of control rather than change in itself. Employee consultation aims to ensure organisations at the very least communicate fully and properly with employees, but also seeks to give back some control through the opportunity to propose different solutions. OD principles do this as a matter of course, giving people a much higher degree of control than is possible in traditional approaches to project and change management.

Ensuring Efficient and Effective Implementation

Finally, these programmes are of strategic importance and competitive value and organisations rightly want them undertaken with efficiency and effectiveness. Lest we forget, OD is not simply about engagement, involvement, pleasant conversations and a 'wait and see what happens' approach. Further direction and impetus is usually necessary. When I asked Aimie Chapple, Managing Director UKI Accenture Management Consulting, she explained, 'Someone has to care about how you turn strategy into reality. Whether this is an individual OD Director, covered by another related leadership role, such as the Strategy Director, or an overall leadership competence, will depend on the organisation'.

In addition, we should not dismiss the tools and techniques offered by traditional project and change management. Good OD will blend the task focus and efficiency achieved through project management approaches, with the human interaction and behaviour change supported by change management approaches throughout the life cycle of the change programme. When determining the right blend of approaches some key questions to ask are:

- Is the change already determined?

- How many people are affected?

- Is there only one way forward or can a problem statement be articulated to engender ideas from employees?

- Can the solution be developed in stages involving more people with each level of detail?

- How many distinct 'tasks' need to be completed and how can they be completed most efficiently?

- What is the level of behaviour change required and what is required to encourage and incentivise it?

Conclusion

Traditionally, complex change programmes have employed project management as the overarching discipline and used the project plan as the road-map to guide the whole change. Change management provided interventions along the way to ensure people move along the commitment curve. Continuing this traditional evolution OD was viewed as an aspirational end state that the organisation hoped to achieve (à la Senge's Learning Organisation concept (Senge et al., 1994)).

I believe we are now turning that completely on its head. OD is now becoming the overarching approach, with change management providing the tools and techniques to involve and engage people, and project management used to manage specific tasks. All approaches have their place and the chosen approach ultimately needs to be pragmatic, realistic and achievable, not least so that it can be 'sold' to leadership.

A Thought to Leave you with

Why do organisations exist? Certainly to produce products, provide services and make money. However, organisations evolved from our ancestors' realisation that survival was much improved by people working together. Are today's organisations not ultimately a modern manifestation of this, providing a living for their employees and enhancing the lives of their stakeholders and customers? In which case, why would organisational change not be focused first and foremost on people?

References

Bridges, W. 1980. *Transitions: Making Sense of Life's Changes*. Da Capro Press.
Cameron, E. and Green, M. 2004. *Making Sense of Change Management*. Kogan Page Limited.
Chartered Institute of Personnel and Development (CIPD) 2011. Factsheets – Human capital. London: Chartered Institute of Personnel and Development.

Available at http://www.cipd.co.uk/hr-resources/factsheets/human-capital. aspx [accessed: 8 February 2012].

Conner, D.R. 1993. *Managing at the Speed of Change*. John Wiley & Sons.

Conner, D.R. February 22 2011. The Eight Stages of Building Commitment. Available at http://changethinking.net/commitment-in-change/the-eight-stages-of-building-commitment [accessed: 8 February 2012].

Hiatt, J. and Creasey, T. no date. The Definition and History of Change Management, Change Management Tutorial Series. Available at http://www.change-management.com/tutorial-definition-history.htm [accessed: 8 February 2012].

Keller, S. and Aiken, C. 2008. The Inconvenient Truth about Change Management, McKinsey and Company. Available at http://www.mckinsey.com/App_Media/Reports/Financial_Services/The_Inconvenient_Truth_About_Change_Management.pdf [accessed 8 February 2012].

Kotter, J. March–April 1995. Leading change: why transformation efforts fail, *Harvard Business Review*, 1.

Kotter, J. 1996. *Leading Change*. Harvard Business School Press.

Kübler-Ross, E. 1969. *On Death and Dying*. London: Routledge.

LeMarsh, J. 1995. *Changing the Way we Change*. Prentice Hall PTR.

Rankins, G.J. no date. The Yin and Yang of Project Management: Comparing PMBoK and PRINCE2 (again). Australian Institute for Project Management. Available at http://www.aipm.com.au/resource/RANKIN_-_FULL_PAPER_AIPM2007_0018_Comparing_PMBoK_and_PRINCE2_V1.0.pdf [accessed 8 February 2012].

Senge, P., Kleiner, A., Roberts, C., Ross, R.B. and Smith, B.J. 1994. *The Fifth Discipline Fieldbook: Strategies and Tools for Building a Learning Organization*. New York. Currency Doubleday.

Stevens, M. 2002. *Project Management Pathways*. APM Publishing Limited.

The National Archives. PRINCE2: What is it?/How does it work?. Available at: http://webarchive.nationalarchives.gov.uk/20110822131357/http://www.ogc.gov.uk/methods_prince_2__whatisit.asp [accessed: 8 February 2012].

The National Archives. PRINCE2: Benefits. Available at: http://webarchive.nationalarchives.gov.uk/20110822131357/http://www.ogc.gov.uk/methods_prince_2__benefits.asp [accessed: 8 February 2012].

Witzel, M. 2003. *Fifty Key Figures in Management*. London: Routledge, 96–101.

11

Working with External Consultants: Smart Contracting and Consulting

Kate Mulcahy

Introduction

The stakes are high when engaging an external consultant to undertake Organisation Development (OD) work. Not only must an organisation bear the cost of consultancy fees, but the cost of poor advice or expertise could ultimately be much greater than this. With The National Audit Office report into spending on external consultants across UK central government (Oct 2010) noting that a number of departments had 'not been acting as intelligent customers', it's time to provide internal practitioners with more guidance about how to effectively buy in external OD support.

Much has been written about the steps that an internal or external consultant goes through in order to create an effective consultancy relationship with their clients. But there has been much less focus on the dynamics of the relationship between the internal client buying OD services for their organisation and the external consultant engaged to provide them, and how their working relationship contributes to the effectiveness of the external consultant within that organisation.

The aim of this chapter is to look at the role the internal client plays in setting up an external consultant for success when providing OD services to their organisation. It will highlight some practical steps that can be taken to ensure that the external consultant is effectively supported by the internal client throughout their relationship with an organisation, and highlight some of the potential pitfalls that need to be avoided at key stages of their relationship, to ensure that personal agendas do not compete with the broader intentions of the organisation.

Beyond the Operating Model

During research for this book, when asked the question 'why do you work with external consultants?' the typical response from internal practitioners was 'we have to, we don't have the resource to do everything ourselves'. Many organisations consciously create an operating model which relies on external partners to deliver OD work so that they can keep permanent headcount and costs down, but in addition to the obvious cost benefits of more flexible resourcing there will be additional value that can be gained from working with external consultants as well. For example, it's not likely that an internal client can always be a prophet in their own organisation; sometimes it takes an external consultant to really ensure a message can be heard internally. By their very nature, an external consultant is not part of the make-up of the organisation and so will not be subject to group think. What they will offer the organisation instead is objective observation, fresh insight and challenge.

However, even when an organisation design consciously advocates the intention to partner with external consultants, experience shows that it's the human elements such as the personal beliefs and behaviours of individuals working within this organisation structure that can make or break this way of working.

Myles Downey (2003) provides an interesting perspective on this with his adaptation of Ken Wilber's Four Quadrants (*A Brief History of Everything* by Ken Wilber) to provide a lens through which to look at organisational life.

Downey believes that every organisation and every individual within that organisation, has an 'inner' (something that may not be seen on the surface) and an 'outer' (something that is very much visible to others). Plotting the inner/outer against the individual/organisation creates a framework of four distinct quadrants (see Figure 11.1).

The four quadrants provide a useful lens through which to view what happens in organisations:

- The top left quadrant focuses on the internal motivation of an individual: their sense of purpose, attitudes and beliefs, aspirations and personal values.

- The top right quadrant focuses on how the concerns of the top left quadrant manifest in how that individual goes about his/her daily

	INNER	OUTER	
	Sense of purpose/meaning		Goals
	Aspirations		Plans
	Desires		Skills
	Attitudes		
	Beliefs		
	Personal Values		Behaviours
INDIVIDUAL			

ORGANISATIONAL			
	Mission		Vision
			Organisational Goals
			Strategy
	Culture		Behavioural Norms
	Organisation Values		Code of Conduct
			Performance Management Systems
	Corporate Mindset		Management Information Systems

Figure 11.1   The four quadrants

business: the individual's goals and supporting plans, their skills and behaviours, even their mannerisms.

- The bottom left quadrant focuses on the corporate mindset of the organisation: its culture and organisational values, what people believe is possible or not.

- The bottom right quadrant focuses on the external representation of the bottom left: the shared vision of the organisation, its supporting goals and strategies, the systems and processes that are in place to manage the organisation towards these goals, and of course, the operating model.

Downey's point about the quadrants was that none of them can happen in isolation and that a successful outcome for the organisation depends on there being congruence across the quadrants.

Consider a situation where an organisation has articulated a strategy (bottom right) to partner with an external OD consultant, but the following circumstances exist:

- A 'not invented here' mindset prevails in the organisation culture (bottom left): The consultant may experience difficulty in introducing new ideas and innovative ways of working to the organisation. There may be a reluctance to share information openly with an outsider, which may also make effective diagnosis difficult.

- Individual values of the internal client (top left) are that of independence and autonomy: The client may choose to engage the consultant on a 'pet project' that is out of step with overall organisation priorities. This means the work may not be sustainable in the organisation when the individual client moves on.

- Individual skills and behaviours (top right) have not been developed towards managing effective partnerships: The consultant may find it difficult to establish trust with key stakeholders because the client wants to manage internal relationships personally.

What are the chances of an external consultant being truly successful in any of these situations? Slim to the say the least. For an external consultant to be effectively engaged by an organisation the framework indicates that all four quadrants need to be congruent with this intention, but in reality there are many challenges with this. An organisation is a myriad of individual needs, aspirations and drivers, and sub-cultures are likely to exist where individuals with the same views form groups, not to mention the many privately and publicly stated objectives that will exist across the organisation. The odds of congruence across all four quadrants are not good!

The organisational landscape that the internal client and external consultant work in is not likely to be conducive to success and so their challenge is to work together to create as much congruence as possible.

For greater congruence to be achieved, it makes sense to start in the top right quadrant with the skills and behaviours of the internal client, as they have insight about the organisation that the external consultant won't have. Developing the skill of an internal client to look at their organisational context through the lens of the four quadrants will raise their awareness of some of the issues that sit beneath the surface both organisationally and within themselves. Building on this awareness, if the client is then able to develop skills and behaviours for more effectively managing their own needs (top left) and the various organisational factors at play (bottom left), they will be making a significant contribution to the likely success of the external consultant they are engaging.

This chapter aims to highlight some of the key skills and behaviours that an internal client can usefully employ when looking to engage an external consultant. Some of these skills and behaviours will come into play before an external consultant is engaged in the first place because the internal client has an important role to play in creating greater organisational readiness for working with an external consultant. Other skills and behaviours will be important in establishing and maintaining an effective working relationship with the consultant once their work has commenced.

Creating Organisational Readiness

The likely success of an external consultant is partly determined by the degree of ground work that has been done before the consultant walks through the door. Based within the organisation, the internal client is knowledgeable about its goals and intentions (bottom right), and cultural norms that underpin how things actually get done internally (bottom left), which means they are ideally placed to carry out initial diagnosis work before the OD work in question is commenced. The extent to which this groundwork is completed relies on the ability of the internal client to do the following.

Start with the End in Mind

A highly skilled internal client understands the distinction between an 'outcome' and a 'deliverable' and will be focusing internal attention towards the business benefits that need to be derived from an OD intervention before an external consultant is engaged.

Consider the following brief that was created by an internal client before sourcing an OD consultant for some skills development work:

> We require Internal Consultancy Skills training for our HR, IT, legal and finance departments. We require a 2-day course to be delivered by 2 trainers for up to 15 participants. We would like 4 of these workshops to run during October at our in-house training site. The training must provide participants with a thorough understanding of the consultancy cycle, communication techniques including rapport and listening skills, effective questioning techniques as well as ways to influence others. We would like all participants to complete some online learning modules before attending the workshop.

This example highlights a common problem when organisations seek to engage external consultants; it focuses on the key *deliverables* of the project, that is, the preferred approach, methodology and frameworks the client wants to see. It makes no reference to the *outcomes* of the project, that is, the change in behaviour they want to see from participants attending the course and the business benefit this will bring.

In this example, by creating a brief that focuses predominantly on deliverables and not outcomes, the internal client will be limiting their organisation in a number of ways. Firstly, by having no clear outcomes identified up front, it will be difficult for the organisation to really evaluate success of the project (unless it's more important to have delivered something/anything rather than the impact the deliverable has). Secondly, by being prescriptive about the deliverables, the client may inadvertently be restricting any innovation that an external consultant and a fresh approach could bring to the situation. Thirdly, it leaves the way wide open for an external consultant to shape measures of success to suit their own agenda.

There are some simple but pertinent questions that an organisation should expect to be able to answer if intending to engage an external consultant. For example:

- Why are we embarking on this piece of work?

- How will it contribute to overall organisation effectiveness?

- What do we want as a result of this piece of work?

- How will we know when we've been successful?

- What do we want to see that isn't there now?

- What don't we want to see that is there now?

- How will we sustain the work once the external consultant has gone?

The answers to these questions are always within the domain of the organisation and are essential for creating common purpose and a clear sense of end result. A highly skilled client will operate in a manner that ensures these questions are addressed prior to the arrival of the external consultant, as they may shape the decision about which consultant to engage in the first place.

Of course, despite the apparent simplicity of these questions, it may not be a simple task for the internal client to elicit a consistent and agreed response from across the organisation. This will partly depend on their ability to do the following:

Manage Internal Stakeholders

A highly skilled consultant knows how to effectively navigate their organisation and is actively managing the political landscape and their various stakeholder relationships productively. They will know who the key decision makers are, versus those who simply need to be informed about the piece of work, and will be actively working with them to socialise them towards the engagement of an external consultant.

Managing internal stakeholders in readiness for an external consultant requires the internal client to clearly set expectations with internal stakeholders regarding their personal contribution towards the success of the project. This requires the internal client to be adept at recognising where the power really lies at any given point. Some stakeholders may think they have the power to make decisions, but don't really. Stakeholders who do have power may not be wielding it appropriately. Other stakeholders may not even realise that power is an issue. The objective of the internal client is to ensure that that the organisation will be using the external consultant as an appropriate resource rather than duplicating effort, and also that necessary internal support is firmly in place to enable the work to be successful.

An external consultant was recently asked by an organisation to lead an internal conference for 100 people to engage them in a big business transformation process across several countries. The brief from the client was that the event needed to be fully interactive and experiential and so the external consultant designed a highly creative and practical programme of events. Unfortunately, the internal client had not engaged early enough with the internal team responsible for venue booking and the organisation was already under contract to a lecture hall venue with limited breakout space. Budget limitations made it impossible to back out of the venue arrangement and so the programme objectives had to be significantly downgraded as a result.

In this example, the desired outcome of the work was not possible because a stakeholder who really should have been informed about the piece of work early on had by now assumed a decision-making position.

Managing internal stakeholders before the external consultant is engaged requires the internal client to be personally resilient enough to have some tough conversations internally. They may need to challenge internal inconsistencies that exist during the various conversations about intended outcomes – if the organisation cannot agree on what success looks like, how can any external consultant be deemed successful? Recognising that the top team cannot agree on a desired outcome for a piece of work may need the intervention of an external consultant in its own right anyway, but it's about clarifying that this is the situation, rather than pressing on with a piece of work when there is considerable internal confusion or resistance.

The internal client may also need to surface and challenge some of the hidden aspirations and desires (top left) of senior stakeholders involved in decision making. It's not unusual for senior executives to bring an external consultant in because they have an existing relationship with them, but will they necessarily be the best fit for the job on this occasion? Likewise, in an organisation that is unfamiliar with partnering with external consultants, the internal client may need to actively surface an unhealthy corporate mindset (bottom left) towards working with external consultants, for example, a desire to undermine them. Without this kind of intervention up front, the external consultant may waste too much energy in battling organisation politics rather than getting on with the task in hand.

In large organisations, one of the biggest challenges can simply be the sheer volume of internal relationships that need to be managed before an external consultant can be selected.

A client organisation required a management development programme for approx 250 team leaders and first line managers in one of its three business units. Knowing that the organisation was highly consensus driven, the internal client meticulously sought input and involvement from various representatives from HR and the business to ensure a shared understanding of objectives was in place. Having taken several weeks to complete this process, she invited six external consultants to take part in a competitive tender. The final stage of the selection process involved no fewer than 14 managers and representatives from HR dedicating a whole day to observing shortlisted suppliers delivering a presentation. Coordinating so many diaries meant that the project moved slowly but eventually a decision was made and the client was confident she'd found an external supplier that the organisation could really buy into. A week later, she was informed by procurement that a more senior stakeholder in one of the other three business units had already signed an exclusive contract with a lower priced supplier to provide all HR/OD related services right across the organisation for the next two years. She was told to abandon her external consultant and work with this other supplier instead. Several wasted weeks and an external supplier who was not really supported by her stakeholders was all she had to show for her efforts.

A highly skilled internal client will be mining their organisational network for information about other projects to ensure they are able to build on progress already made elsewhere and learn from previous success stories. Simply by starting the process of engaging with the wider organisation and creating a beauty parade of potential external consultants, the internal client will be surfacing all kinds of issues that may be as important for the organisation to address as the presenting OD issue itself.

Key questions for an internal client to consider at this stage are:

- Who internally needs to be informed that I am about to engage an external consultant? Who else?

- Who do I need to consult with internally? Who else?

- Who can advise me on this internally? Who else?

- Who internally will contribute to the success of the external consultant? Who else?

- What elements of our organisation might help/hinder this piece of work?

- What do I need to do internally now to ensure success with the external consultant later?

- Who cares? Who can? Who will?

Where an internal client invests time in robust internal stakeholder management before engaging an external consultant, problems are less likely to occur later on in the work. It's important to recognise that internal stakeholder management such as this requires personal energy, resilience, commitment and time. Given the many operational demands already on their time, not to mention the fact they will have their own set of personal aspirations and beliefs (top left) about how they want to be perceived in the organisation, it's not surprising that some internal clients ignore the need to manage their internal stakeholders up front. If internal stakeholders have not been managed effectively, it's more likely that the incoming external consultant will have to spend time and energy managing internal politics and will likely be a scapegoat when the project is not a success.

Right Consultant, Right Now

A highly skilled internal client is able to combine their knowledge of the organisation's desired outcomes, preferences of key stakeholders and cultural style, and match these needs with an external consultant who has the capability to complete the work and will also be a good cultural fit. This may not always be as straightforward as it sounds. Firstly, on the internal side of things, the internal client may need to decide which set of selection criteria are most important. For example, is it more important to engage a consultant who will meet the procurement department's objective of global reach and scalability, or is it more important that they go with a consultant who is a good cultural fit for the local team commencing the work? Secondly, as they look out on to the market place for external OD consultants, the internal client will find a huge volume of potential consultants which they will need to carefully select from (a Google search for 'OD consultant' at time of writing identified several thousand links worldwide).

A useful starting point is for the internal client to consider what role the organisation needs the external consultant to play at any given time. Schein (1988) identifies three roles – pair of hands, expert and partner – that a consultant can potentially play. Schein very much focuses on process consultation as the underpinning approach for OD consultancy, with the internal client and external consultant each in the in the role of equal partner. Here, the internal client brings knowledge of the organisation's issues and business, and the external consultant brings techniques, new ways of thinking and practices that can solve the problem.

In reality, the client organisation may not share the same understanding of the term OD consultancy and may be expecting the external consultant to play an expert or pair of hands role. A mismatch of role expectations can cause real problems later on. For example, bringing in a process consultant to be a pair of hands on an internal project that simply requires additional resource will be frustrating for the external consultant who is used to working in partnership, and may mean the organisation is overpaying for their services. Or working with a 'pair of hands' on a project that has become increasingly complex may mean that the organisation is losing out on OD expertise that process consultation would bring. Ongoing role clarity is an important part of an effective working relationship with an external consultant, and a skilled internal client will ensure that it is regularly discussed throughout a long-term contract.

A potential pitfall when seeking the right external consultant is that despite its strategic impact on organisation effectiveness, external OD consultancy is an area which is often managed quite reactively by organisations. It's not unusual to be called by a potential client about a piece of OD work that's been on the internal agenda for several months, which now has to be completed immediately. In such a situation, the internal client may end up working with whichever external consultant is available, rather than the best external consultant for the work. When time is an issue, the easy option is to engage someone you've worked with before rather than take time to source someone new.

A highly skilled internal client will be continually keeping an eye on the marketplace for external OD consultants and be informed about new thinking and latest trends. Rather than engaging with external consultants as a reaction to operational requests from the organisation, they will be actively seeking external OD perspective so that they are able to offer their organisation fresh new thinking.

Useful questions for an internal client to ask themselves are:

- What's my own working definition of 'OD consultancy'?

- What have I done this week, this month, this quarter to improve my network of external OD consultants?

- When was the last time I tried partnering with an OD consultant who is untried and untested in my organisation?

Establishing a Working Relationship with an External Consultant

Having identified some of the skills and behaviours that an internal client will benefit from employing in order to ensure organisation readiness for an external consultant, we can now turn our attention to the role of the internal

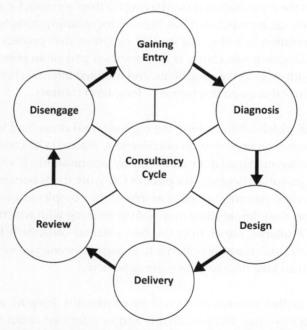

Figure 11.2   The consultancy cycle: Adapted from *Flawless Consulting*
Source: Peter Block, 1981.

client in establishing and maintaining an effective working relationship with an external consultant.

The consultancy cycle provides a useful framework for considering the phases the internal client and external consultant will go through as their working relationship develops.

Equally applicable to a long-term working relationship with an organisation as to a one-off short-term project, the consultancy cycle highlights the need for the internal client to be able to utilise different skills and behaviours at particular times, in order that the working relationship can effectively progress and the external consultant can be successfully engaged by the organisation.

Gaining Entry

'Gaining Entry' is a critical first stage in the consultancy cycle. It is where credibility is established and expectations managed. If done well, it will create a solid foundation for successful completion of the work. If done poorly, it is likely to mean that the external consultant will experience difficulties at later stages of the work.

A skilled internal client will recognise that there are many 'characters' involved in the organisation system and that the external consultant will want to gain entry in their own right with each of these individuals. Typically for OD interventions, the initial 'client' will be an HR Business Partner or internal Learning and Development or OD consultant but they may not be the ultimate decision maker; neither will they be the only stakeholder to be consulted on for the piece of work. As the initial point of entry into the organisation for the external consultant, the internal client plays a vital 'gatekeeper' role to the wider organisation and will determine the degree of access (or not) that the external consultant will experience with these other key stakeholders. For this reason, it's essential that the external consultant can gain entry with the internal client and that the relationship between the two of them is a strong one.

Despite the importance of establishing an effective working relationship between internal client and external consultant from day one, there are a number of issues that mean this is not always an easy task. For example:

- Time: We've already highlighted the reactive approach to sourcing external consultants and when this is the case, there will be an immediate time pressure within the client organisation to get straight into delivering results. This can create difficulties for the external consultant when trying to properly establish a working relationship based on trust and mutual understanding, as the internal client may perceive conversations about the working relationship to be wasting time.

- Perceived Involvement of Supply Chain: There may be an organisational preference that all contract-related discussions are held with supply chain rather than the internal client engaging the external consultant for the piece of work. This can lead an internal client to want to skip over any informal contracting conversations in the belief that a formal contract will cover the important stuff. Conversations immediately focus on 'task' without time being invested up front on the qualities of an effective working relationship for each party.

- Preconceptions: Another difficulty can be dealing with the preconceptions that internal clients hold about how external consultants behave. Most internal clients have experienced uninvited approaches from external consultants who try to drum up business internally without the client's consent. The legacy of such bad experiences with external consultants can lead internal clients to adopt unproductive practices with external consultants moving forward, to keep them on a tight leash. A common example is the HR Business Partner who insists on being involved in every single meeting between the external consultant and the business manager commissioning the piece of work. This can cause enormous delays whilst diaries are synchronised and significantly limit the degree of openness between external consultant and manager when discussions take place.

A central issue in the early stages of the relationship between internal client and external consultant is certainly that of trust. Charles Green (2007) provides a useful insight into the key components of trust in his 'Trust Equation':

$$\text{Trust} = \frac{\text{credibility} + \text{reliability} + \text{intimacy}}{\text{self-orientation}}$$

He proposes that there are three core components of trust; credibility, reliability and intimacy. By credibility he refers to the personal and professional impact that an individual brings to a situation. Reliability is demonstrated over time – it's about a track record for being dependable for what you say you will do. Intimacy is the ability to create genuine personal connections with people, establish rapport and respect confidentiality. His theory is that these three components combined are *diminished* by the degree of self-orientation that exists within an individual. If someone is highly self-oriented they cannot really focus on the needs of the other person.

This provides an interesting perspective on the relationship between internal client and external consultant. Each is likely to have a degree of self-orientation that is not openly shared with the other, which could hinder the relationship. For example:

Internal Client:

I need to protect and enhance my personal and professional reputation and so it's important that I am associated with the right pieces of work in the right manner.

I'm worried the external consultant will screw this up and it will reflect badly on me.

I'm afraid that my internal customers will rate the external consultant more highly than me.

I don't feel confident to do this myself and don't want to be exposed.

I feel completely capable of completing this work myself and am frustrated that the organisation wants us to partner externally.

External Consultant:

I need to protect and enhance my personal and professional reputation and so it's important that I am associated with the right pieces of work in the right manner.

I want to establish my reputation with the major budget holders in the organisation.

I hope this will lead to more interesting projects here.

I want to find an opportunity to test my latest ideas/thinking.

These points of self-interest are entirely valid given the different perspectives of the internal client and external consultant. What's interesting to note is that as soon as the external consultant enters the organisational landscape, they will bring with them their own personal drivers (top left and top right) which potentially create further incongruence in the system.

When self-interest on either side remains unspoken it can be damaging to the relationship between internal client and external consultant because it may promote behaviours that are perceived by the other party as game playing. Such behaviours are most likely to occur when either party feels vulnerable. The recent economic downturn surfaced some particularly unhealthy behaviours amongst internal clients and external consultants alike as organisations faced some tough decisions and individuals felt increasingly vulnerable about the longevity of their role.

A highly skilled internal client will be aware of the points in the working relationship where either the internal client or external consultant is likely to feel more vulnerable than the other, and use this awareness to consciously role-model behaviours that will serve to minimise this vulnerability and prevent perceived game playing from polluting the working relationship.

Figure 11.3, on the opposite page, maps out what could be considered a 'typical' early relationship between an internal client and external consultant.

At the point of initial contact between potential client and potential external consultant, they are in the 'neutral zone' as neither party is more vulnerable than the other. The internal client has identified an organisational need that needs resourcing and will have a degree of professional and personal vulnerability until they have been successful in finding the right consultant. Equally, an initial conversation about the organisation's requirements will pique the interest of the external consultant, who will also now develop a degree of vulnerability if they are attracted to the work on offer.

It is likely that the internal client will invite the external consultant to take part in a selection process in order to establish their degree of fit for

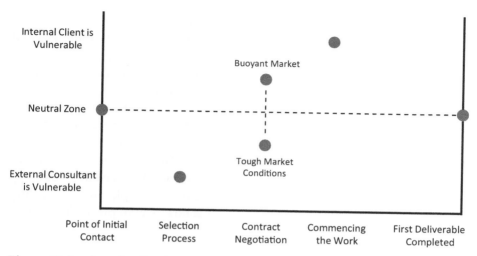

Figure 11.3   Levels of vulnerability as early relationship develops

the work. The external consultant is likely to experience some anxiety about how they are perceived by decision makers, and whether or not they will be successful. As time elapses, the consultant may place a commercial value on the work or simply build more personal interest in the project. They are now more vulnerable than before. The danger is that this increased vulnerability can lead to some unhealthy behaviour from the consultant, for example pushing the client too hard for a decision, trying too hard to promote themselves and their suitability – paradoxically the very behaviours that are likely to push a client away. At this stage in the relationship, the internal client holds the cards – information and decision-making responsibility. By making a conscious decision to work in an open and timely way as the selection process continues, the internal client can reduce the feeling of vulnerability the consultant might have, and avoid the unhealthy behaviour it often promotes.

Contract negotiation stage will be another point at which one party may feel more vulnerable than the other. The health of the prevailing business environment may determine which party feels most vulnerable here. In a tough climate the external consultant is likely to feel vulnerable because if they don't agree to the contractual requirements of the organisation, they risk losing the work. The internal client may look to exploit this vulnerability by driving the best commercial arrangement they can, which may manifest in seeking aggressive reductions in fees or other such demands. The whole process can set an unpleasant tone to a fledgling relationship and leave the external consultant less trusting of the client and potentially less engaged in the piece of work. Conversely, in a buoyant market, the external consultant may not feel vulnerable because they are confident they have other lucrative work. In this situation it may now be the internal client who is vulnerable, because they fear losing out on the services of a good consultant. At this stage it's really a case of whose needs are best served by a decision to engage the external consultant. The person with the greatest need will be the most vulnerable. A skilled internal client will recognise that contract negotiation is a sensitive point in a developing relationship and seek to agree working principles in person, early on, rather than rely on an email exchange of contracts with procurement once the work has commenced.

Once the external consultant commences work and becomes established in the organisation, it may now be the internal client who feels vulnerable. The external consultant may be cementing relationships with the internal client's own stakeholders and have access to information that is not known to the internal client. An external consultant who has a genuine desire to establish and maintain a relationship based on trust will recognise this vulnerability and look to promote some simple working practices that ensure that the internal client feels included throughout the work. For example, building in regular update conversations, ensuring queries are run by them first, etc.

Once the first deliverable has been successfully completed, they're likely to return to the 'neutral zone' where neither party is more vulnerable than the other. The internal client will feel confident they've introduced an external consultant to the organisation who is deemed successful, and the external consultant will now feel more trusted by the internal client.

In summary, Gaining Entry is an important part of the working relationship between internal client and external consultant and there are a few simple steps the internal client can take to ensure this goes well:

- Invest time in building a genuine relationship based on trust and understanding.

- Be open about personal aspirations and any previous experiences (good and bad) with external consultants.

- Personally discuss informal and formal contract issues before passing them over to procurement.

Diagnosis

The diagnosis stage of the consultancy cycle is the first place where the trust that has been created between internal client and external consultant is put to the test. Effective diagnosis is about being able to answer the question, 'What's really going on?' before going any further with the work.

Role clarity between internal client and external consultant is important here. The internal client will have engaged in some important initial diagnosis before the external consultant arrived as a way of creating organisation readiness and determining what external consultant to engage in the first place. Diagnosis is often seen by internal clients as an interesting part of their role, an opportunity to practise some real consultancy skills internally and a chance to establish relationships at a senior level. All of these top left quadrant issues can drive them to want to do more of it. The difficulty is that organisations do not always invest in developing the diagnostic capability of their internal people, which means the quality of internal diagnosis may be poor. It's also highly likely that internal politics and personal agendas will prevent issues from being surfaced openly with an internal client.

Where too much diagnosis is owned by the internal client, it may also indicate that they are not defining the role of the OD consultant in the same way as the external consultant. They may perceive the external consultant as a pair of hands who is simply going to implement a solution of the organisation's choosing, or an expert who will simply advise them on what to do once they have identified their own problem.

The process of diagnosis is an important part of the external consultant building relationships and establishing credibility with key stakeholders in their own right. If they're perceived by these stakeholders to be going over ground already covered by the internal client, their diagnosis may be considered a waste of time and resources. Also, if the external consultant is not fully involved in the diagnosis process, they are relying on receiving issues second hand as interpreted by their internal client. This may limit the objectivity that an external consultant can bring.

The internal client can do a number of things to ensure diagnosis is managed well:

- Facilitate access to all stakeholders for the external consultant.

- Be part of the diagnosis process by contributing personal observations and opinions.

- Be a sounding board for what the external consultant is noticing throughout this phase.

Design

The design phase is where decisions are made about how best to proceed with the work, given the issues that have been surfaced during diagnosis. This is a point in the working relationship where the internal client can really reap the benefits of their decision to work with an external consultant.

As a result of diagnosis, it's sometimes the case that stakeholders commissioning the piece of work are a large part of the presenting problem themselves, or that what they say they want is not actually what the organisation needs. In either case, there may be the requirement for some robust conversations, which are sometimes easier to do if you are from outside the organisation.

A highly skilled internal client can support the external consultant at this stage by:

- Acting as a sounding board for key messages they plan to deliver to stakeholders.

- Being quietly supportive of the external consultant to ensure that difficult messages are reinforced and not simply buried.

Delivery

The delivery stage of the consultancy work can be another phase of the working relationship that potentially highlights some interesting dynamics between internal client and external consultant. Once work is underway in the organisation, it could be said that the internal client and external consultant enter into a triangular relationship, with the organisation stakeholder(s) becoming the third point in the triangle.

As work proceeds, the internal client, external consultant and organisation stakeholder(s) may well start to take on the roles identified in the Drama Triangle (Stephen B. Karpman, M.D., 1968). Take, for example, a situation where something goes wrong. The organisation stakeholder may take on the role of 'persecutor' by blaming the external consultant, who is treated as 'victim'. The internal client may choose to side with the external consultant, taking on the role of 'rescuer'. Alternatively, organisation stakeholder(s) might cast themselves as 'victims' of a difficult message being delivered by the external consultant whom they now perceive to be a 'persecutor', and the internal client may seek to 'rescue' the stakeholder, in the process becoming a persecutor of the external consultant themselves.

During the course of OD consultancy work, there are likely to be points where the external consultant and the organisation stakeholder(s) may not be in agreement. A highly skilled internal client will alleviate this situation by:

- Remaining focused on the overall organisation outcomes identified at the beginning of the work.

- Avoiding siding with the external consultant or the stakeholder.

Review

Once a piece of work has been delivered it's useful to make time for a formal review so that learning can be fed back into the organisation. An effective review will focus on completion of the task as well as the working relationship between external consultant and the organisation.

In reality, this process is not always as straightforward as it sounds. Often, the internal client has moved on before the work is completed, which means there may no longer be anyone with a vested interest in reviewing something that is deemed to be successfully 'delivered'. This is particularly common in highly operational organisations. Alternatively, the internal client may not feel confident at giving the external consultant feedback – perhaps they feel intimidated by their perceived expertise or have become accustomed to working in an environment where difficult feedback is avoided.

A highly skilled internal client can improve the review stage of the working relationship by:

- Scheduling review meetings at regular points in the relationship.

- Actively encouraging feedback between themselves and the external consultant from the beginning of their relationship.

Disengage

This stage is about leaving the organisation with something that is sustainable once the external consultant has moved on.

A highly skilled internal client will ensure that the issue of long-term sustainability is on the agenda from the beginning of the piece of work so that it is clear about when/how and to whom, things will be handed over. This is important in terms of managing expectations effectively with the external consultant so that there are no surprises on either side. It's also about ensuring the work does not suffer in any way once the external consultant leaves.

Ensuring the external consultant can disengage smoothly requires forward planning and structure. (As opposed to what happens when an internal consultant moves on to another role internally and they're still picking up queries from the old job months down the line!) For long-term projects it can be useful to include internal sustainability as one of the key deliverables up front. This means that the internal resources to continue the piece of work can be identified early, involved in the work and coached/trained on an ongoing basis, ensuring a solid understanding and history of the work remains in the organisation. This isn't the case where internal resources are identified at the eleventh hour to take something over.

It's possible that the external consultant may have aspirations to extend their involvement in the work (top left). It's important that the internal client is clear about roles and remaining requirements of the work so that the organisation is not picking up the cost of an external OD consultant taking on remaining 'pair of hands' activity. Equally, it can be detrimental to the work if things are handed over too quickly to less experienced internal resources.

A highly skilled internal client will:

- Ensure that the question of long-term sustainability is addressed at the beginning of the work and a plan agreed.

- Clearly set the expectations of the external consultant if the long-term plan is to manage the work internally.

Conclusion

Organisations are complicated places with a host of personal and organisational agendas, aspirations and drivers that may or may not be visible to the external consultant. The internal client has a pivotal role to play in working with the external consultant to create as much congruence as possible in their working environment, to ensure the best conditions for their success.

A highly skilled internal client will do the following things to promote success when engaging an external consultant:

- Prepare the groundwork before the external consultant arrives to ensure that outcomes are clear and stakeholders effectively managed.

- Personally invest time in establishing a working relationship based on mutual trust and understanding.

- Ensure that organisational needs are prioritised above personal drivers.

- Plan the exit strategy for when the external consultant disengages.

References

Block, P. 1981. *Flawless Consulting: A Guide to Getting your Expertise used.* San Francisco, CA: Jossey-Bass/Pfeiffer

Downey, M. 2003. Effective coaching: Lessons from the coach's coach. In K. Wilber, *A Brief History of Everything.* Shambhala Publications Inc.

Green, C. 2007. *Trust in Business: The Core Concepts.* Trusted Advisor Associates LLC.

Karpman, Stephen B., M.D. 1968. Fairy tales and script drama analysis. *Transactional Analysis Bulletin 7.*

Schein, E. 1988. *Process Consultation,* Vol. 1. Reading, MA: Addison-Wesley series on OD.

National Audit Office. October 14 2010. Report by the Comptroller and Auditor General. *Central Government's Use of Consultants and Interims.*

12

Measuring and Evaluating OD: Return on Investment?

Liz Finney and Jo Hennessy

Introduction

In this chapter we will examine the challenges, the benefits and the practicalities of measuring and assessing the success of Organisation Development (OD) interventions. The chapter is adapted from a research report published by Roffey Park Institute, *Best Practice in OD Evaluation* (Finney and Jefkins, 2009). Roffey Park owns the copyright for this report and we are grateful that they have allowed us to reproduce substantial parts of it here.

We know that there are people in the OD community who will view a chapter on evaluation with some scepticism. There are many practitioners who believe that the systemic nature of OD makes it hard to measure; some say it's inappropriate even to try (Garrow et al., 2009). The very word 'evaluation' carries connotations of bureaucratic box-ticking, defensive budget justification and the mechanistic cramming of complex human systems into rigid, numerical formulae. Some practitioners talk about the evaluation of OD interventions as a 'holy grail', perhaps implying that to seek it would be a hopeless quest. Evaluation is something which is often overlooked, avoided, or included only as an afterthought when an OD intervention has already taken place.

But if you're not evaluating, might you be missing opportunities to add value to your work? To improve your practice? To enhance the credibility of the discipline of OD? Developers who embed an evaluation element into their proposals show themselves to be accountable for the results they deliver. As we emerge into a post-recession world, this accountability will, we believe, give practitioners a competitive edge in a challenging market. In fact, without it there may be a risk that OD seems to those outside it a nebulous discipline, its impact unproven. Without evaluation we believe that OD is less likely to be seen and trusted as an established profession that is still influential in 20 years' time.

Evaluating within complex living systems isn't straightforward, but we would argue that it is critically important. We believe that being able and willing to demonstrate the impact of OD will be imperative if the discipline is to maintain and increase its credibility.

As part of our research at Roffey Park Institute we interviewed over 20 experienced practitioners, in order to explore best practice in OD evaluation. Based on our findings, as well as on our own experience as researchers, we would suggest that there are six main reasons why more formal evaluation does not take place:

1 – Clients may not see it as a valuable use of time or resources
Formal evaluation requires an investment of time, resources and (usually) money by the client organisation, and this needs to be weighed against the perceived benefits. Sometimes, if the client can see and feel change happening around them they don't feel the need to support (or perhaps challenge) these perceptions with additional reporting.

2 – Organisations are focused on moving forward, not looking back
Many clients, inclined to be more future-focused than reflective, may not be pressing for evaluation. Evaluation of outcomes, whether at an interim stage or at a later or final stage of an OD intervention, requires a review of what has gone before and what point has been reached. But things move on, circumstances change, and decision-makers in organisations are primarily concerned with the set of problems facing them today and in the future. Interestingly, our own recent experience of working in Asia Pacific on behalf of Roffey Park has suggested more appetite in countries like Singapore for evaluation than reported by UK and US practitioners when discussing their client organisations.

3 – Practitioners don't have the right expertise, or enough guidance
When we began our research into OD evaluation we were aware of relatively few relevant (or recent) sources of information on the subject. Our literature search confirmed that little is available, and we concluded that OD evaluation is a complicated topic in which there is a lack of clear, practical guidance for the OD practitioner.

Some people assume that evaluation is based primarily on quantitative measurement, complicated quasi-experimental research designs and statistical analysis. Practitioners without training in these methodologies can feel paralysed.

4 – Evaluating in complex, emergent systems is problematic
Many OD interventions (especially those at a large-system level) are complex and often involve several interrelated changes. Many take considerable time to produce desired outcomes. Results may not emerge when, or as, predicted. The longer a change programme goes on, the greater are the chances that factors other than the intervention will emerge to affect the results. It becomes impossible to separate the effects of OD from these other influences; in research terms, to establish causality.

5 – Practitioners have little interest in, or appetite for, formal evaluation
Evaluation, particularly the 'hard' or quantitative methodologies, is often at odds with the skills and preferences of the practitioner. Many OD practitioners prefer to be working in and with organisations to create change. Evaluation can feel less interesting and rewarding than other work; the 'poor relation' in the OD portfolio.

6 – Practitioners or clients feel threatened by evaluation
What if your evaluation delivers bad news? What if you find that the results of your work are not what you hoped for? How will it reflect on your relationship with your client; on your personal credibility? After a big investment of time and resources, both client and practitioner may find it hard to hear that the intervention has not had the effect they anticipated.

It's important to acknowledge these barriers. But as we show in the remainder of this chapter, the benefits of evaluation outweigh its challenges. We also offer some practical tips to help practitioners to get maximum benefit from OD evaluation, whilst avoiding its pitfalls.

WHAT ARE THE MOST EFFECTIVE WAYS OF EVALUATING OD INTERVENTIONS?

Just as every OD intervention is unique, there is no one-size-fits-all formula for OD evaluation. Every evaluation will require an element of problem-solving and thought, analysis and creativity. The simple flowchart shown in Figure 12.1, on the next page, is designed to help practitioners design meaningful ways of measuring their work.

What is the desired or planned outcome?
What will the milestones be on the road to this outcome?
What will success look like?

What emergent or unexpected outcomes may occur?

How short term – or long term – are the outcomes you will be evaluating?
In the short term, are there problems that need to be eliminated?
In the long term, how effectuve has a new organisational strategy proved to be?

What is the scale of the intervention?
Does it involve the whole organisation or parts of it?

What evaluation methods will you choose and why?
Will they measure what you want to measure?
What existing data sources can you tap into?
What new information to you need to collect?

What is the timescale of the evaluation?
Are you measuring at the right points during the programme? Before? During? After?

Have you got the practical resources in place to collect and analyse your data?

How wll you report the findings?
How can they be presented so that they are relevant and meaningful?

Figure 12.1   Planning an OD evaluation

Source: Finney and Jefkins 2009. © Roffey Park Institute.

As Figure 12.1 shows, the first, crucial step in planning an evaluation is to agree with senior stakeholders what you're setting out to do. No matter how socially constructed your world, there will be a reason you're doing the work and there will be some outcomes you and your clients are hoping for. Are they to do with customer service? A change in culture or relationships? What will success look like? What will have changed? Your initial objectives might shift as the intervention progresses, but you can still plan to evaluate emergent outcomes and goals. Having a good conversation about 'what success looks like' becomes a critical part of the intervention at its earliest stage.

It is also important to consider the key drivers of the outcomes you are aiming for. OD is often about changing people's behaviour as a way of influencing other outcomes. For example, encouraging a greater focus on quality may improve products, and thence customer satisfaction, and subsequently sales. So, evaluating the extent to which quality is a core focus may be a valid measurement of a key business driver.

Few OD interventions reach their goals in one step. Along the way there will be a number of milestones, and evaluation at these points can help determine if the intervention is going in the right direction, or if some reassessment is called for. It is useful to determine what these milestones might be at the outset.

There will often be long- and short-term aspects to an OD intervention. In the short term there may be specific problems that need to be ironed out before the organisation can progress. What are they and how will you know when they've been addressed? In the longer term there may be changes in strategy or behaviour than can take some time to become embedded in the system. What indicators will help you track these changes?

Based on these success measures you will need to choose which methodologies will deliver the data you are looking for, working within the resources at your disposal. Don't forget that there may be existing measurements within the organisation that you can tap into, or you may need to collect new data. The toolkit described in this chapter will help here; or you may want to bring in some research expertise from elsewhere.

Then there are some practical considerations; do you have the resources and expertise in place to collect and analyse the data you need?

Finally, in what format will you report the data, so that it is of practical use both to you and the client? How will you present your data so that it is clear and accessible, highlighting the outcomes of the intervention and their relevance to the organisation? How can you use it as a learning resource?

Figure 12.1 can be used as a high-level checklist.

TIMING IS EVERYTHING

Timing is crucial, and needs to tie in with the milestones you have identified. If you are running pre-test/post-test comparisons you need to make sure your measurement is in place before and after the elements of the intervention you are assessing.

To identify a shift from an original state, it is first necessary to understand what the original state was. Pre-test/post-test comparisons allow you to detect changes in opinion, behaviour or systems between two given points in time.

As with all evaluation, this requires the identification of intended outcomes. Measures need to be created that will capture these outcomes. These measures can be administered before and after an intervention. Just asking the same question at different times can tell a powerful story about the way that an organisational system has shifted. This, in turn, requires some planning right at the start of your evaluation. If it occurs as an afterthought it will be too late.

Table 12.1   Ten top tips for OD evaluation

1	*Talk about evaluation early on and ask the right questions* Early conversations are essential for identifying success criteria and encouraging buy-in and support from key sponsors. Key questions are 'What does success look like?' and 'How will we know when we've reached our destination?'
2	*Flex your approach to suit culture and context* When designing an evaluation toolkit, one size does not fit all. Each intervention will require a different approach, based on culture and preferences within the organisation, and the scale and nature of the intervention.
3	*Keep it simple – don't try to boil the ocean* It isn't always easy to come up with a set of simple, tangible measures because of the complexity and unpredictability of OD work. However, it is important to be able to repeat an evaluation exercise for comparison purposes. An over-complicated methodology may make this difficult or even impossible.
4	*Secure the support of an influential sponsor* Evaluation can be both costly and labour intensive; it requires the participation of busy people, some of whom may not see the value of the exercise. The support of a senior sponsor can help to unlock resource and encourage participation where it is required.

Table 12.1   Continued

5	**Educate yourself about evaluation** Few OD practitioners are currently expert in evaluation techniques. We recommend not only training in evaluation methodology and basic statistics, but also in business metrics. This can serve both as a way to develop consultants' practice and as a way of increasing the credibility of OD with its sponsors.
6	**Use evaluation to drive improvement and learning** One of the key benefits of the OD evaluation is to drive up standards of practice and enhance the credibility of the discipline. In order to do this it is important to use the results of an evaluation, not as a box-ticking exercise, but as a resource for improvement and learning, and to inform future interventions.
7	**Focus on measuring the right things, not the easiest** In evaluating an intervention, focus on the information that will be most helpful to the organisation and identify the best way to access that information. Try to resist the temptation to measure what is easily accessible or acceptable, rather than what is most relevant and helpful.
8	**Get help if it's needed** There are many sources of help, both from inside the organisations in which practitioners are working, and from specialist external consultants, who can either help carry out the evaluation or act as a learning resource for the practitioner.
9	**Look for new solutions – 'normal science' may not work** In the absence of evaluation methodologies specifically designed to deal with the complexity and ambiguity of organisational change, be creative in developing evaluation techniques that attempt to accommodate the emergent, the nuanced or the intangible impacts of OD.
10	**Move towards more accountability as practitioners** The development of good practice in evaluation will make practitioners more accountable and increase clarity of understanding of the value OD can bring to an organisation. This may lead to increased credibility both for practitioners and for OD as a discipline. This, in turn, can make it easier to evaluate OD interventions.

WHAT ARE THE BENEFITS TO OD OF EVALUATION?

Evaluating OD is not just about justifying expenditure; it can also be about learning, improving and increasing understanding, as well as recognising and celebrating success. Financial justification aside, its primary purpose should (paraphrasing Mark Easterby-Smith) be not to prove, but to improve our practice. From the reflections of our research participants we identified a number of real benefits which evaluation can deliver.

Evaluation As a Diagnostic Tool

Talking about evaluation can help to clarify desired outcomes up front and informs the choice and design of interventions – often for the better.

Planning an evaluation requires us to specify where we are now and where we want to be. This entails a thorough diagnosis of the current situation and definition of the aim of the intervention, with clear links to organisational goals. Thinking about how we might see, note and measure when desired outcomes are achieved is a way of shaping them in specific and tangible ways.

Evaluation as 'GPS'

Evaluation during an OD intervention often helps to keep it on track, refocus, reassess possibilities, or spot and act on unexpected effects. Evaluation data can act as a 'temperature check' to help make sure the intervention is on the right track. One of the interviewees in our Roffey Park study likened evaluation to a GPS system: on a long journey it's a good idea to check where you are, how much further you have to go and whether you're still taking the right route.

Evaluation As Intervention

It is worth remembering that evaluation can be a valuable OD intervention in its own right, reinforcing or complementing the other work going on. Evaluation can be seen as a form of Action Research, in which we learn about organisations by trying to create change in them. This can be a cyclical process, where a change is first planned and acted upon. What happens as a result of the change is observed and reflected upon and then further action is planned in light of this. Thus the cycle repeats itself. The very process of evaluation can highlight the areas in need of change and focus people's attention on them.

Evaluation As Learning

Evaluation enables learning about how OD interventions impact on organisations, and how they can be developed or improved. Evaluation can provide evidence on which to base decisions about what works, what doesn't and what could be done differently next time. It can also determine whether unforeseen problems or by-products have arisen as a consequence of the intervention.

Engaging and Energising

The process of evaluation can enhance relationships and energise and inspire both participants and practitioners. Being asked for their views and experiences as part of an OD evaluation can be a positive and engaging experience for participants and practitioners alike. Creating energy and engagement with the intervention can help develop interest, trust and commitment.

Building a Body of Evidence for OD

Evaluation can help to develop OD as a discipline, adding to its credibility and to clients' understanding of what it can deliver. It can add to our understanding of organisational change. Building a body of solid evidence for the 'results' of OD enhances its reputation and helps to ensure it is taken seriously as a discipline.

Demonstrating Return on Investment

Evaluation can demonstrate that investment in OD was worthwhile. It helps to ensure clients 'get what they pay for'. Are the expected results being achieved? Is the investment of time, money and resources delivering a return? Our data suggest that the practitioner's credibility grows if they are able to provide a reporting system that tracks the return on investment being delivered by the intervention.

Recognising and Celebrating Success

Evaluation provides information that can be fed back to participants in OD programmes, informing them about progress, increasing engagement and recognising their contribution. By collecting, recording and publicising people's stories, the practitioners can create 'functional myths' which propagate a positive narrative about a change programme.

Professional Development for Practitioners

Evaluation can provide practitioners with valuable learning to help them develop and improve their own professional practice. By paying attention to what has worked and what hasn't, the practitioner can use evaluation data to deepen their own expertise.

Winning Business

Finally, evaluation can be a powerful tool in helping OD practitioners to develop their own business and secure new client contracts. Not only can practitioners refer to previous evaluations as supporting evidence for the quality of their work, they can also offer evaluation as part of their service to clients. In the current climate, where budgets are under great pressure, this may increasingly be the deciding factor in winning business. For OD practitioners working within organisations, evaluation data can help win the confidence of sceptical colleagues.

Key Theories, Thinkers and Shapers

BORROWING AND ADAPTING FROM OTHER DISCIPLINES

Mee-Yan Cheung-Judge, an influential practitioner and writer working in OD today (and one of our interviewees in the research study), describes OD as a 'magpie discipline' and OD practitioners as 'intellectual scavengers', and nowhere is this more apparent than in the field of evaluation. In the absence of theoretical frameworks or evaluation tools specifically designed for OD, practitioners have created, borrowed and adapted a wide range of methodologies, often from learning and development, and also from project management and marketing.

Perhaps the best known evaluation framework, designed to assess learning and development programmes, is that introduced by Donald L Kirkpatrick in the 1950s and developed in his 1975 book *Evaluating Training Programs*, now revised (Kirkpatrick, 1998). Briefly, the four levels of evaluation measure:

- Student or participant reaction – what they thought and felt about the training.

- Learning – the resulting increase in knowledge or capability.

- Behaviour – the extent of behaviour and capability improvement and implementation/application.

- Results – the effects on the business or environment resulting from the trainee's performance.

Subsequent writers have suggested a fifth level, measuring return on investment. This is often seen as 'the holy grail', very hard to prove, given the many different variables that relate to business success, of which a learning and development or OD intervention may be just one factor.

In OD, evaluation can be informed by the four or five levels described by Kirkpatrick. It should also go beyond these to look at the intended and the unintended outcomes; the positive and the negative; the tangible and the intangible. In recognition of this complexity, The Centre for Conscious Leadership in South Africa has created the Measurement Cube shown in Figure 12.2 below, onto whose six sides are plotted the light and 'shadow side' of OD's impact.

Another widely recognised and used theoretical framework is the Burke-Litwin model of organisational performance and change, developed by George

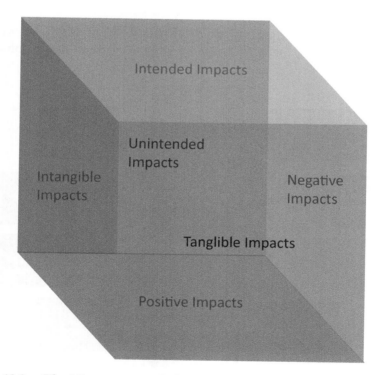

Figure 12.2   The Measurement Cube, showing the 'shadow side' impacts of OD

Litwin and Warner Burke (Burke and Litwin, 1992). The model examines organisational change and performance, providing a link between an assessment of the wider institutional context and the nature and process of change within an organisation. It can be used for organisational diagnosis, and for a 'temperature read' of current organisational health. It can also, therefore, be used to identify the most likely impact of interventions, as well as recognising organisations as systems in which one change may affect all parts of the system.

In addition to these three more commonly used frameworks, *Best Practice in OD Evaluation* (Finney and Jefkins, 2009) also describes how a number of practitioners are developing their own approaches based on a range of academic writing and theory related to their specific area of intervention. The value of drawing on academic theory to inform practice is that it enables the practitioner to form hypotheses that can be tested out in OD interventions and their evaluations.

Exploring an OD Evaluation Toolkit

In the spirit of providing practical guidelines for the OD practitioner, we offer, in Figure 12.3, below, this toolkit of commonly used – and not so commonly

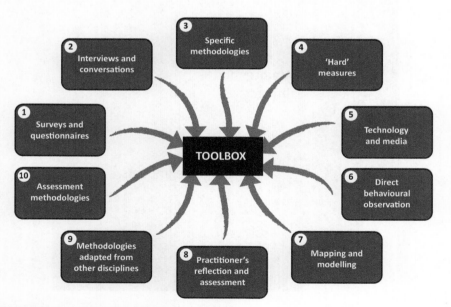

Figure 12.3   An OD evaluation toolkit
Source: Finney and Jefkins 2009. © Roffey Park Institute.

used – evaluation techniques and theoretical frameworks. Whilst this is not an evaluation textbook, the toolkit is intended to provide an overview of some of the methodologies a practitioner might consider when designing an evaluation, with some practical considerations to help incorporate evaluation into OD work.

1 – Surveys and Questionnaires

Survey research is one of the most widely used measurement tools in evaluation, both in OD and elsewhere. This broad area of research encompasses any measurement procedures that involve asking the same questions of multiple respondents.

The value of a survey is the collection of multiple responses to the same question. Questions can be open or closed, giving the evaluator the opportunity to collect either qualitative or quantitative data, or both.

Survey design is a specialist skill; the way that questions are framed can have a dramatic effect on the quality of data they elicit. It is also important that desired or expected outcomes are clearly defined to make sure the survey is investigating the right things. In Table 12.2, on the following page, we summarise some of the most commonly used forms of survey research.

2 – Interviews and Conversations

Some practitioners argue that both the process and the evaluation of an OD intervention centres on conversations, and certainly conversations can be a powerful tool for keeping track of progress.

These conversations take many forms, from the structured to the informal; from work with individuals to work with groups. They can be used to collect anecdotes and to explain and enrich quantitative data. They can also be used to form an assessment of the overall effectiveness of an intervention and to track the progress of ongoing work.

SEMI-STRUCTURED OR STRUCTURED INTERVIEWS

A semi-structured interview is one in which the interviewer has a series of questions in the form of an interview schedule, but is able to vary the sequence

Table 12.2   Commonly used surveys and psychometrics

	How they work	Benefits
'Happy Sheets' and Reactionnaires	Typically use closed questions to capture the reactions of participants to their experience in the training room or group activity.	Dismissed by some as too simplistic to offer a useful measure, they nonetheless are a useful way to look at the immediate impact of an event, offering fairly uncontaminated data. Can be used to plot the extent of a shift in attitude or alignment as a result of specific activity.
Interactive audience response and voting technology	Dedicated voting keypads are used to capture individual responses from large groups.	Can provide a powerful and immediate picture of a shift in attitude or alignment. Voting results can be quickly analysed and projected onto a screen so that groups can witness such shifts themselves.
Employee engagement surveys	Widely used staff surveys in which responses are analysed to provide engagement scores, often broken down into subscales that measure engagement with different aspects of the organisation and job role.	The relationship between management behaviour and employee engagement is widely recognised and these surveys can be used to identify areas of concern or improvement in interventions with a focus on management behaviour. Engagement surveys can be valuable in surfacing issues and keeping them under discussion. They can also be run on a regular basis to monitor improvement in the experience of a group of employees.
360° or multi-rater feedback	Provides information on an individual from a number of sources; their peers, their direct reports, their seniors and, increasingly, from external contacts and customers. Often, the subject also assesses their own performance using the same questionnaire.	A useful indicator of management behaviour. Can help translate agreed strategy and values into the behaviours that support them, particularly in relation to the impact these behaviours have on employee performance.
Emotional Intelligence questionnaires	A number of assessment tools are available to measure an individual's social and emotional strengths and weaknesses.	Useful where an aim of the intervention is to encourage greater emotional intelligence among the leadership population of an organisation. Tested before and after a number of coaching sessions, managers who opt for coaching may show higher emotional intelligence scores than those who have not had coaching. This data may in itself provide an incentive for managers to sign up for coaching sessions.
Organisational culture	A number of models exist to assess organisational culture using questionnaires.	Useful as a diagnostic as well as to measure culture change by administering questionnaires at different points in a change process.

of questions or to probe what seem to be significant responses. Questions tend to be more general in their frame of reference than in a structured interview.

In structured interviews, all respondents are asked the same questions, both in form and in sequence, so that their replies can be aggregated. Questions are specific and often closed, offering the interviewee a fixed range of answers.

Using a predetermined set of questions can help the practitioner elicit specific and comparable information from respondents, and this information can be used in a variety of ways during an intervention. Structured or semi-structured interviews can be used to gain a better understanding of any quantitative data you may have collected.

UNSTRUCTURED INTERVIEWS, INFORMAL MEETINGS AND CONVERSATIONS

An unstructured interview can be defined as one in which the interviewer has a list of topics and issues, but varies the phrasing and sequence of questions. These conversations can be used both to identify the changes that people perceive within the organisation and to help determine the direction of the intervention as it progresses.

GROUP DISCUSSIONS

Focus groups typically address a specific issue or topic, which is explored in depth. The process of data gathering from a group is quite different from that of an individual interview. In focus groups, the facilitator observes the way people respond to each other's views and builds a communal view out of the interaction that takes place.

ANECDOTAL EVIDENCE, STORYTELLING, USE OF METAPHOR

The collection of stories and anecdotal evidence may not form part of a more traditional evaluation toolkit, and may have little or no 'objective' validity. However, the stories people tell, the language they use to tell them and the metaphors they use to describe change can be a powerful tool for the evaluator. Organisational culture is sometimes defined as the stories people tell one another. A measure of success could be that the stories have changed, or the way they are told.

SUCCESS CASE METHODOLOGY

Evaluation specialists we interviewed reported that they had used the Success Case Method, developed by Robert O Brinkerhoff (2003). This methodology aims to harness the power of storytelling, but balances it with the principles of rigorous evaluative enquiry and research to underpin and validate the stories that are collected. It recognises that storytelling taps deep collective emotions and commands attention, but can also be seen as suspicious or questionable; a 'story' can be another word for a 'lie'.

3 – Specific Methodologies

APPRECIATIVE INQUIRY

Appreciative Inquiry (AI) as an approach was first described in an article entitled *Appreciative Inquiry into Organisational Life* (Cooperrider and Srivastva, 1987) and has since been developed and used by many academics and practitioners. The proposition of AI is that problem-solving and 'deficit-based' forms of analysis are incapable of inspiring growth and development in people, and that they stifle innovation.

AI can be summarised as the art and practice of asking questions that strengthen a system's capacity to apprehend, anticipate, and heighten positive potential. It seeks to identify possibilities, not problems. From an evaluation perspective, AI can be used to identify success criteria, the focus for interventions and learning at key stages.

ACTION RESEARCH

Many writers on action research trace its origins to the work of Kurt Lewin in the 1940s (Lewin, 1946). It has since been developed by a number of other researchers. Lewin argued that if people are active in decisions that affect them, they are more likely to embrace and accept change.

Action research focuses on the relationship between power and knowledge. It considers how knowledge exists in the context of the perspectives and biases of the individual. Within organisations, much of the power resides at the top, so what is presented as 'truth' may, in reality, be the personal perspective of the organisation's leaders.

4 – 'Hard' Measures

These are the quantitative measures; the numbers and statistics that, whilst they may not capture the full and complex story of an OD intervention, are valuable components in the evaluation toolkit. As we describe on page 270, quantitative measures interact with qualitative data to point to trends and shifts and to provide base-level information on some of the issues that need to be tackled. A few basic statistics can help distinguish insignificant smaller shifts from real change, and add rigour to 'softer' methodologies.

QUANTITATIVE MEASURES OF BEHAVIOUR

A useful component in the evaluation of an OD intervention can be to look at quantitative behaviour measurements; in other words, looking at how many times a particular behaviour takes place. This might include, for example, the number of times teams write or use an action plan; the number of participants in specific events or programmes; the number of website hits or contributions to an 'ideas' web page.

SPECIFIC BUSINESS MEASURES

Most organisations have easily accessible measures that can be used as part of a wider evaluation by OD professionals. They can be used both to evaluate the work of the OD professional and to define success criteria at the outset of an intervention. These measures might include staff retention statistics, sales figures, customer satisfaction surveys and service level agreements.

5 – Technology and Media

DIGITAL VOTING AND SURVEY TECHNOLOGY

As mentioned previously in this chapter, OD practitioners have found that new audience voting technology can bring immediacy and impact to group events. Certainly real time feedback is a useful and highly relevant evaluation tool, and can be used to monitor progress against key objectives by specific stakeholder groups.

SOCIAL MEDIA

The dizzying rise of social media; Twitter, Facebook, LinkedIn and the like, is making its mark, and some practitioners are investigating how this powerful phenomenon can be harnessed for evaluation purposes. Marketing professionals are using social media to collect data, customer feedback and opinion and some OD practitioners are drawing on this expertise to explore new ways of understanding behavioural and attitudinal change.

6 – Direct Behavioural Observation

From their position on the periphery of an organisation OD practitioners are often able to observe people at work and pay attention to changes that occur during an intervention. For example, a practitioner might sit in on management meetings and observe the interactions that take place, sometimes offering feedback as part of the intervention, but at other times simply noting how behaviour has changed.

As researchers we would add that good note-taking, analysis and write-up can turn behavioural observation into a powerful evaluation tool. Analytical techniques such as template analysis can equally apply to this kind of observational practice.

7 – Mapping and Modelling

The pictorial representation of a change process can be useful in presenting the elements of a multi-faceted intervention and facilitating the identification and evaluation of its component elements.

PROCESS MAPPING

First introduced in the 1920s as process flowcharts, process mapping has developed with the emergence of software tools that can attach 'meta-data' to activities, drivers and triggers to provide a more complete understanding of processes.

FORCE FIELD ANALYSIS

This principle, developed by Kurt Lewin (1943), is another way to visualise a change process and assess its components. It provides a framework for looking at the factors, or forces, that influence a situation. It looks at forces that are either driving movement towards a goal ('driving forces') or blocking movement towards a goal ('restraining forces').

8 – Practitioner's Reflection and Assessment

OD practitioners attend to the intangible characteristics of an organisation – its atmosphere and mood. The practitioner's own assessment of this may be the most sensitive 'instrument' with which to pick up these nuances and has a part to play in tracking change and identifying potential threats.

However, we would argue that reflection and practitioner assessment alone are not enough to populate the evaluation toolkit. Better practice, in our view, would be to use this personal radar to help identify what data needs to be collected through other methods to evaluate what is really going on.

9 – Methodologies Adapted from Other Disciplines

In the absence of tools specifically developed for the evaluation of OD initiatives, several practitioners reported that they have adapted methodologies from other disciplines, especially project management, to provide a framework in which to track their work.

For example, a traffic light system can act as a tracking mechanism for an intervention, helping the practitioner focus on reaching milestones and reassessing strategy if necessary.

10 – Assessment Methodologies

OD's focus on human behaviour is well served, in terms of evaluation, by a number of assessment methodologies. Specialist leadership assessment consultancies, for example, can put leaders through a benchmarking and development process to assess their competencies against leaders in comparable organisations.

A number of capability matrices exist which can measure and track a management or leadership population's behaviour. Similarly, competency frameworks provide a behavioural model against which managers and leaders can be assessed.

Interaction Between Quantitative and Qualitative Approaches

OD evaluation is a topic on which there are some strong and opposing views among practitioners, rooted in quite fundamental differences in philosophy and approach. Many OD practitioners have a preference for either qualitative or quantitative evaluation methods, based on their background and training, personal philosophy and world view. The relative merits and differences between the two have been hotly debated among social researchers for many years. But based on our research and on our own experience in the field of evaluation we would advocate the fertile middle ground of a mixed approach, combining both qualitative and quantitative methods.

As Figure 12.4 illustrates, the relationship between qualitative and quantitative research is, at its best, symbiotic and cyclical. One approach feeds off the other, enriching and clarifying the stories each is telling. Some

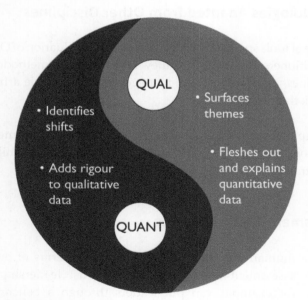

Figure 12.4   How mixed methodology can add value
Source: Finney and Jefkins 2009. © Roffey Park Institute.

researchers argue that the difference between qualitative and quantitative is quite small. All qualitative data can be quantitatively coded using a number of different techniques without detracting from the qualitative information. Likewise all quantitative data can be said to be based on qualitative judgements; you can't interpret numbers without understanding the assumptions which underlie them.

Quantitative methods alone will rarely give you the whole story about the success – or otherwise – of an OD intervention. However, they can alert you to important shifts and guide you to areas where a qualitative study will flesh out and explain your data. Similarly, qualitative research can surface important trends and themes which can be tested with quantitative techniques to add rigour to the data.

We choose not to take sides in the qualitative-quantitative debate; indeed we're not convinced that it is a valid debate to have. Both methods have their strengths and weaknesses, and each has their place, depending on what you are trying to measure. Used judiciously in combination, we believe they can be greater than the sum of their parts.

Building on Research and Best Practice to Create a Culture of Evaluation in OD

The thinking and practice of the leading OD practitioners we have interviewed, summarised in Roffey Park's research findings, are beginning to build not only a range of methodologies suited to the measurement of OD impact, but also a culture of evaluation within the OD discipline, in which it becomes an integral part of professional practice.

Conclusion

So how can the OD community make evaluation a more significant part of its work? Firstly, we believe practitioners should continue to debate the topic in order to raise the profile of the issue and focus people's attention on it: at conferences, through online forums, journal articles and professional networks.

Secondly, we would encourage the sharing of best practice among organisational OD practitioners. Support and challenge from peers could help practitioners to refine and develop their ideas about how to evaluate their work.

Thirdly, we would welcome more accessible and relevant training in research techniques, for example, what if formal qualifications in OD were to include evaluation methodologies? More broadly, we would like to see some formal professional standards for OD, perhaps in the context of a professional body for the discipline.

Finally, we believe there needs to be a shift in culture in the OD community towards a greater focus on evaluation, with individual practitioners committing to making it a greater part of their practice.

Evaluation is undoubtedly set to become a bigger part of OD practice, and this will be a challenging professional assignment for the OD community. We hope Roffey Park's research findings will act as a catalyst to stimulate discussion and debate, and provide some ideas for action, both in the current economic crisis and beyond. We look forward to being part of the debate, and to supporting OD professionals in showing the impact that their work has in organisations across the world.

References

Brinkerhoff, R.O. 2003. *The Success Case Method: Find out Quickly What's Working and What's Not*. San Francisco, CA: Berrett-Koehler.

Burke, W. and Litwin, G.L. 1992. A causal model of organisational performance and change. *Journal of Management*, 18, 523–45.

Cooperrider, D.L. and Srivastva, S. 1987. Appreciative inquiry in organisational life. In *Research in Organisational Change and Development: Volume 1*, edited by R. Woodman and W. Pasmore. Greenwich, CT: JAI Press, 129–69.

Finney, L. and Jefkins, C. 2009. *Best Practice in OD Evaluation: Understanding the Impact of Organisational Development*. Horsham: Roffey Park Institute.

Garrow, V., Varney, S. and Lloyd C. 2009. Fish or Bird? Perspectives on Organisational Development. (OD) Research Report 463, Brighton: Institute for Employment Studies.

Goffee, R. and Jones, G. 2003. *The Character of a Corporation: How Your Company's Culture Can Make or Break Your Business*. Profile Books.

Kirkpatrick, D.L. 1998. *Evaluating Training Programs: The Four Levels*. 2nd edition. San Francisco: Berrett-Koehler Publishers Inc.

Lewin, K. 1943. Defining the 'Field at a Given Time'. *Psychological Review*, 50, 292–310. Republished in *Resolving Social Conflicts & Field Theory in Social Science*. Washington, DC: American Psychological Association, 1997.

Lewin, K. 1946. Action research and minority problems. *J Soc. Issues*, 2(4), 34–46.

Tamkin P., Yarnall J. and Kerrin M. 2002. Kirkpatrick & Beyond: A Review of Models of Training Evaluation. Report 392. Brighton: Institute for Employment Studies.

Index

For Product Safety Concerns and Information please contact our
EU representative GPSR@taylorandfrancis.com Taylor & Francis
Verlag GmbH, Kaufingerstraße 24, 80331 München, Germany